DAILY PREPARATIONS FOR PERFECTION

A Daily Devotional
by Gwen R. Shaw

Engeltal Press
P.O. Box 447
Jasper, ARK 72641 U.S.A.

Copyright 1983 by Gwen R. Shaw
End-Time Handmaidens, Inc.
Engeltal
P.O. Box 447
Jasper, ARK 72641
U.S.A.

Second edition, 1986
Fourth printing, 1996

Printed in the United States of America

FOREWORD

The days of fiery testing have come upon the Christians all over the world. These are days when many will be tempted to turn back and deny the Lord. The love of many shall wax cold, and old friendships will fall apart. We are at the threshold of the Great Tribulation.

Because of the dark days ahead, God sees that we need a special word to strengthen us and encourage us to press on. Through the years that I have served my God on the mission fields I have always been helped, comforted and blessed by some of the great daily devotional books. God would speak to me out of the pages and often give me guidance for that very day.

In the past year the Lord has been speaking to me many mornings (and sometimes in the evenings). I felt I should share these words with you. I know they will help you as they have helped me.

Sometimes the Lord rebuked me, sometimes He exhorted me. Then there were times He taught me and revealed hidden truths to me. I have shared it all. If you feel parts do not apply to your life, put it to the side; let God speak to you where He can.

His one desire is to daily give us the preparations we need so that we may be perfected to be counted worthy to be His bride.

"Watch ye therefore, and pray always, that ye may be accounted worthy to escape all these things that shall come to pass, and to stand before the Son of man." (Luke 21:36)

Gwen R. Shaw

FOREWORD TO THE SECOND EDITION

My heart has been overwhelmed at the tremendous response I have received from all the dear ones who have read the first edition of this devotional. Many have told me that it was as though God Himself spoke to them out of its pages every day. It always seemed to fit their need for the hour.

I give God all the glory. He is the true Author of this book. I am glad He used me as His scribe to comfort many hearts.

Gwen R. Shaw

January 1

CHERISH THE SILENCE

Scripture Reading — Mark 1:32-39

"And in the morning, rising up a great while before day, he went out, and departed into a solitary place, and there prayed." (Mark 1:35)

At the threshold of any new assignment get alone. Ask Me to give you solitude. It is one of the greatest gifts I have for My children. Those who know Me and love Me enjoy My presence in such a great way that they begrudge any interruption even from those who are their loved ones.

In the silence, the music of heaven draws close and is heard. Do not clutter your life with a lot of noise. Cherish the silence. It is in the silence you can hear My still, small voice.

The more busy your life is, the more you need the balance of silence. Get away from the noise and the pressure — the telephone, the voices — and let your every nerve be put to rest. It is healing.

The secret of finding time is EARLY. This is because very few are awake. While others are sleeping, they cannot interrupt your solitude. You have the key to privacy when those around you are sleeping.

Take that key and use it. The older you get, the more you need it. Get alone with Me. Meditate and read, and meditate and talk to Me, and listen, and I will speak My secrets to you. And you will be given strength to face that day.

They will seek you out like Simon sought Me out — but then you will be ready for them. Because you have been alone with Me, you can face the crowd.

January 2

DON'T TURN THEM AWAY

Scripture Reading — Mark 2:1-4

"And it was noised that he was in the house. And straightway many were gathered together, insomuch that there was no room to receive them, no, not so much as about the door: and he preached the word unto them...they uncovered the roof..." (Mark 2:1,2,4a)

There are so many hungry, needy, weak and troubled people. They are like little children looking for help. They need someone who cares about them. If they find that someone loves them they will come running from all directions.

Word will be carried from mouth to mouth that someone has come who cares for them. You will see them crowd around you because they will feel My love in you.

Don't try to keep them from coming. They are desperate people with desperate needs. They will find a way. If they cannot get in the door (the usual) they will uncover the roof. They will break through the laws of man to be in My presence.

Today, I still have a hungry, desperate, needy people — looking for love, looking for help. They will come to where there is help. Again, I say — don't turn them away. Open your heart to them. Feel their heartbreak. Cry with them, laugh with them. Share with them, pray for them. Don't cut yourself off. Stop and listen — and then preach — preach the Word unto them. Give them My Word, even the word of commanding faith that releases miracles and meets their every need.

January 3

GRIEVED FOR THE HARDNESS OF THEIR HEARTS

Scripture Reading — Mark 3:1-15

"And when he had looked round about on them with anger, being grieved for the hardness of their hearts, he saith unto the man, Stretch forth thine hand. And he stretched it out: and his hand was restored whole as the other." (Mark 3:5)

There is more hardness of heart among My very own children than among those who do not know Me. Their hearts are in ignorance, but they often are not in a state of hardness because ignorance and hardness are two different things. The latter is worse than the former. It comes about by constantly refusing the Word and by rejecting the leadings and guidance of the Holy Spirit, even while one "acts" spiritual or religious.

The hardness of heart grieves Me and it angers Me, for My children profess to know Me but they know not My will or My ways, neither do they follow Me, nor sacrifice to do what I desire. They do not what I desire. They do not know what is best for them and so they often miss it by seeking to please their flesh or refusing to hear My voice.

My child, My will is to make the lame arms whole, so they can reach out their hands to bless and help others. So many are crippled in spirit because no one has shown them love. But if you will look past the hardness of heart in the synagogues of the righteous, and bring cures and healing to the needy who come for help, you will see My glory. But do not let the hardness of others hinder you from giving the needy My love and help.

January 4

YOU CAN KNOW THE MYSTERIES OF THE KINGDOM

Scripture Reading — Mark 4:1-13

"And he said unto them, Unto you it is given to know the mystery of the kingdom of God: but unto them that are without, all these things are done in parables." (Mark 4:11)

Yes, My beloved, the mystery of the Kingdom is yours to know, yours to possess because it is ordained from the foundation of the earth that you understand the secrets that are hidden from the world.

You do not need to continue in ignorance, not understanding the great truths of the Kingdom of God. The time has come for these truths to be revealed to the children of the Kingdom. Do not feel that you are unworthy, or that you do not have the ability to know these truths, or that you are somehow going to work for them, so that one day you will become "righteous" enough to be given these truths.

No, My daughter. You already have the right to know all these great truths which are hidden from the world, simply because you are a child of the King, and as such, you are brought up and trained in the protocol of the royal family to take your place on the throne when your hour to reign will come.

The secrets of your Father belong to you. Open your heart and He will teach you all you need to know and all you long to learn.

January 5

"GO HOME AND TELL THEM!"

Scripture Reading — Mark 5:1-20

"...Go home to thy friends, and tell them how great things the Lord hath done for thee, and hath had compassion on thee." (Mark 5:19)

My beloved child, the last ones to know what great things I have done are the ones at home. The family you belong to is the last to awaken to the miraculous touch of your God in your life.

Have I not said, "No prophet is without honour, except in his own country and among his own people"? My own family did not know who I was. My brothers mocked me, even as they had mocked David when he was anointed by Samuel.

Vanya's very own brother denied Me and became a betrayer to the family. Judas was a member of My inner circle and he betrayed Me.

You will find your worst opponents in "the family." You will also find those who will doubt and be indifferent and ridicule. Nevertheless, go home and tell them what great things I have done for you. Let the indifferent, unbelieving, careless members of your family know and see that I am alive in you. And let them know My great compassion for you. Let them know the great love that I have for you. For everything that you have received is out of My love for you. You are My most precious and beloved, and your family needs to bear witness to the fact that I love you and have blessed you.

> Go back and tell them one more time
> All that I've done for thee.
> If they don't listen, still they'll know
> That you have been with Me.

January 6

"COME APART AND REST A WHILE!"

Scripture Reading — Mark 6:30-32

"And he said unto them, Come ye yourselves apart into a desert place, and rest a while: for there were many coming and going, and they had no leisure so much as to eat." (Mark 6:31)

Yes, we were busy. I well remember those days. But they were happy days. My strength was poured out hour after hour. My disciples who did not have the same dedication that I had were more exhausted than I was, for zeal and dedication to a purpose gives one a strength which is above the normal. Besides being busy, we were not eating properly. We snatched a morsel here and a morsel there. There is much strength given to My people when they sit together in communion while they eat. Always take time to eat together with those who love God.

Besides this, all of us were broken of heart because of the cruel and treacherous act of John's death. It was right that he should have the honour of sealing his testimony with martyrdom. The greater the testimony, the greater the death should be! But the deplorable weakness of Herod, a king, and Herodias' cruel, conniving, Satan-inspired spirit, together with the innocent and ignorant, foolish teen-aged daughter was sickening to the souls of all of us who loved and honoured John. We had just buried him and we knew, in spite of the multitudes who loved us and followed us and who praised us and seemed to honour us, that persecution was in the land.

John was an example to us. Even as we followed him in preaching repentance, we would shortly have to follow him in laying down our lives.

Never let the glamour or seeming popularity of your calling blind you to the fact that if you are truly dedicated to Me, you are a living martyr. You must always anticipate the opportunity to lay your life down for the glory of God.

These crowds never give you strength. They drain it from you. You must always seek to escape from their false and empty flattery and praise.

And so I counselled My followers, as I counsel you after a great and exhausting time of ministry, after strong opposition and persecution, "Come apart and rest for a while."

Do not let the busybody, Satan, condemn you for a few days of rest. I call you to do absolutely **nothing** for at least the space of 24 hours — every once in a while. Stop measuring time by hours, days and weeks. Stop thinking that when you are not working or talking nothing is being accomplished. For while you rest, your heavenly Father is working for you, and so much is accomplished then also. Now, I call you to separate yourself from all and rest a while in My presence.

January 7

LOVE DOES NOT FIND FAULT

Scripture Reading — Mark 7:1-23

"They found fault." (Mark 7:2)

"This people honoureth me with their lips, but their heart is far from me." (Mark 7:6)

It is so easy to find fault where there is no love. Love is light and glory. When it fills the heart it sees the best in everyone and in every situation. But when the heart forsakes its commandment of God (to love), it must find another substitute — the tradition of man.

The traditions of man bring death and destruction because they come from a love-rejecting heart. They are the law of the negative and not the law of the positive. They are created out of a love-rejecting spirit — and so they only can see the negative in others.

I am God — I walked among men, perfect. Yet they found fault with Me. I tried to teach men the law of God, the law of love — but they preferred the law of men, the law of fault-finding.

With their lips they honoured Me, but with their deeds they put Me to shame and disgrace. The churches and synagogues of today are filled with fault-finders. Their heart is far from Me.

Because of this they reject the command to love. Love is giving something of yourself. Where there is no love — one cannot give. So one makes another law — one of fault-finding.

You cannot keep both concepts. You cannot live by the law of God, to love, and the tradition of man, to find fault.

You are called to live by My law, even the law of purity and holiness of heart which is based on love.

It is not what you eat or what you drink that defiles you. All that comes out in the draught. It is only what happens to your mind when you are under the influence of harmful drugs or alcohol that defiles you, for it is in the mind that you are defiled.

Therefore keep your mind pure. When you participate in gossip and slander or fault-finding of your neighbours, then your mind is eating of the forbidden fruit which brings death. When you give forth these evils to others you are as the serpent who tempted Eve to eat of the forbidden fruit.

Love only blesses. Love only forgives. Love only leaves a fragrance. The tradition of the elders is not love; the tradition of the elders is to find fault with the imperfection of others. And though the "elders" (those who think they are wise but are fools) parade as religious, their hearts are far from Me, for they teach not My commandment to love, but the command to find fault. I came to break their traditions; I have sent you to do the same.

January 8

HEED NOT MAN'S REBUKES

Scripture Reading — Mark 8:31-38

"And he spake that saying openly. And Peter took him, and began to rebuke him." (Mark 8:32)

"Whosoever therefore shall be ashamed of me and of my words in this adulterous and sinful generation; of him also shall the Son of man be ashamed, when he cometh in the glory of his Father with the holy angels." (Mark 8:38)

My child, never let Satan condemn you for the words of truth you speak. I came speaking words of light and life, love and liberty which the self-righteous, adulterous generation could not accept, for self-righteousness is the most hardening and blinding of all sins. It makes its victim appear perfect and everyone else faulty.

Peter, My very close companion, wanted to silence Me. He did not want Me to tell the people truth because he saw that they were offended by it. Some forsook Me when I revealed the truth to them. Peter did not want to lose any adherents to our cause.

It is hard for the "Peters" to see others drop out from our vision. They are severely tempted to do the same. "Peters" are valuable to the Kingdom because they are easily influenced. I can influence them to great good — Satan knows that. He can influence them to great evil. That is why, when people who followed Me were offended by My words and left Me, I said to Peter and the twelve, "Will ye also go away?" (John 6:67) Peter knew the truth however, for he said, "Lord to whom shall we go? Thou hast the words of eternal life."

I want to speak these same words of eternal life through you to others who blindly follow the rules of religion. Not all will be able to receive it. Those whose "toes you walk on" will hate you viciously, even as they hated Me. They will try to kill you. They will scream, "We have a law..."

I have a law too, a law of grace and truth; I came teaching and living this law. They accused Me of gluttony and drunkenness, of friendship with swindlers and whores. What do you think they will do with you when you teach and live grace and truth? Do you really think they will accept you when they rejected Me? Are not these same self-righteous demons in the world today?

Do not try to save your skin by refusing to speak truth. This is the generation of which I said, "And then shall many be offended, and shall betray one another, and shall hate one another....the love of many shall wax cold. But he that shall endure unto the end, the same shall be saved." (Matthew 24:10-13) "Every one that is of the truth heareth my voice." (John 18:37)

> Go, tell the truth of grace and love
> To all who will truth hear;
> You need not fear for truth to die
> If truth you do hold dear.

January 9

IT IS IN THE BLUEPRINT – YOU MUST SUFFER

Scripture Reading – Mark 9:11-13

"And how it is written of the Son of man, that he must suffer many things, and be set at nought." (Mark 9:12)

My beloved, because you are very close to Me you must share My life. Not only will you know My joy and My peace, My love and My courage, My zeal and My vision, you will also know My suffering. There is much suffering for those who live close to Me. Every pain that I feel, they also feel. Every nail that pierces Me, pierces them.

If you seek to escape suffering, you will find yourself far from Me. If you walk with Me, you will find yourself in the garden of betrayal and the halls of condemnation. Others, less great than yourself, shall condemn you and pass judgment on you.

Beloved, they do this because they do not know Me. If they knew Me, they would surely know you like I know you and they would love you like I love you.

It was written of My forerunner that he must suffer, and he accomplished it and fulfilled his blueprint. It was decreed that I come as man's son and suffer all that is humanly possible to suffer. I fulfilled this blueprint. It is decreed of you, as My close followers, to also drink My cup and know My bitterness and rejection. To this day you have fulfilled this pattern.

My child, time on earth is very short. The time of suffering seems to endure forever. But when it is over you will rejoice that you were counted worthy to know Me in the fellowship of My suffering. For all who know Me in this fellowship of suffering shall also know Me in the power of My resurrection.

It was written I would suffer much, I would be set at nought. Rejoice when you are set at nought. It means you are rejected by My "rejects," for they have not only rejected Me; they have also been rejected by Me, when they rejected My truth. I cannot be separated from My truth.

The truth you teach is love. This truth is set at nought, together with you, by those who do not love because their hearts are full of anger, bitterness, unforgiveness and hate.

January 10

YOU WILL RECEIVE AN 100-FOLD

Scripture Reading – Mark 10:17-31

"But he shall receive an hundredfold now in this time, houses, and brethren, and sisters, and mothers, and children, and lands, with persecutions; and in the world to come eternal life." (Mark 10:30)

My beloved, have I not kept My promise to you? Have I not blessed and multiplied you and all that you have?

Yes, I have given to you all these blessings even when you didn't have anything of material things to give to Me.

But you left your home to follow Me. You left your children, brothers, sisters, parents and homeland and I will always stand by My Word to prove I am no man's debtor. No one can outgive Me. You must know if you give Me a handful, My hand is 100 times bigger than yours. You have left one homeland to obey my call. Do not only claim one nation in return. Claim 100 nations. Believe Me to send you to all the lands and to give you all the lands that I have promised. Strive to work out My promises to you.

And as you see My promises fulfilled in you, without striving the persecutions will come. Yes, you will suffer equally to the glory that there might be a balance in your life which is eternal.

January 11

I WILL PROVIDE TRANSPORT

Scripture Reading – Mark 11:1-11

"And saith unto them, Go your way into the village over against you: and as soon as ye be entered into it, ye shall find a colt tied, whereon never man sat; loose him, and bring him. And if any man say unto you, Why do ye this? say ye that the Lord hath need of him; and straightway he will send him hither." (Mark 11:2,3)

I know how to commandeer and provide all means of transport. I am able to release for you and provide for you an ass, a horse, a camel, a bicycle, a car, a train, or plane or bus, or whatever the need of transport may be. I know the need and I know the source of supply. Both are predestined from the beginning of time.

Remember how it was decreed, "Rejoice greatly, O daughter of Zion; shout, O daughter of Jerusalem: behold, thy King cometh unto thee: he is just, and having salvation; lowly, and riding upon an ass, and upon a colt the foal of an ass." (Zechariah 9:9)

My Word was spoken five centuries before it was performed. I gave the command to My children to rejoice. It is time now, only to rejoice in anticipation of the Lord's glorious provision, for surely He will provide. Surely He will not fail. It is not your need. It is the Lord's need.

You are doing His work. You are fulfilling His commission. He needs to send you here, He needs to send you there. He will provide for His ambassador the vehicle of transport. He will move the hearts of owners to release it to Me, for I have need of it.

January 12

LOVE WILL CAST IN ALL

Scripture Reading – Mark 12:28-44

"And thou shalt love the Lord thy God with all thy heart, and with all thy soul, and with all thy mind, and with all thy strength: this is the first commandment. And the second is like, namely this, Thou shalt love thy neighbour as thyself. There is none other commandment greater than these." (Mark 12:30,31)

"And to love him with all the heart, and with all the understanding, and with all the soul, and with all the strength, and to love his neighbour as himself, is more than all whole burnt offerings and sacrifices." (Mark 12:33)

"For all they did cast in of their abundance; but she of her want did cast in all that she had, even all her living." (Mark 12:44)

"All!" Yes, that is what perfect love is. It is giving to the limit. Giving until there is nothing left.

If you have perfect love you will not be able to hold back from giving your all. I have many who give. Even this last week throughout the churches, temples, synagogues and houses of worship they came with their tithes envelopes, their cheques and their pennies and they gave with pride of their faithfulness, they gave with feelings of responsibility, as pillars of their certain organizations. Some gave because they knew the church secretary would add it up at the end of the year and every bit given would be carefully noted down. Others gave because they were afraid of great economic crises to come to them if they did not give. But a very small number gave out of sheer love.

If My children all gave out of sheer love, there would be no lack. That is how they gave in the early church, in the heat and passion of first love. They sold out to give and there was no lack. (Acts 4:34, 35)

You will always have Ananiases and Sapphiras among you who will pretend to give all, that they may have the approval of My leaders, but they are withholding because their love is imperfect. They do not have the true spirit of Christ. Their love is not pure, perfect, complete love. They not only are on dangerous ground, they will be a danger to My work.

A hypocrite is one who pretends to love, but is only making a pretence, for without love the heart has no strength to give.

I measure your love by the way you give to Me, My child, for you will give as you love. If you love Me with all your heart, you will give as the widow gave — her all.

Never be afraid to love completely. I am the treasurer of the bank of heaven and I keep your finances "in the black."

January 13

YOU ARE RESPONSIBLE TO USE YOUR AUTHORITY

Scripture Reading — Mark 13:24-37

"For the Son of man is as a man taking a far journey, who left his house, and gave authority to his servants, and to every man his work, and commanded the porter to watch." (Mark 13:34)

Yes, I have gone away and you are all My servants and handmaidens. As My handmaiden, I give you My authority. You are representing Me. You must use the authority I give you. Just as you delegate others to be in charge when you go away, and are dismayed if you return and find that they have not acted with the authority you gave them, but have allowed others to control them, so I am grieved when you do not use the authority I give you. Even as you would remove the servant who failed to stay in control of the situation, so I will remove you and put another in your place who will carry out all My orders, if you fail your chain of command.

As a handmaiden in a place of authority it is your responsibility to always know My will in every situation and to stand firmly until it is carried out. Do not let opposition from difficulties or from people dismay you or keep you from fulfilling all your duties. You have not only authority, you also have responsibility.

Every man has his own job to do. Everyone is appointed to his own particular task. Do not try to do someone else's work – only what is allotted to you. You can help someone with their task, but you have your own task. And while you work the porter will stand with you, helping you to stay alert, and will watch what you are doing and record it all in the heavenly records.

January 14

POUR OUT YOUR OINTMENT

Scripture Reading – Mark 14:3-11

"And there were some that had indignation within themselves, and said, Why was this waste of the ointment made? For it might have been sold for more than three hundred pence, and have been given to the poor. And they murmured against her." (Mark 14:4,5)

"And Judas Iscariot, one of the twelve, went unto the chief priests, to betray him unto them." (Mark 14:10)

There are always those who are very critical of the way finances are used. They make it their responsibility to keep a watch on the handling of all finances. It does not mean that they themselves are honest. In fact, My child, they are the very ones who are **not** honest in the giving of their tithes and offerings and the handling of the finances in their care. They look for faults in others to justify their own weakness by murmuring loudly against My Marys who dare to break the alabaster box and pour out the ointment of love upon My body.

So angry did Judas become, that he used this excuse to justify the evil of his heart. He knew the value of the perfume was 300 pence ($60.00). Because he couldn't get his hands on it (because that which is poured out is unretrievable) he sold Me (with the perfume on My head) for 30 pieces of silver. He was truly an anarchist. He was saving finances for the overthrow of the Roman dominion, intending now to set himself up as leader because I was not the political agitator he had thought I was when he had joined Me. He felt I had betrayed "the cause of Israel" — and because the religious leaders despised Rome (though they pretended to be co-operative and sympathetic to them) he went to them, for he knew that they would finance his cause as they not only were angry with Me because I did not speak against Caesar, but because I was a threat to their powerful position. They despised the truth in Me and the words I taught, for the people were now more ready to overthrow the powerful adulterous priesthood of Israel (the source of their inner bondage) than the dominion of Rome (which was only an outward bondage). So the priesthood had to get rid of Me.

Therefore they were glad to pay out the 30 pieces of silver in order to secure the victim of their hate and prejudice. And Judas felt justified in selling Me and accepting the money, for he "kept the bag" (John 12:6), that is, the finances for the revolution. For he said in himself he was doing this for the poor.

Every revolutionary cry is "For the Poor!" That is because the leaders want to awaken the sympathy of the sleeping masses. Judas was angry with Mary who poured out her love gift on Me, but even more angry with Me because I justified her and rebuked him when I said, "The poor you always will have with you." (John 12:8) Revolution cannot eliminate the poor — it only makes more poor. Love, not hate, can lift. Pour out your love on My children. Pour out your finances on My body. Know this, that if anyone objects, it is only because they are revolutionists with political designs of their own, and not because they truly care for the poor. Don't be intimidated by the Judases who are in every ministry. Go, get your ointment and pour it out. It shall be recorded for all ages by the recording angel. **The good you do is never wasted.**

January 15

TRUTH HIDDEN IN MOCKERY

Scripture Reading — Mark 15:16-38

"And the superscription of his accusation was written over, THE KING OF THE JEWS." (Mark 15:26)

"Likewise also the chief priests mocking said among themselves with the scribes, He saved others; himself he cannot save. Let Christ the King of Israel descend now from the cross, that we may see and believe. And they that were crucified with him reviled him." (Mark 15:31,32)

Beloved, have you ever noticed how people will reveal their heart by the things which they say when they tease and when they mock. It is strange that Rome called Me "King of the Jews" in mockery and the chief priests called Me "Christ, the King of Israel." They all did it in mockery, yet it was pure truth.

God has planted truth in the deepest recesses of the heart, and even though the mind will not accept it, when one is mocking, often the truth escapes.

It had to be that both Rome and Israel would confess Me, and they did — to the glory of God. The chief priests went one step further. They confessed Me not only as King of Israel, but as their Messiah when they addressed Me as Christ. This was the pronouncement that I needed. Only My death and extreme suffering, their hatred of Me fully vented upon Me, and their exaltation of having finished Me off, could release these very important words from their mouths. They, as the religious authority of all Israel, had to confirm by utterance that I was their Messiah and their King.

They were snared by the words of their mouths. It was now a decree established in the political and the religious world. Let us together accept our suffering that God may be glorified.

January 16

DIVINE AND HUMAN MESSENGERS

Scripture Reading — Mark 16:1-20

"And when they looked, they saw that the stone was rolled away: for it was very great. And entering into the sepulchre, they saw a young man sitting on the right side, clothed in a long white garment; and they were affrighted. And he saith unto them, Be not affrighted: Ye seek Jesus of Nazareth, which was crucified: he is risen; he is not here: behold the place where they laid him. But go your way, tell his disciples and Peter that he goeth before you into Galilee: there shall ye see him, as he said unto you." (Mark 16:4-7)

This angel messenger, this "young man," never announced his name, and yet he was given the greatest honour of saints and mortals — to roll the stone away and make it possible for My daughters of Zion to see the empty tomb. Jacob rolled the stone from the well for Rachel and she loved him. I need "young men" on earth to roll stones away, to bring joy to My daughters. There are certain things only My sons can do, and until they do them many shall suffer.

The heavenly messenger I sent first calmed their troubled hearts. You must bring peace wherever you go before you can do My works. Then he instructed them visually of the fact of the resurrection. You must be convinced that I am risen. He then commanded them (My daughters) to go and tell the resurrection story to the brethren. You must tell others. He revealed that I go before My very own at all times. I always go before you. He foretold that they would see Me, because My father had instructed him to give them this information. They have a task to:

1. Roll away the stone — physical labour
2. Bring comfort to the fearful
3. Speak the Resurrection Truth
4. Command others to go and tell of My Resurrection
5. Promise them that I will go before them and am with them always
6. They will see Me, face to face, as they journey forward in My will.

Do this, and you do the work of My heavenly messengers. Besides this, you have no other commission.

January 17

HIS NAME SHALL BE KNOWN THROUGHOUT THE EARTH

Scripture Reading — Malachi 1:1-14

"For from the rising of the sun even unto the going down of the same my name shall be great among the Gentiles; and in every place incense shall be offered unto my name, and a pure offering: for my name shall be great among the heathen, saith the Lord of hosts." (Malachi 1:11)

I have decreed the great end-time missionary thrust even through my servant and prophet Malachi. The world has yet to see the mighty outpouring of My Spirit over the whole world. It will bring a great change in the hearts because it is a heart-religion and not an outward form of religion of traditions and ceremonies.

My name shall be great among all the nations — Tibet, Burma, China, Africa, Russia, Egypt, Israel. My very own name, Jesus, will be the greatest name spoken on their lips and I will be the object of their love.

And throughout the world the incense of praise and the pure offering of holy prayers will be offered unto Me. It will bring Me close to man, and it will bring you close to Me until it will seem that I am walking among you.

Even now, as you, my handmaidens and servants are fasting and in chains of prayer, you are bringing Me very close to you. This amount of prayer and fasting has never been since the beginning of time. Don't be afraid to call more into these circles of prayer. These vigils of intercession are very mighty and will do more than save your beloved: they will bring changes on this entire earth. For prayers and fastings are a pure offering unto Me.

January 18

GOD'S COVENANT WITH LEVI

Scripture Reading — Malachi 2:1-7

"And ye shall know that I have sent this commandment unto

you, that my covenant might be with Levi, saith the Lord of hosts." (Malachi 2:4)

My child, you have not chosen Me, but I have chosen you and ordained you into My priestly family. While it is true that not many wise, mighty and noble (after the flesh) are called, I do have credentials which must be fulfilled. If they are not, then you are disqualified from being My messengers.

You are My Levi. Look again at the qualifications of My Priesthood. They are not difficult to attain unto, but they are absolutely vital, both then and now.

First: Give Glory unto My Name (vs. 2). You must always give the glory to Me. Never accredit yourself with having done anything. It is My strength in you, My wisdom, My ability, My opportunity. I will have done it through your vessel. Give Me the glory for the smallest things you can do for Me today and tomorrow I will do greater things. Do not insist on complaining of being worthless, useless, a wasted life. You are where I want you. Give glory to Me for **everything**.

Second: Covenant of Peace (vs. 5). Know that I have made a covenant of eternal life and of deep peace with you. Walk in that peace and you will have eternal life. Many lives are cut short by infirmities of the flesh which are brought on by a troubled and anxious spirit that has not permitted its heart to be at rest.

Third: Law of Truth (vs. 6). Keep the law of truth and honesty in your mouth by keeping your heart honest through much self-examination. Do not let your heart lie to yourself and your mouth will not lie to others.

Fourth: Walk in Peace (vs. 6). Walk with Me in Peace. You must know that if you walk alone, you cannot have peace. Only as you keep close to Me and walk with Me can you have peace. In so doing you will turn many to righteousness.

Fifth: Live a Life of Equity (vs. 6.) I demand equity. This is vital. Many of my messengers have lost their equity. They tell lies, they steal My money and My time; they give wrong judgment in cases that pertain to My children that they might buy for themselves influence and popularity. I will not allow this. I could have won the favour of the high priests; I chose rather to be spat upon.

Six: Priest's Lips Should Keep Knowledge (vs. 7). Speak only My words. Keep a holy watch before your lips. Let the knowledge of My Word pour out of your mouth. Let your words be rich in My Word that many will seek and hunger for My Word because they will have a taste of it from you.

Seven: For He is the Lord's Messenger (vs. 7). Always remember, you are not your own. You are My messenger.

January 19

THE BOOK OF REMEMBRANCE

Scripture Reading — Malachi 3:16-18

"Then they that feared the Lord spake often one to another: and the Lord hearkened, and heard it, and a book of remembrance was written before him for them that feared the Lord, and that thought upon his name. And they shall be mine, saith the Lord of hosts, in that day when I make up my jewels; and I will spare them, as a man spareth his own son that serveth him." (Malachi 3:16,17)

If you fear and honour Me, then speak often about the things that you want Me to hear. I am listening to your words when you talk about Me. I love to hear the way you give glory to Me and honour Me.

Do not spend your precious time (you have so little of it on earth in comparison to eternity) to talk about people in a negative way. You are wasting precious, precious time. Also you are making a negative recording. All negative recordings fill the earth with negative vibrations.

It is better that you make positive recordings, for then you will fill the earth with the good sound.

You must sing more. Sing My happy songs. Rejoice, and make others to be joyful.

The only mourning I permit is the travailing of the Holy Spirit. But that is positive and not negative. Do not speak of death as death, but of eternal life in My presence. Soon there will be no more death. Old things are passing away. All things are becoming new, new, new.

Talk about the new things I am even now preparing and beginning to do. Talk about it and rejoice. Live in anticipation and expectation of My sudden appearance in My temple.

Israel is building a great temple for Me now, in anticipation of My coming into that temple. But they have rejected Me then and would now, because they still are blind, but I am coming into the temple of the hearts of My very own who accept Me and talk about Me with love.

A record has been kept of your life. The purer your words, and the more loving your thoughts, the sooner I come. I come to select you as My jewel for My temple above.

January 20

GOD'S CALL TO THE FATHERS

Scripture Reading — Malachi 4:1-6

"And he shall turn the heart of the fathers to the children, and the heart of the children to their fathers, lest I come and smite the earth with a curse." (Malachi 4:6)

My beloved, I am calling, calling, calling for the fathers to turn towards their children in compassion and love. This generation of men has sired children whom they do not even regard as their own offspring. There is no compassion in the hearts of the fathers for their little ones. There is no true father-heart in them.

This is the generation Malachi spoke about.
1. A generation that gives Me its cast-off sacrifices (1:8,13)
2. That serves Me for a salary (1:10)
3. That dealeth treacherously with the wife of its youth (2:14)
4. That covers its sins of unfaithfulness (2:16)
5. That robbeth Me of My tithes and offerings (3:8,9).

This is even that rebellious, proud, greedy and lustful generation which will burn up as the grass is burnt by the prairie fire, leaving neither branch nor root, unless it repents.

I will send the sun of righteousness to shine upon this generation, even **this** weak and miserable generation. And I will pour out of My

Spirit upon it, one more time in a mightier way than ever before.

I will kindle love in the hearts of all of those who will receive it. This love must come to the fathers. Pray for the fathers. I am calling for the fathers. They must turn and love their sons and their daughters, lest I smite the world with a curse. What I will do depends now on the fathers.

January 21

SET FREE TO FREE OTHERS

Scripture Reading — Galatians 1:1-24

"Who gave himself for our sins, that he might deliver us from this present evil world, according to the will of God and our Father:" (Galatians 1:4)

My child, this is how I loved you. I did not love you because you were perfect or because you loved Me. I loved you with unconditional love.

I saw you as a helpless victim of the evil one. You were a prisoner in a prison with no ability to save yourself out of it. Satan possessed your body, soul and spirit. He had even convinced you in your mind that you were enjoying your captivity and bondage. You were so duped that you looked out through your prison bars and mocked those who were free. You were helpless since your birth.

But I saw what you could be through My power to deliver and change you, and change you, and change you until you would come into My likeness and image as the Father first intended you to be before the Fall.

My Father and I first created the world perfect, then we created man perfect, but man became evil and made the world like himself.

I came to redeem this evil world and the people in it. It is not enough to empty out the prison and slave camps of an evil nation. I must change the whole nation and deliver it out of slavery and bondage. For this purpose am I come, that I can deliver you from every single trait of the bondages of yesterday, that there be no trace of your former life found in you, and you become like Me.

When you become what I am, you will be able to deliver others also from their bondages. Until you are free, you cannot be a blessing.

Many of My children have been released out of prison, but they are still walking about with the chains of former habits and sins rattling with every move they make.

I came, and sacrificed all, that you might be free. Do not be content with one trace of yesterday's bondages upon you when I have paid the price for your **full** release and deliverance —body, soul, spirit.

January 22

FALSE TEACHING CAUSES BONDAGE

Scripture Reading — Galatians 2:1-21

"And that because of false brethren unawares brought in, who came in privily to spy out our liberty which we have in Christ Jesus, that they might bring us into bondage:" (Galatians 2:4)

Man, because of his impurity has sought through the centuries to make himself righteous in his own strength. He has said "I sinned, so I will make myself righteous."

All his attempts to perfect himself only made him self-righteous. It made him proud of his self-denial, his outward showing of holiness. This made him critical of others who did not attain unto his standards of what he called "holy." He sat on his pedestal of self-praise and sought to impress others to copy him. If they were not impressed, he ordered them to copy him first by gentle persuasion, then by coercion, then by scare and shunning and finally by fiery sermons of wrath and judgment.

These are false brethren who want you to be brought into their same bondage because they are not right with God through faith in Me alone. Neither are they holy in the inward parts. They are of the circumcision and cut off the outward and leave the inner defiled. Many sincere Barnabases are carried away by their hypocrisy. Even leading apostles like My son Peter are intimidated and fearful of confrontation with them because of their strong influence on other weak ones who are swayed about by every wind of doctrine.

My child, your righteousness is from Me. I am your righteousness. You have no other, but Me. If you can attain righteousness in any other way, by doing this, or not doing that, then I have died in vain for your sins.

You have only one act to perform to be perfect and that is to be crucified with Me. Die to self-perfection, self-esteem, self-vindication, self-righteousness, self-preservation, self-love, and you will live by My Spirit, My righteousness and My perfection. For the more you die to self, the more I can live My life through you till you can say with My servant Paul, "I am crucified with Christ: nevertheless I live; yet not I, but Christ liveth in me; and the life which I now live in the flesh I live by the faith of the Son of God, who loved me, and gave himself for me." (vs. 20)

January 23

IN THEE ALL THE NATIONS SHALL BE BLESSED

Scripture Reading – Galatians 3:1-29

"Know ye therefore that they which are of faith, the same are the children of Abraham. And the scripture, foreseeing that God would justify the heathen through faith, preached before the gospel unto Abraham, saying, In thee shall all nations be blessed. So then they which be of faith are blessed with faithful Abraham." (Galatians 3:7,8,9)

The first great recorded revelation after the Antedeluvian Age was My revelation of faith which I gave to My obedient servant and disciple, Abraham. I came to him because of his father's search for Me, and his father's life of prayer and I revealed Myself to him, that I might call out a family from all the families of the earth. It was at the time of new beginnings when I was taking families and turning them into nations.

The revelation I gave the family of Terah, descendents of Shem, was revolutionary. Revelation is nothing, if it does not revolutionize a person's way of thinking and thus his life and the lives of others.

The revelation of righteousness through simple faith and trust based on love to Me was new to those post-deluvians who still only had the memory of an angry God who had destroyed the inhabitants of the earth (except for the family of Noah).

That they could become righteous by faith in My revelation to them was revolutionary to their understanding. Of all the families of the earth only the family of Terah received it.

After that came the law, because man's mind was contaminated by centuries of slavery and the millions of idols of Egypt. I had to pull out the memory of those many idols which they had seen in Egypt. This was a great work. I gave a strict law against all idols, that they might know the shame and evil of this worship of demons and spirits of the past. After I had uprooted idolatry I could again give the descendents of Abraham the revelation of faith when I came to earth and died for their sins.

I sent My servant and the great prophet, Paul, to take them back to the original, perfect way, the Abrahamic way of faith in Me alone. Most of Abraham's family refused to come. The descendents of Jacob preferred the works of the law because they had no love. Without love there is no faith.

But the families of the earth, outside of Israel, accepted what Abraham had lived by, **faith in Me**. And they were grafted into Abraham's family tree by faith, and not by flesh.

I had decreed that through Abraham, because of his faith walk, all the nations of the earth would be blessed. (Genesis 12:3) He brought light and salvation to the Gentiles two millenia later through his seed, Jesus.

You have inherited the family inheritance of Abraham, which is to walk by faith and bless the nations, not just one or two, but **all** the nations. "Ask of me, and I shall give thee the heathen for thine inheritance, and the uttermost parts of the earth for thy possession." (Psalm 2:8)

Abraham's promise to bless the nations is your promise. Take it, possess it, don't be cheated of your rightful inheritance.

January 24

EVERYTHING IS ON DIVINE SCHEDULE!

Scripture Reading — Galatians 4:1-31

"But when the fulness of the time was come, God sent forth his Son, made of a woman, made under the law, To redeem them that were under the law, that we might receive the adoption of sons. And because ye are sons, God hath sent forth the Spirit of his Son into your hearts, crying, Abba, Father. Wherefore thou art no more a servant, but a son; and if a son, then an heir of God through Christ." (Galatians 4:4-7)

Beloved, I have a perfect schedule for everything in your life. It leaves you enough hours to sleep, to eat, to visit with friends, to talk to Me, to do all that is required of you.

There is no need to rush about and worry. Neither need you lack your needed hours of rest, because I have a schedule for your whole life.

I knew what time you would need to leave or arrive at a certain place, even from before you were born.

You too were born in the fulness of time to be called to serve Me in the nations, to be sent to the nations one by one in the fullness of time, to go and to return to your home in the fulness of time, to seek My face to be prepared to hear My call to be raised up to call out others in the fullness of time, that all might be fulfilled according to My perfect plan.

January 25

THE SPIRIT-FILLED LIFE VS. THE FLESH-LIFE

Scripture Reading — Galatians 5:1-26

"This I say then, Walk in the Spirit, and ye shall not fulfil the lust of the flesh." (vs. 16)

"And they that are Christ's have crucified the flesh with the affections and lusts. If we live in the Spirit, let us also walk in the Spirit." (vs. 24,25)

My beloved, there are only two kinds of life, the life in the Spirit, which is pure and holy and pleasing to Me, or the life that is built to fulfil the lusts of the flesh.

To be born again means that one has left the flesh-life behind, one has a rebirthing, one has a new mind, a new desire, a new emotion, and a complete new life.

To pass from the flesh-life to the Spirit-life one must be reborn. One cannot be reborn without first dying. The old "you" that was born in sin must be put to death. The old "you" must be crucified with Me, or you will be lost, even though you take on a religious form, observe religious rules, and live by a new code of ethics. As long as the old flesh-desires burn in you, you are still living in the flesh realm and you will destroy yourself and cast your own soul into hell.

You must crucify the old life. You must be radical with yourself, despise your weakness and forsake it. Don't cover it with excuses of weakness. My grace is sufficient!

Walk in the Spirit. The Spirit-life is divided from the flesh life and there is no bondage in the Spirit-life. In heaven there are no bondages, as mentioned in Galatians 5:19-21. These things do not belong to the Kingdom of God. You have been called to the Kingdom life, which is the life of the Spirit. Make soul-examination. Do any of these evils control you? Then you are under the law and the curse. For these evils belong to the laws of the earth that destroy nations of people.

I was "lifted up" to lift you up above the earth realm. You must be lifted up through crucifixion. Forsake the worldly life of the past or you will perish and will lose your inheritance. You will be left out of the Kingdom of God to continue to exist with these earth-lusts and passions consuming you for eternity. Neither will the fires of your hell go out forever.

Cry desperately unto Me for deliverance. Mortify the deeds of the flesh. Put the deeds of the flesh to death by godly living.

Time is short. Many are receiving their LAST and final call to godliness through these words.

All of the old life must go — the wrong acts, the wrong thoughts, the wrong affections, and all lusts. Self-love and rebellion must be crucified. For rebellion is as witchcraft. (I Samuel 15:23) And I will not suffer a witch to live. (Exodus 22:18)

January 26

NEVER TIRE OF DOING ACTS OF KINDNESS

Scripture Reading — Galatians 6:1-18

"And let us not be weary in well doing: for in due season we shall reap, if we faint not. As we have therefore opportunity, let us do good unto all men, especially unto them who are of the household of faith." (Galatians 6:9,10)

The greatest thing that you can do is to do acts of kindness to others.

Many of My children try to please Me by performing great deeds which bring them fame and reknown. They make sacrifices of tremendous magnitude, but they never do one kind thing for one of My children. This is not pleasing to Me. I call on you to love — not to do. Love will make you perfect and love will get your perspective perfect.

Many of My children try to please Me by writing volumes of books which do not edify the body of Christ. Others build churches to propagate their religious beliefs. Some even die to prove their courage. But I only call you to love all men and do good to them. Let your heart be kind and tender. Let it care for others. Let it feel what Mine feels.

The loving heart does not need to force itself to show kindness to others. It is not looking for a reward for its kind and good deeds. The loving heart only wants to do kind deeds because of the joy it gets from doing good to others. Some begin, out of their own limited love, to do good, but they faint on the way because they feel no one appreciates them, and they get bitter; thus they lose their reward.

My child, I have not called you to be a great famous preacher, teacher, evangelist or missionary. I have called you to be a mother to My children, to love them, succour them, and help them to find their way.

Do good to all men, Buddhist, Moslem, Hindu, Atheist, but especially to those who belong to your family of faith. Be loyal to your own family. Be kind to those who belong to you.

Don't let them carry their burden alone. Try to help them carry their load. Look not for ways to get out of responsibilities and work, but for ways to help each other. Don't let your vocabulary be "you do it," but rather, "let me do it."

The way to greatness is through service. You will reap your reward in due season. The reward will far exceed every act of kindness you have performed.

If you could see the rewards for every act of loving kindness, you would hasten to perform acts of kindness with every opportunity — a smile, a sympathetic tear, an ear that listens to a broken heart, a word of encouragement, a cold drink on a hot day, or a hot drink on a cold day, a coin in the hand outstretched, a warm blanket for a beggar on the side of the road, a bed for the traveller, a quick response to each request, a carrying of the cross for the one about to fall under its weight. All are acts of kindness. DO THEM!

January 27

SHE KEPT CLOSE TO NAOMI

Scripture Reading — Ruth 1:1-22

"And Ruth said, Intreat me not to leave thee, or to return from following after thee: for whither thou goest, I will go; and where thou lodgest, I will lodge: thy people shall be my people, and thy God my God: Where thou diest, will I die, and there will I be buried: the Lord do so to me, and more also, if ought but death part thee and me." (Ruth 1:16,17)

It takes this kind of complete abandonment, generated by love, to be a chosen vessel unto Me. This handmaiden from Moab had very high and loyal qualifications. This is why I chose her.

I look beyond the family lineage when I choose those who shall do great things for Me. I look deeper than customs and traditional habits. I look into the heart.

With Ruth I saw a woman who, through love, had risen above the rank and file of the women of Moab. Moab was the corrupt seed. They were destined to destruction. But I chose out of that evil race a jewel and grafted her into My holy race of Israel, thus preserving a token of that race in My son Jesus and every one of His followers, for Ruth is your spiritual mother, ye descendents of Jesus, ye seed of grace.

Take upon you her qualifications of abandonment, loyalty and love. My son inherited these graces from a woman, Ruth, and another woman, Mary, as well as Rahab and many others.

You are the chosen seed of Israel's race, you are ransomed from the fall. You are an heir He has purchased to bring into His glory. My child, you are a child of Ruth by faith through the rebirth. Look at Ruth your mother, and practice these graces of love, dedication, loyalty, faithfulness, abandonment in your life and you shall be great in the Kingdom of God.

January 28

RUTH KEPT CLOSE TO THE HARVESTERS

Scripture Reading — Ruth 2:1-23

"Then said Boaz unto Ruth, Hearest thou not, my daughter? Go not to glean in another field, neither go from hence, but abide here fast by my maidens: Let thine eyes be on the field that they do reap, and go thou after them: have I not charged the young men that they shall not touch thee? and when thou art athirst, go unto the vessels, and drink of that which the young men have drawn." (Ruth 2:8,9)

"And Ruth the Moabitess said, He said unto me also, Thou shalt keep fast by my young men, until they have ended all my harvest. And Naomi said unto Ruth her daughter in law, It is good, my daughter, that thou go out with his maidens, that they meet thee not in any other field. So she kept fast by the maidens of Boaz to glean unto the end of barley harvest and of wheat harvest; and dwelt with her mother in law." (Ruth 2:21-23)

There is an allotted place for you to bring in the harvest. I have appointed to every one of My handmaidens a certain field, a certain harvest.

My child, you will many times be tempted to think that another field would be more profitable. Many of My harvesters are tempted by the evil one to leave the harvest field that I have appointed for them, and go off by themselves somewhere. They do not want to stick fast by My other maidens where there is a covering and protection. They are too proud to follow behind My maidens who have gone out ahead of them. Even though they are late-comers on the harvest field — and strangers to My calling in that they lack experience — they want to be leaders and they search for a field where they can have the whole harvest to themselves and not follow behind those who went out before them. They have forgotten My grace, that I will not let them suffer lack. I will command that there be let fall for them some handfuls on purpose so that in the end their blessing will be equal to the leaders.

Do not let greed for more, desire for independence, pride and rebellion keep you from your appointed field of harvest.

Stay close to the handmaidens who have gone out before you. After the barley harvest, there is a wheat harvest. You will always have a place to serve Me.

Be careful to stay under the covering and protection of My other handmaidens. I have commanded the young men not to hurt you, but to allow you to bring in the harvest.

Satan would seek to separate you from My handmaidens who have gone out before you and who have experience. He will accuse the handmaidens to you. But you must not let him divide you. If you are driven out and become a loner, you will suffer much and will come into great danger of your soul.

Satan is wise. He would accuse My earlier handmaidens (who have gone before you and learned his wiles) of being organized by the evil one to harm or keep you from My best. This is not true. They are not an organization unto evil, but a fellowship of companionship unto help, comfort and safety.

Don't let Satan put pride and a wrong spirit of rebellion in your heart to cause you to be separated from My handmaidens who went out before you. Stay close by My appointed and experienced handmaidens, for if you be found in any other field, it shall be dangerous for you, for you shall have gone out from under your appointed covering.

January 29

SHE STUCK CLOSE TO BOAZ

Scripture Reading – Ruth 3:1-18

"And it came to pass at midnight, that the man was afraid, and turned himself: and, behold, a woman lay at his feet. And he said, Who art thou? And she answered, I am Ruth thine handmaid: spread therefore thy skirt over thine handmaid; for thou art a near kinsman." (Ruth 3:8,9)

Ruth had the ability to cleave to the promises of God. In chapter 1:14 "Ruth **clave** unto Naomi." In chapter 2 she **stayed with the harvesters** in the fields of Boaz and refused to look to another harvest field.

If you want the best that I have for you, then you must hold fast to God's promises. You will not be able to receive your inheritance if you desire it one day and reject it another.

James, My servant said, "But let him ask in faith, nothing wavering. For he that wavereth is like a wave of the sea driven with the wind and tossed. For let not that man think that he shall receive anything of the Lord. A double minded man is unstable in all his ways." (James 1:6-8)

Instability is a character trait of many in these days. You cannot trust people unless they sign their name to a document, and even then, they haven't got the stability to be faithful. It requires faith to be faithful. This is the generation of which I said, "When I come, shall I find faith upon the earth?"

Ruth had faith in the words of Naomi. At her request she moved. She did not question the wisdom and advice of this godly older woman, who was a mother in Israel.

To cleave to a promise requires only one thing—that is, to sit still in faith until you see Me work it out for you.

She laid herself down at the feet of Boaz and waited until morning. Rest at the foot of the promise. Abide at the cross. That is where all powers of Satan were broken. That is where all the blessings of heaven were released to you. You must abide at the cross. Stay where the Lord can work it out for you. Keep your eyes on your crucified Saviour. He will work out every problem for you.

Lay yourself down at His bleeding feet. When morning begins to break you will have His promise to do to you all that you require. And you shall receive the earnest of the inheritance, even six measures.

Benjamin, the favoured son, received five portions, but My faithful handmaiden who perseveres, endures, tarries and holds on, receives six portions.

Yea, six portions were poured into her veil, the veil of her widowhood. The symbol of her sorrow was filled with the earnest of the inheritance.

Do not reject your veil of sorrow, for that is what your beloved Boaz will fill with blessings. Some have nothing with which to hold the blessing because they have rejected the sorrows of life and refuse to abide by the cross. Their life is empty. Accept your cross and cling to it. You will exchange it some day for a crown.

January 30

RAISE UP RIGHTEOUS SEED FOR YOUR BROTHER

Scripture Reading — Ruth 4:1-22

"And the kinsman said, I cannot redeem it for myself, lest I mar mine own inheritance: redeem thou my right to thyself; for I cannot redeem it. Now this was the manner in former time in Israel concerning redeeming and concerning changing, for to confirm all things; a man plucked off his shoe, and gave it to his neighbour: and this was a testimony in Israel. Therefore the kinsman said unto Boaz, Buy it for thee. So he drew off his shoe." (Ruth 4:6-8)

"Arise, walk through the land in the length of it and in the breadth of it; for I will give it unto thee." (Genesis 13:17)

"Every place that the sole of your foot shall tread upon, that have I given unto you, as I said unto Moses." (Joshua 1:3)

"If brethren dwell together, and one of them die, and have no child, the wife of the dead shall not marry without unto a stranger: her husband's brother shall go in unto her, and take her to him to wife, and perform the duty of an husband's brother unto her. And it shall be, that the firstborn which she beareth shall succeed in the name of his brother which is dead, that his name be not put out of Israel. And if the man like not to take his brother's wife, then let his brother's wife go up to the gate unto the elders, and say, My husband's brother refuseth to raise up unto his brother a name in Israel, he will not perform the duty of my husband's brother. Then the elders of his city shall call him, and speak unto him: and if he stand to it, and say, I like not to take her; Then shall his brother's wife come unto him in the presence of the elders, and loose his shoe from off his foot, and spit in his face, and shall answer and say, So shall it be done unto that man that will not build up his brother's house. And his name shall be called in Israel, The house of him that hath his shoe loosed." (Deuteronomy 25:5-10)

"I cannot redeem it for myself, lest I mar mine own inheritance." Many are so afraid of marring "their own" inheritance that they lose the inheritance which I, the Lord want to give them.

To redeem costs a price. The kinsman who rejected the inheritance of Naomi did not want to pay the price. He would gladly have inherited the land, but he did not want to pay the price that it would cost him, that is, that he had to take Ruth, My handmaiden, and raise up seed through her unto the name of another.

So many want to acquire homes and lands in their own name and build up their own kingdom and possess their own possessions, but they are not willing to sell out and make an investment for Me. They do not want to give their strength for the raising up of righteous seed in the name of their brother, Jesus.

Many only build and work for themselves and not for Me, or My name. I am that brother who died. Now you go and take My lands where I have not been and raise up seed in those nations unto Me. Take My inheritance, accept what is rightfully yours. Do not refuse it and thus lose your blessing. The woman rejected was humiliated and put to open shame before the elders. So I gave her a command for her to loose the kinsman's shoe and spit upon his face before all witnesses saying, "So shall it be done unto that man that will not build up his brother's house." (Deuteronomy 25:9)

This rejected woman is commanded by Me to put the sign of rejection on the one who rejected her.

Self-preservation has kept many from receiving the best I have for them, and they do not know that in rejecting My "Ruths" they have rejected the only inheritance that is worthwhile. This kinsman would have been an ancestor of the Messiah and his name would have been engraved in the hall of eternal fame, as the grandfather of the great King David. But he did not accept what was rightfully his because he had **his own** inheritance for which he was building, planning and working.

Do not pour out your life for **your own** inheritance. Sell out to Me. Don't reject My blessing, lest I come and loosen your shoe. Then, if your shoe is loosened how can you walk through the length and breadth of the land that I want to give you?

Many of My children have been born to inherit great blessings from Me, but they are handicapped because their shoe has been loosened when they want to do their own thing, rather than My will.

Moreover, the woman, who is a type of My true bride, the church, will spit on his face, and he must live with the mark of rejection upon him to his shame and disgrace, because he has put himself and not My will first.

Many are already spat upon and covered with shame, because they have refused to give their strength to raise up seed unto Me, the holy and rightful heir, who died for them.

Do not lose My best for you, beloved child. If you continue to build up "your own" inheritance you are losing the inheritance I want to give you — to be great in My kingdom.

How far will you go with your loosened shoe? How many will see you and mock you with spit on your face? The price you pay if you don't have My best is too great!

> I "spit" on all that's not your best;
> I hate your "spotted" feasts,
> Reject your luke-warm worshippings,
> For men have hearts like beasts.
> Come now and show true sacrifice;
> The last will not be least.

January 31

SONS OF WISDOM – SONS OF SUFFERING

Scripture Reading – Daniel 1:1-21

"As for these four children, God gave them knowledge and skill in all learning and wisdom: and Daniel had understanding in all visions and dreams." (Daniel 1:17)

"And in all matters of wisdom and understanding, that the king enquired of them, he found them ten times better than all the magicians and astrologers that were in all his realm." (Daniel 1:20)

"And Pharaoh said unto Joseph, See, I have set thee over all the land of Egypt." (Genesis 41:41)

These two servants of Mine, Daniel and Joseph, paid a price for the gift of wisdom and knowledge that I gave to them. Joseph was hated of his brothers, sold into slavery in a foreign land, held as prisoner in chains, tempted in the flesh and separated from his brothers.

Daniel was captured in the seige of Jerusalem, carried as a captive to a foreign land, kept as a slave, rendered an eunuch, tempted by the King's dainties and separated from the brethren.

Joseph knew I was the source of his wisdom (Genesis 41:16) and so did Daniel (Daniel 2:23).

Because neither of them took the credit or the praise for what I did in their lives and through their ministry, they were able to bear the burden of greatness.

Not many can bear the burden of power, honour, gifts, and greatness. It is a terrible burden. If they do not give Me the credit for all I do in their lives, then they will be destroyed by these very same things.

It is My desire for all My children to have all these things, but many are not able to bear the burden of greatness and wealth. Pride enters their hearts and they boast that they have made themselves great and wise and wealthy. They have forgotten that I said, "But thou shalt remember the Lord thy God: for it is he that giveth thee power to get wealth, that he may establish his covenant which he sware unto thy fathers, as it is this day." (Deuteronomy 8:18) Read again Deuteronomy, chapter 8.

This is your hour to be raised up into sonship and glory. I want to make you victorious and give you the fulfilment of all ages. I am preparing you for your eternal position in the heavenlies.

The Holy Spirit is working in you through hurts, rejection, pains, and suffering to prepare you to be the bride of Christ. The wedding will soon take place. You shall receive the royal crown which only the bride can wear.

Do not be overcome by your testings. Those I use to test you have been tested and have fallen from My grace. Now, look away from them and look to Me. I am preparing you to stand before Pharaohs and kings. If you do not forget the hurts, you will become hurt to the core of your heart. Accept your hurts as works of grace. You have always been able to forgive your enemies. Do it now!

February 1

GOD REVEALS SECRETS

Scripture Reading — Daniel 2:1-49

"But there is a God in heaven that revealeth secrets, and maketh known to the king Nebuchadnezzar what shall be in the latter days." (Daniel 2:28)

Yea, I am the mighty and omnipotent God. I am in full control of the universe. I have measured and divided the nations and I have ordained their rulers. None can be in offices of power except by My permission. Each one has his allotted time.

I speak to whom I will. I could have bypassed Nebuchadnezzar and given this dream to Daniel, but I wanted the king to be shaken to the depths of his soul, so I gave it to him. He had great riches and great power. He was this head of gold. After him came other kingdoms and America is the end-time nation of mixed clay and iron — a mingling of many nations which cannot endure because there is corruption in its heart. It is the weakest of all.

But the time has come when the Stone is being cut out of the Mount of God which shall destroy these kingdoms, grind them to powder, and the wind of the Holy Spirit shall blow them away.

I am the revealer of all secrets of the darkness because light is in Me. I am light. You also are lights in the world. Let the light in you reveal to you the secrets of the deep and the secrets of the darkness, so that you will not be ignorant concerning all these things. As you abide in Me I will reveal to you the hidden secrets of the hearts of men. None shall be able to deceive you.

February 2

HE IS WITH YOU IN THE FIRE

Scripture Reading — Daniel 3:1-30

"Nebuchadnezzar spake and said unto them, Is it true, O Shadrach, Meshach, and Abednego, do not ye serve my gods, nor worship the golden image which I have set up? Now if ye be ready that at what time ye hear the sound of the cornet, flute, harp, sackbut, psaltery, and dulcimer, and all kinds of musick, ye fall down and worship the image which I have made; well: but if ye worship not, ye shall be cast the same hour into the midst of a burning fiery furnace; and who is that God that shall deliver you out of my hands?" (Daniel 3:14,15)

Every self-centred person who sets himself up as a "golden image" wants to control people and force them to live according to his rules and his laws. "Serve MY gods! Worship MY image! Fall down before MY image which I have made! Who can deliver you out of MY hands!" Self-centred religion is idolatry. It has a controlling spirit and seeks to control the lives of others by threats and revenge on all who refuse to be intimidated.

"Shadrach, Meshach, and Abednego, answered and said to the king, O Nebuchadnezzar, we are not careful to answer thee in this matter. If it be so, our God whom we serve is able to deliver us from the burning fiery furnace, and he will deliver us out of thine hand, O king. But if not, be it known unto thee, O king, that we will not serve thy gods, nor worship the golden image which thou hast set up." (Daniel 3:16-18)

My child, don't be afraid to stand against these religious demon spirits of self-righteousness. Don't bow down to the self-image of gold for one minute. Recognize money for what it is — it has the image of the one who created it. You cannot bow before any man-created god, nor can you give any place to it for one hour.

"Then was Nebuchadnezzar full of fury, and the form of his visage was changed against Shadrach, Meshach, and Abednego: therefore he spake, and commanded that they should heat the furnace one seven times more than it was wont to be heated. And he commanded the most mighty men that were in his army to bind Shadrach, Meshach, and Abednego, and to cast them into the burning fiery furnace. Then these men were bound in their coats, their hosen, and their hats, and their other garments, and were cast into the midst of the burning fiery furnace." (vs. 19-21)

There is no fury like the fury of a religious spirit when it has lost its power to intimidate and control either by threats or so-called prophecies. You will soon see the "faces" change and reveal the hidden anger and hatred if you stand up against them.

Do not make friends with the spirit of Nebuchadnezzar which stoneth the prophet. For tomorrow they will turn on you when they have finished using you to their advantage and they will throw you in a fiery furnace. So angry is the religious spirit that its fury is seven times greater than that of any other demon spirit.

"Therefore because the king's commandment was urgent, and the furnace exceeding hot, the flame of the fire slew those men that took up Shadrach, Meshach, and Abednego." (vs. 22) But the very heat of their fury will slay them and the "strong men" they use to try to destroy you. If anyone becomes even an innocent agent to destroy a righteous, anointed prophet, that one will also be destroyed. Stay away from Nebuchadnezzar's revenge and fury. Have nothing to do with his evil ways.

"...Lo, I see four men loose, walking in the midst of the fire, and they have no hurt; and the form of the fourth is like the Son of God. Then Nebuchadnezzar came near to the mouth of the burning fiery furnace, and spake, and said, Shadrach, Meshach, and Abednego, ye servants of the most high God, come forth, and come hither. Then Shadrach, Meshach, and Abednego, came forth of the midst of the fire. (vs. 25-26)

Yes, you will come out of the furnace of revenge. Because I will enter the furnace with you. I will walk with you in the fire. I stand with the accused, not the accuser. I will only burn off the bondages man put on you. I will set you free from all man's controlling, hindering chains. The fire they make in their fury has no power to hurt you. Nor will the stench of their smoke even remain with you.

I will send My angel to "change your body" so that the evil accusers cannot harm or destroy you in any way. Rather there shall be glory and praise and honour to My true servant who worships Me in spirit and in truth.

February 3

THE WATCHERS ARE WATCHING

Scripture Reading — Daniel 4:1-37

"I saw in the visions of my head upon my bed, and, behold, a watcher and an holy one came down from heaven;" (Daniel 4:13)

There are many "watchers." These "watchers" are the same investigating angels who went down to spy out Sodom and Gomorrah and gave Me a report on it. They investigate nations, cities and individual persons. They also investigate communities. They see all things. Nothing happens at any time, day or night, which they do not know about. They see all the acts, hear all the words spoken, and feel all the vibrations. They know what thoughts you are thinking now. They are heaven's secret police and security system. If you live right, they are your friends and work for you. If not, they are your most deadly adversaries and enemies.

"And whereas the king saw a watcher and an holy one coming down from heaven, and saying, Hew the tree down, and destroy it; yet leave the stump of the roots thereof in the earth, even with a band of iron and brass, in the tender grass of the field; and let it be wet with the dew of heaven, and let his portion be with the beasts of the field, till seven times pass over him." (vs. 23)

Not only do they see and know all things, both good and evil, they are able to pass righteous judgment on all situations at all times. They hew down the mightiest trees, determine the length of sentence and change the hard heart of a human into the heart of a beast.

Nebuchadnezzar's diet was changed from kingly, royal, scrumptious feasting to grass just because his heart changed. You eat what your heart longs for. If your heart is pure you will eat My flesh and drink My blood. But if your heart is a beast's heart you will eat what beasts eat. And you will become like a beast.

"Wherefore, O king, let my counsel be acceptable unto thee, and break off thy sins by righteousness, and thine iniquities by shewing mercy to the poor; if it may be a lengthening of thy tranquillity." (vs. 27)

Even in the most evil and wicked cases I give opportunity for the transgressor to repent. If he will break off sinning by righteousness, and by showing mercy to the poor, I can and will stay the judgment. Even wicked sinners who do good deeds and show mercy to the poor often escape great judgment in this life. They are given mercy because their good deeds outweigh their evil. The smallest good deed will outweigh great sin. When the watchers pass judgment they take into account all these things.

"At the end of twelve months he walked in the palace of the kingdom of Babylon. The king spake, and said, Is not this great Babylon, that I have built for the house of the kingdom by the might of my power, and for the honour of my majesty? While the word was in the king's mouth, there fell a voice from heaven, saying, O king Nebuchadnezzar, to thee it is spoken; The kingdom is departed from thee." (vs. 29-31)

The greatest evil of king Nebuchadnezzar, the thing that finally brought My wrath upon him was his proud, boastful spirit. "Is not this great Babylon, that I have built for the house of the kingdom by the might of my power, and for the honour of my majesty?" (vs. 30) He took the credit and the praise for all I had given him. He did not acknowledge that it was I who had raised him up and given him all this great empire of Babylon, which reached from the river Euphrates to Egypt.

"While the word was in the king's mouth, there fell a voice from heaven, saying, O king Nebuchadnezzar, to thee it is spoken; The kingdom is departed from thee." (vs. 31) The watchers passed the sentence and in that hour it was fulfilled. Even as he spoke those words of boasting and bragging and did not acknowledge Me, his heart began to change, his mind became that of a beast and his posture became that of a beast as he began to walk on all fours and not upright as a man.

For seven years he existed out in the wilds roaring like a beast because his speech and reasoning was taken from him. He even desired to co-habit with other beasts, for he lusted with the lust of a beast. He thought himself an ox and lived with the oxen. He defecated like an ox and could not be kept in a house. His hair became mangled and like eagles' feathers for length, and his nails like eagles' claws.

For seven years he was an ox in his heart. He had heated the fire seven times hotter for My children to pass through and his judgment was for seven years.

"And at the end of the days I Nebuchadnezzar lifted up mine eyes unto heaven, and mine understanding returned unto me, and I blessed the most High, and I praised and honoured him that liveth for ever, whose dominion is an everlasting dominion, and his kingdom is from generation to generation: And all the inhabitants of the earth are reputed as nothing: and he doeth according to his will in the army of heaven, and among the inhabitants of the earth: and none can stay his hand, or say unto him, What doest thou? At the same time my reason returned unto me; and for the glory of my kingdom, mine honour and brightness returned unto me; and my counsellors and my lords sought unto me; and I was established in my kingdom, and excellent majesty was added unto me. Now I Nebuchadnezzar praise and extol and honour the King of heaven, all whose works are truth, and his ways judgment: and those that walk in pride he is able to abase." (vs. 34-37)

I gave him an opportunity to repent, I gave him a mind. When his eyes were lifted towards heaven, his reasoning returned to him. He gave glory to Me. I restored his kingdom with its glory, honour and brightness.

Look to heaven. Keep your eyes on God above. Give Me alone the glory for all I have done for you and great will be your restoration. For the watchers are watching you.

February 4

WHEN GOD FINISHES IT, IT IS FINISHED

Scripture Reading – Daniel 5:1-31

"In the same hour came forth fingers of a man's hand, and wrote over against the candlestick upon the plaister of the wall of the king's palace: and the king saw the part of the hand that wrote." (Daniel 5:5)

Belshazzar inherited a mighty kingdom which he had not fought for. He inherited power, wealth and glory, but not honour. One can never, ever inherit honour. One must earn honour by what one is on the inside.

Too much was given to this spoiled son of a king. He had come into too great power too early. He was a playboy, his life was one of debauchery and reckless living.

Never be reckless and indifferent with the talents, gifts and callings God has given you. Do not waste the opportunity to do good and to serve Him.

Belshazzar knew the great and terrible experiences of his grandfather, Nebuchadnezzar, but he did not know Me. It is not enough for your parents and grandparents to know Me. You need to know Me yourself. I will hold each one responsible for the testimony and witness which their parents have given to them.

Belshazzar knew how the pride of Nebuchadnezzar had brought My judgment on him, yet Belshazzar refused to walk in humility and reverence. He borrowed the sacred and holy, dedicated vessels and used them in a common way. This was his final act of pride and mockery to Me. It is the same sin as mocking My dedicated vessels who are My children today. When he held in his hand My holy vessels and praised the demon spirits that were represented by gold, silver, brass, iron, wood and stone, his cup of iniquity was running over. My watcher began to write on the wall. The same watcher who had watched Nebuchadnezzar and had judged him, was now watching Belshazzar and judging him and his kingdom.

"And this is the writing that was written, MENE, MENE, TEKEL, UPHARSIN. This is the interpretation of the thing: MENE; God hath numbered thy kingdom, and finished it." (vs. 25, 26)

It was with great courage and bravery that My servant, Daniel, stood before this heathen king and told him the truth. But it was made easier because he knew that I, the Lord, gave him every word and that Belshazzar was finished as a king. His power had been taken from him, his kingdom had come to an end. When I have numbered anyone's days of usefulness and finished them, they are finished. You never need to fear anyone whose kingdom is finished.

"TEKEL; Thou art weighed in the balances, and art found wanting." (vs. 27) Not only was his kingdom finished (the greatest on earth), but he himself was found wanting. There was not enough good in him for Me to spare him any longer. If anyone does not fulfil his calling, I put that one on the side and call another to take his place.

"PERES; Thy kingdom is divided, and given to the Medes and Persians." (vs. 28) What Daniel said was absolute treason and he could have died for it, but the king rewarded him for the truth because of the hopeless fear and condemnation of his heart. That night he was killed in his bed by conspirators and his kingdom was handed over to King Darius of the Medes and Persians. When I have finished a thing, then it is finished. When I have taken away a man's position, power and office, he has lost it forever. I never anoint two for the same position at one time.

February 5

THE WATCHERS WATCHED DANIEL

Scripture Reading — Daniel 6:1-28

"And when he came to the den, he cried with a lamentable voice unto Daniel: and the king spake and said to Daniel, O Daniel, servant of the living God, is thy God, whom thou servest continually, able to deliver thee from the lions? Then said Daniel unto the king, O king, live for ever. My God hath sent his angel, and hath shut the lions' mouths, that they have not hurt me: forasmuch as before him innocency was found in me; and also before thee, O king, have I done no hurt. Then was the king exceeding glad for him, and commanded that they should take Daniel up out of the den. So Daniel was taken up out of the den, and no manner of hurt was found upon him, because he believed in his God." (Daniel 6:20-23)

Daniel knew that the only way that the mouths of those hungry lions could be stopped was that a mighty angel would enter the den and take dominion over them.

Yes, the "watchers" had been watching Daniel. They had also

watched his jealous and evil enemies who had conspired to destroy him. But when they brought the evil charges against him, the angels who were watching, saw Daniel being watched by his enemies. Your God is always spying on those who are spying on you.

If you live right, you never need fear the watchers. They will be watching out for you and will accompany you in all places and situations.

When Daniel was thrown into the lion's den, the watcher went into the den with him, and in his mighty presence, the lions passed the night in the Kingdom age when the spirit of the lion shall be changed, and he shall lie down with the lamb and he shall eat only grass. The lions had no appetite for flesh in the hours of that night.

Daniel's faith in Me made him perfect before the heavenly witnesses and all of creation. No manner of hurt was found on him. He came out as he went in — flawless before Me.

Pay no heed to your accusers. Only live so that the watchers are on your side. Read Psalm 57.

February 6

WHEN THE BOOKS ARE OPENED, THE SAINTS ARE CHOSEN

Scripture Reading — Daniel 7:1-28

"I beheld till the thrones were cast down, and the Ancient of days did sit, whose garment was white as snow, and the hair of his head like the pure wool: his throne was like the fiery flame, and his wheels as burning fire....And the kingdom and dominion, and the greatness of the kingdom under the whole heaven, shall be given to the people of the saints of the most High, whose kingdom is an everlasting kingdom, and all dominions shall serve and obey him." (vs. 9, 27)

Daniel was given a peek into the future. He saw only the most powerful empires of the times of the Gentiles. Nebuchadnezzar saw until the Roman Empire fell. But Daniel saw into this hour, and the winding up of all things. Both saw the last world power, the world government under the control of a devastating and evil influence which shall last only a short while (3½ years — vs. 25) and shall then be handed over to the Almighty God, the Ancient of Days, for the great judgment. The books shall be opened. All records revealed full and final punishment from which none shall escape.

Jesus Christ, the Son of man, shall be given dominion and power over all people, nations and languages, forever and ever. The saints of the most high God who have suffered from the evil one shall take the kingdom out of the power of the evil one and they shall possess it in the name of the Almighty forever. They will co-operate with the Son of man and rule the Kingdom according to His Governorship. They will be under His command.

My child, I am now training you for this great day. Satan knows that you will be given great power and authority to rule under My Command. He hates you because he sees what you are being trained for. He is making war on the saints now and he is prevailing against them. Few have been able to conquer him or defeat him. He has defeated small and great, man and woman.

But there is a holy company, ruled by love, under the control of My Holy Spirit whom Satan has not defeated. Their spirits are clean, their motives true, their hearts pure. To them shall be given authority to rule, under My command, all people, nations and languages (races, nations and tribes). They shall be a pure race, who have come through the fire and have overcome the evil nature.

This holy company will be revealed when the books are opened. Every act which the watchers have seen is recorded in these books. They are those who hate sin and wickedness. They are obedient to My every command. They have been trained in the fires of suffering, they are humble and submissive to Me. They are chosen by the watchers. They love the nations over which they shall rule and will be given Divine appointment over the nations like Joseph and Daniel were.

The time is very close. Do not let Satan wear you out, lest you lose your heavenly, eternal destiny. You have an appointment to rule. Don't miss it My child! If you pay the price you will end in victory!

> I'm choosing now My army
> From among the ranks of men
> Who've come through sword and fire
> And served Me till the end.

February 7

FAINTING AT THE DARK TRIBULATION AHEAD

Scripture Reading — Daniel 8:1-27

"And I Daniel fainted, and was sick certain days; afterward I rose up, and did the king's business; and I was astonished at the vision, but none understood it." (Daniel 8:27)

Daniel saw into two different periods of time, one which has been fulfilled in the Mede and Persian and Greek dynasties, and another which has been, and is being fulfilled in the greatness of the British Empire and its extension, the United States of America (the ram and the he goat).

He saw something else which made him sick, something which pertains to the end-time. "Out of one of them (Mede and Persia) came forth a little horn (power), which waxed exceeding great." This is out of what is now Iran. The "little horn" is an evil one who rises up in the anti-Christ demonic spirit from Iran. Out of nothing he becomes exceeding great. "Towards the south" indicates he is supported by the southern area of Iran (where the oil wells are) and "from the east" also indicates the Middle East where the oil is. He turns against Israel, the pleasant land.

"And it waxed great, even to the host of heaven." (vs. 10) He will continue to destroy and defeat other leaders and kings. The Shah is one, but will not be the last. He will go further east and more shall fall. Sadat fell before his evil power.

"Yea, he magnified himself even to the prince of the host, and by him the daily sacrifice was taken away, and the place of his sanctuary was cast down. And an host was given him against the daily sacrifice by reason of transgression, and it cast down the truth to the ground; and it practised, and prospered. Then I heard one saint speaking, and another saint said unto that certain saint which spake, How long shall be the vision concerning the daily sacrifice, and the transgression of desolation, to give both the sanctuary and the host to be trodden under foot? And he said unto me, Unto two thousand and three hundred days; then shall the sanctuary be cleansed." (vs. 11-14)

This is the abomination of desolation which has taken control of the holy place, the site of the temple. It has been there since Mohammed conquered Jerusalem in the year A.D. 637 and the first wooden mosque was built on the site in A.D. 644. Satan has long desired to possess this site because he knows that it is My chosen place where Abraham prepared to offer Isaac and where Solomon built the temple. Even as Lucifer is prince of the world, he is squatting on My most holy site.

Daniel saw this in the vision. He knew the importance of this place. This is what made him sick in his soul. He saw the place of the holy sanctuary trodden under foot for a long time — 2300 days. Satan's time is long, but it is limited.

Gabriel is qualified to explain the whole thing because Mohammed said Gabriel gave him the Koran. (vs. 16) He explains to Daniel that this vision is for the end-time. (vs. 17-19)

"And in the latter time of their kingdom, when the transgressors are come to the full, a king of fierce countenance, and understanding dark sentences, shall stand up." (vs. 23) He has already stood up. He is fierce of countenance. Hebrew for "fierce" is *az*, meaning "strong, impudent, rebellious, greedy." Dark is *chiydah* in Hebrew which means "puzzles, tricks, intrigue, occult, fortune telling." He works through the power of witchcraft and satanic darkness.

"And his power shall be mighty, but not by his own power: and he shall destroy wonderfully, and shall prosper, and practise, and shall destroy the mighty and the holy people." (vs. 24) Many, throughout the world shall come under the control of his great power. He shall corrupt through the power of oil in a world-wide sphere. He shall prosper through the wealth of oil. The prince of darkness and deception who rivals for power with the Prince of Light (Jesus Christ) is the demon prince of Allah and his prophet is Mohammed. Allah is not Me, the Lord God Jehovah. My name is not Allah. I have given My names to My prophets and patriarchs. I never gave the name of Allah. Allah will destroy the mighty in the world; even great nations shall bow to his power through oil. Russia too will tremble before the spirit of Allah and his oil power. The holy people, natural and spiritual Israel, are his deadly enemies and the Moslem spirit will turn on them to try to destroy them, hating with a vengeance both Israel and all Christian nations.

"And through his policy also he shall cause craft to prosper in his hand; and he shall magnify himself in his heart, and by peace shall destroy many: he shall also stand up against the Prince of princes; but he shall be broken without hand." (vs. 25) When he is at his height of power and evil, I Myself will cut him off. Only I will be able to destroy him, for he will have trampled the whole world under his feet through his powers of oil, wealth and satanic witchcraft and sorcery.

"And the vision of the evening and the morning which was told is true: wherefore shut thou up the vision; for it shall be for many days." (vs. 26) This vision has been shut up for the end-time, waiting for the revival of Moslemism. It is now coming into fulfilment. May all saints understand it and beware!

February 8

UNDERSTAND AND SET YOUR FACE

Scripture Reading — Daniel 9:1-27

"In the first year of his reign I Daniel understood by books the number of years, whereof the word of the Lord came to Jeremiah the prophet, that he would accomplish seventy years in the desolations of Jerusalem. And I set my face unto the Lord God, to seek by prayer and supplications, with fasting, and sackcloth, and ashes:" (vs. 2,3)

It is time that My children search out My Word and understand prophecy. The secret concerning My plans for the future is hidden in My Word, but very few understand.

Daniel prepared his heart to hear My instruction by prayer, travail, fasting, humility and confession of sins, not only his sins, but the sins of his people. (vs. 3-6)

Daniel set his face unto Me. This is the secret of praying through. You must learn and know how to pray through. You cannot get anything if you do not set your face. It is the same as when the pilot of the plane sets the auto-pilot in the exact direction of where he is going.

There will be many interferences and distractions that Satan will use to try to keep you from your goal, but as you fast, you will be able to overcome many of these hindrances and you will see in the Spirit the true reason behind all things.

Fasting helps you to see in the Spirit, to make true confession of all sins, not only your own, but those of others also. You will find others in the Spirit, and when you do, you will not only see their weakness, but why they are weak. You will be able to make true confession for them. Without honest confession, there can be no dealing with the sins, and no Divine help from Me.

You must rise above the weakness of others. A true intercessor does not take delight in Me judging another for his sins.

A true intercessor pleads to Me for mercy towards the cruel, and seeks to show Me why the guilty one should not be judged. He tries to gain My forgiveness, not by hiding the transgressor's sins, but by standing before Me in proxy (in place of the sinner), like My Son Jesus died in proxy for the transgressor.

This is the true intercessor, who can move heaven and earth.
1. Know My will by the study of My Word (vs. 2).
2. Set your face toward heaven (your goal).
3. Pray and intercede.
4. Fast.
5. Walk in humility.
6. Make your confessions (vs. 4-15).
7. Plead for mercy (vs. 16-19).

Daniel prayed through. The mighty archangel Gabriel immediately responded, and not only did he get what he asked for, but much more. He was told he was greatly beloved and given understanding concerning the times. This is your true key to greatness.

February 9

FAST FOR MY CHOSEN VESSELS

Scripture Reading — Daniel 10:1-21

"...Cyrus, He is my shepherd, and shall perform all my pleasure: even saying to Jerusalem, Thou shalt be built; and to the temple, Thy foundation shall be laid." (Isaiah 44:28)

Cyrus was My special, chosen vessel. 176 years earlier My prophet Isaiah had foretold his mission, which was to open the doors of bondage, and let My people return to their land. He stood against the powerful demon spirits of Persia. I stirred up his soul (II Chronicles 36:22-23) and I used My servant Ezra, My scribe, who went up from Babylon to Jerusalem in answer to God's call, to teach God's Word to the people who returned. (Ezra 7:6,10)

But all these wonderful things could not have happened if Daniel had not fasted and prayed through. Daniel knew, from Jeremiah 25:11,12, that the time of captivity was 70 years. But he also knew that the time was now up and there was no sign of the Jews returning, and he began a "Daniel fast" for 21 days.

The heavenly messenger from glory appeared. He spoke to Daniel and told him he had come from the time Daniel had started fasting, but he had wrestled with the prince of the Kingdom of Persia for 21 days. This is the prince of darkness who rules over the Persian empire and who has been revived in these last days in the spirit of fanatical Islam.

Michael, the great archangel who is the prince of Israel, came and helped this heavenly messenger to fight against this dark prince for 21 days.

When you fast, you are at war against strong demon spirits who have ruled over you in your past life. At that time mighty angels come down and begin warfare against these demons on your behalf because the warfare is in the heavenlies.

For we wrestle not against flesh and blood, but against principalities, against powers, against the rulers of the darkness of this world, against spiritual wickedness in high places. (Ephesians 6:12)

The messenger strengthened Daniel and spoke to him, telling him that this vision (chapter 8), which had completely devastated Daniel, was for the latter days.

Then the messenger returned to fight with the prince of Persia, with the aid of Prince Michael.

When you fast, you send the armies of heaven into spiritual warfare. Strong demons are made powerless. If My people knew the power of fasting, they would fast much, much more than they do.

February 10

STRONG TO DO EXPLOITS

Scripture Reading — Daniel 11:1-45

"...but the people that do know their God shall be strong, and do exploits." (Daniel 11:32)

There will not be many strong people in those days of war, treachery, conspiracy and intrigue. It will take a very special person to stand up against the godless confusion, rebellion, anarchy, and warring spirit that prevails all through this chapter. The angel was speaking to Daniel all about wars and rumours of wars. This prophecy is about the time of the Gentiles, their destruction of the holy land, their coming and going until the end-time when the anti-Christ will arise, who will have only one desire and one love, and that is the god of armament. He will live to make wars.

In the midst of all this warfare, the falling of nation after nation, I will have a strong people who will do mighty works in My name because they know Me. (vs. 32)

They shall help and instruct many and they shall lay down their lives for Me. There will be many martyrs. (vs. 33)

Many will fail Me and then be restored. This will humble them so that they will know that they are what they are by the grace of God alone. (vs. 35)

February 11

ARCHANGEL MICHAEL SHALL DEFEND YOU

Scripture Reading — Daniel 12:1-13

"And at that time shall Michael stand up, the great prince which standeth for the children of thy people: and there shall be a time of trouble, such as never was since there was a nation even to that same time: and at that time thy people shall be delivered, every one that shall be found written in the book. And many of them that sleep in the dust of the earth shall awake, some to everlasting life, and some to shame and everlasting contempt." (Daniel 12:1,2)

This is that day in which the mighty Prince Michael has stood up to call together Daniel's people and to defend them. These are great and important days. My children, know the hour in which you are living.

These are days of trouble such as never was since there was a nation. There is strife and turmoil everywhere. The evil one is constantly working through those who are weak in faith or who have prejudices and bitterness, to stir up and create negative and quarrelsome situations.

My children, I call you to love, not to warfare. Everyone has a record of his life. Your life is being recorded by the recording angel. Both good and evil is faithfully recorded. On the day of judgment all deeds will be read out. If the record is one that is pure and under My Blood, you shall enter into the blessings of the Lord; if not, there shall be terrible shame and everlasting contempt.

Michael, My prince, is even now active in preparing the stage for this final judgment. As he defends Israel, he will defend you when you are Israel's friend. Behold, there are strong demons who hate Israel with a satanic hatred. All who love Israel are hated by these demons. All who minister to Israel are attacked by these demons. But Michael defends those who minister to Israel. He has many angels under his command. They will work with him for you.

The time of the great resurrection is very close. Keep your records pure by living a holy life, for the names of the righteous and the unrighteous shall all be called to stand before Me. It is a very serious hour. It is an hour to stand with My people, lest you be judged.

February 12

GRACE FOR GRACE

Scripture Reading — John 1:1-51

"And of his fulness have all we received, and grace for grace." (John 1:16)

My child, even when there is no more mercy, when mercy has expired, there is grace, that mysterious extension of My great love.

Without My grace all of mankind would be lost. Grace was manifest in My Son, Jesus. Law came through Moses, Moses represents the ruling authority of man. Moses received the laws from Me. But I make the law and can also make by-laws and amendments.

Jesus came to become the amendment of the law. He came to substitute grace for justice and judgment. He is the overflow of My love and mercy when you didn't deserve it any more. When you were worthy of the whip of punishment, He came and bared His back, receiving the stripes of My anger through the hand of the Romans who represented the laws and justice of the land.

He came to teach you truth, the truth that "as you have received grace, you must give grace." You now live by this new law of absolute truth that only through giving grace can you receive grace. Grace for grace, go and give grace!

February 13

KEEP YOUR MOTIVES PURE

Scripture Reading — John 2:1-25

"And said unto them that sold doves, Take these things hence; make not my Father's house an house of merchandise." (John 2:16)

My child, there are so many who are employed in My house who are not truly dedicated to Me. They are dedicated to the ministry, but that is not the true purpose. They are dedicated to the temple, and this is wrong also. These are false visions. They will lead you to concentrate on the wrong need. They will burden you with the need of finances and the need of finances will cause you to put the emphasis and the pressure and the prayers on the wrong thing.

I want to purify My house of all these things which are drawing your attentions away from the real goal.

Too many ministers turn to business ventures because My people lose the source of supply, which is the anointing, and hence they need to resort to natural resources.

There is a higher source of supply. Tap into that. It is prayer.

Dig a hole in the heart of the greedy man by prayer and you will strike an oil well that will release an unexpected supply.

February 14

HE HAS FREELY GIVEN YOU ALL THINGS

Scripture Reading — John 3:1-36

"For he whom God hath sent speaketh the words of God: for God giveth not the Spirit by measure unto him. The Father loveth the Son, and hath given all things into his hand." (John 3:34,35) Also read John 14:12,13.

My child, you are as precious to Me as My Son, because Jesus has loved you and chosen you and given you into My hands. You are precious to Me because you are precious to Him. He died for you. He paid for you with the greatest treasure of heaven, His very own, precious blood, even His very life.

I have taken of the Spirit which is in My Son and I have put it upon you, even as I did with Moses. (Numbers 11:25) The same Holy Spirit that rested on Him rests on you. You remember that, when the Spirit of Moses fell on the elders of Israel, it affected their speech. They began to prophesy. So with you, My children, it will put holy words in your mouth and you will prophesy. As I gave of the Spirit of Moses to the elders, I also gave of My fulness to My Son. Today you stand in His place, crying out to mankind on My behalf. I will give you of the same great measure of love and power. Yes, I give you not only words, but I put all things into your hands, even the understanding of heaven.

February 15

DOING HIS WILL IS THE SOURCE OF YOUR LIFE

Scripture Reading — John 4:1-54

"Jesus saith unto them, My meat is to do the will of him that sent me, and to finish his work." (John 4:34)

My child, you must always be careful to keep your priorities straight. Many of My servants are overworked simply because they are occupied with doing many things which I have not asked them to do. They become involved with "garbage." I call you not only to do, but to lead. As a leader, your responsibilities are very great. As different as My Son was to Peter or John or James, so much must you be different to those whom you lead. Do not expect the same of them as you know you must give to Me. It would be good for them to give to Me all, even as you give, but it is not in them yet.

Should I remove you and call another to take your place, I would demand of them what I demand of you. Do not judge others in their liberty.

Your "meat" is your life's strength. It is the thing which sustains you. As you do My will, you are sustained. Otherwise, you will die. Without natural "meat" a body deteriorates and dies in two months time. Even so, spiritually, if you do not do My will, you will soon die spiritually. The shell is nothing without the life in it. You must finish My work which I gave you to do.

February 16

BETHESDA, HOUSE OF MERCY, WATERS OF HEALING

Scripture Reading — John 5:1-18

"For an angel went down at a certain season into the pool, and troubled the water: whosoever then first after the troubling of the water stepped in was made whole of whatsoever disease he had." (John 5:4)

This was no superstition. I truly did send My angel down to Bethesda's pool from time to time. Had not this pool been built for just such a reason, to show My mercy to the sinner?

Today I still perform miracles of healing upon the impotent folk, the blind, halt, and withered by the waters of healing.

Some waited years in hope and faith that they would receive the miracle of healing. It was not a great multitude who were healed at one time, but only one case, now and then. Even, when I Myself walked to the pool that day, I the great Creator healed only that one man. I could have healed all, but I healed only that one, because he had no one to help him, no one to pick him up into the healing water.

I love to heal the one who is a hopeless case. I love to save the chiefest of sinners. I love to supply the need of the one who has no means of support in the natural, I love to use the one who is the most rejected, I love to take the weak things of the world to confound those who are mighty in their own eyes. That is why I love to use you!

February 17

TO DO THE WILL OF HIM WHO SENT YOU

Scripture Reading — John 6:22-45

"For I came down from heaven, not to do mine own will, but the will of him that sent me." (John 6:38)

You have no other reason for living. You are here on the earth, in My place, for only one purpose, and that is to do the will of the Father.

The difference between My followers and My disciples is that My disciples will study Me and imitate Me in all My arts and all My character.

For this reason, the Holy Spirit was given to you, that you may have the power from on high to become, not only an imitator, but also a very Christ-child.

But you must lay aside your own will, your own personal ambition, your own understanding. You must put on the mind of Christ, so that you can have the fruit of Christ in your life.

It is the Father who has called you to come to Me. It is the Father who shall teach you (vs. 45). All things shall be revealed to the Christ-ones.

But you must eat My bread, which is to do the will of the Father. My meat is to do My Father's will. Only as you do the Father's will can you exist. For obedience is the bread of heaven and you have no other reason for living.

When you do My will, your spirit is made strong, My words to you are your spirit and your life.

Eat My words (by obedience) so that your spirit may live forever and your life be everlasting.

February 18

YOU CAN'T FOLLOW THE CROWD

Scripture Reading — John 7:1-24

"But when his brethren were gone up, then went he also up unto the feast, not openly, but as it were in secret....Now about the midst of the feast Jesus went up into the temple, and taught." (John 7:10,14)

"He that speaketh of himself seeketh his own glory: but he that seeketh his glory that sent him, the same is true, and no unrighteousness is in him." (John 7:18)

I did not go up to Jerusalem for the first day of the Feast of Tabernacles. I waited until the crowd had gathered. And then I went to Jerusalem, for I was not one of the crowd. I came with a separate mission and a pure message. I came, not because it was "the thing to do" according to custom and tradition, but because My Father commissioned Me. And I let My brethren, who were not a part of My ministry and did not believe in My calling or My vision or My purpose in life, go up by themselves with the crowd. They followed the crowd to the Feast of Tabernacles in Jerusalem, like many will today. But those who were My disciples and who know the Father came up with Me to Jerusalem when I went, not as a part of the crowd, but as a "sent one" with a message.

Had I gone with the crowd, I would have been just one of the crowd, but going alone, I went as a "sent one" to the crowd.

I did not identify with the crowd because I had a message from heaven. My doctrine was not Mine. It did not originate with man. It was the message of the ONE who sent Me to Jerusalem. Not all could receive My message. Only those who did the will of the Father, whose hearts were opened by love and purity, could receive My Father's message. I did not go to Jerusalem for My own glory. I went because the Father sent Me. It was not My own message that I brought to Jerusalem. It was My Father's message. It was His glory that I sought. I only wanted to bring glory to His name.

If you will have this same, pure motive, to only bring glory to the Father, then you will be doing the Father's will and there will be no unrighteousness in you.

Not all who go up to Jerusalem to worship Me have a pure motive. Many go to see the crowd, to be seen of man, to promote their own ministry. This is all unrighteousness and the works of man.

Stand aside from the crowd, My child. You cannot mingle with the seed of man and still have a pure message from the Father.

February 19

GOD DOESN'T LISTEN TO YOUR ACCUSERS

Scripture Reading – John 8:1-11

"...But Jesus stooped down, and with his finger wrote on the ground, as though he heard them not." (John 8:6)

I never listen to accusations that any man brings Me. Neither do I regard them or am influenced by them. Satan has accused you to Me many times. He is the accuser of the brethren.

When I beheld the camp of Israel, I saw only the beauty of their dwellings. (Numbers 24:5) I did not even allow Balaam to see the mistakes of Israel or her shortcomings.

David, My servant, had My Spirit in him when he said, "Tell it not in Gath, publish it not in the streets of Askelon; lest the daughters of the Philistines rejoice, lest the daughters of the uncircumcised triumph." (II Samuel 1:20)

Women have always loved to gossip. Even My daughters have this weakness, but only because their lips speak from an uncircumcised heart. "For out of the abundance of the heart, the mouth speaketh." (Matthew 12:34b)

Let them accuse you. Let them "report" to Me your faults.

These poor, uncircumcised in heart have forgotten that I have covered all your sins with My blood.

They have also forgotten their own sins. By condemning you, they uncover their own sins before My eyes.

These same accusers, who accused this poor lost daughter of Israel and who wanted Me to accuse her, later picked up stones to stone Me. (John 8:59)

The spirit of killing is in the one who accuses you. Today they would stone you, tomorrow they would stone Me. Because they are not My true children. Neither is the God of love their father. If God were their Father, they would love you. (John 8:42) I have no need that anyone should testify against anyone to Me. I know what is in man. (John 2:25)

Do not bring to Me any accusations about any man. Let the Holy Spirit travail through you with intercession in His language, for He knows what is in the depths of man's heart and He does not judge. He only pleads; His prayer is pure and I will answer.

If you bring Me your accusations, I will not hear them. But you will only uncover your own sins and you will not be able to stand before Me.

The place you thought would become another's judgment seat shall become your own.

Daughter of Zion, let Me handle your case. I am still writing today, and I know every man's record.

February 20

GOD'S WORKS MANIFEST IN YOU

Scripture Reading – John 9:1-41

"Jesus answered, Neither hath this man sinned, nor his parents: but that the works of God should be made manifest in him." (John 9:3)

I knew this young man. I had compassion on him, not only

because he was blind, but because I knew his beautiful, strong and courageous character. He had a character even stronger than his parents. They cowered before the Pharisees and feared them greatly, but this son of Israel was fearless before the Pharisees who interrogated him.

He even mocked them, "I have told you already, and ye did not hear: wherefore would ye hear it again? will ye also be his disciples?" (vs. 27).

They interrogated him like tormentors do My followers today. But he stood firm in the same way that they do.

They used the same tactics. They attached Me to him. They called Me, "this fellow of no repute." But the young man tried to reason with them. "Why herein is a marvellous thing, that ye know not from whence he is, and yet he hath opened mine eyes. Now we know that God heareth not sinners: but if any man be a worshipper of God, and doeth his will, him he heareth. Since the world began was it not heard that any man opened the eyes of one that was born blind. If this man were not of God, he could do nothing." (vs. 30-33)

For this defence of the Gospel they threw him out of the synagogue. It was the best thing that could have happened to him. It put him in a state of no compromise. The place of compromise is a dangerous place to be in. You not only have to suffer the accusation of the enemy, but the condemnation of God. And it is impossible to receive further revelation there.

It was after his banishment that I revealed Myself to him. I loved him dearly. I still do. He is with Me today in My Father's house. I revealed truths to him concerning My duty which I did not reveal to many of My followers. I gave him one of the greatest confessions I ever gave to man on earth. "Thou hast both seen him, and it is he that talketh with thee." (vs. 37) He that will defend truth will know truth.

He cried, "Lord, I believe," and I permitted him to worship Me there. Not even My nearest disciples worshipped Me so readily or with such great faith and acceptance. But neither had such a great work of grace been done upon any of them. Did I not know he would become what he became, even before I healed him? Remember I said, "Neither hath this man sinned, nor his parents: but that the works of God should be made manifest in him." (vs. 3) I knew the great works of God would be made manifest not only on him (in that he should receive his sight), but in him (in that he should see the light of salvation and bear bold witness to the truth of God, even before those who mocked Me and hated Me). While they professed to give God glory in their blindness, and they thought they did, yet they called Me, the only begotten Son, a sinner. (vs. 29) Wisely the young man answered them, "Whether he be a sinner or no, I know not: one thing I know, that whereas I was blind, now I see." (vs. 25)

February 21

CHILDREN OF THE MOST HIGH

Scripture Reading — John 10:1-41; Psalm 82:1-8

"Jesus answered them, Is it not written in your law, I said, Ye are gods?" (John 10:34)

My beloved children, you have never even begun to realize your greatness. You are of My line and lineage. I have redeemed and begotten you through My blood.

Yea, not only are you what I am, but even those who were under the law of Moses belonged to the family of their God, Jehovah, for they had His mark and His signature upon them.

I spoke to them in Psalm 82:6 that they were children of the Most High, thus making them of the family of God, but they did not understand.

I told them to judge as I judge, and not be influenced by the power and position or pressure of the wicked.

I told them to defend the poor and fatherless, to do justice to the afflicted and needy and to deliver them out of the hand of the wicked, but they did not understand the authority I gave to them and so they continued to walk in darkness. And because they did walk in ignorance, which is darkness, the foundations of the earth were out of their true course. (Psalm 82:5)

It is only as My sons know who they are in Me and that they are an extension of all I, the Father, am and that they are called to rule in My authority, that the world will return to its original orbit and the seasons, nature and the weather will be at peace and not torment man with misery and agony. Did I not reign above the weather? What do you do with your authority to do the same?

This was not only for a chosen few, but I said, "All of you are children of the Most High." (Psalm 82:6)

But I also warned them that, because of their darkness and ignorance which hinders them from accepting this reality, they would die like mortals and fall from their thrones of authority like earthly princes fall.

You could inherit the nations. Instead you shall inherit the grave, unless you come into your rightful position which I have already promised you.

Let not the religious Pharisee persuade you that you are "making yourself a god." The Father has sanctified you and sent you into the world, even as He sent Me. "Peace be unto you: as my Father hath sent me, even so I send you." (John 20:21)

I promised you, the works that I do shall you do also. (John 14: 12). "And the glory which thou gavest me I have given them;" (John 17:22)

You are a crown prince who has not assumed his throne. You are allowing an usurper to reign in your place. Rise up and take your rightful place, that My Kingdom may come in thee.

February 22

GOD'S REVELATION TO A BUSY WOMAN

Scripture Reading — John 11:1-46; Luke 1:38-42

"She saith unto him, Yea Lord: I believe that thou art the Christ, the Son of God, which should come into the world." (vs. 27)

This was one of the greatest statements of faith ever made by mortals before My resurrection. There are three great things about it.

1. It was made by a woman when women were not expected to know great spiritual truths.

2. It was made before I had done the great miracle of the raising of Lazarus, her brother, and before she had seen My great power in operation.

3. Martha had not sat at My feet like her sister, Mary. She had been busy in the kitchen and taking care of the necessities of life. And yet, in the midst of all her cooking, serving and entertaining, she had received the most important of all revelations and had believed it.

To be busy and helpful to others does not mean that one is insensitive to spiritual things. In fact, sensitivity to the need of others is often the reason some people take no time for themselves, and they neglect their personal, spiritual meditations.

Yet I am, because of their sensitivity to Me, in the midst of activity, able to speak to them. They do not need great miracles in order to believe great truths.

I love My daughters, even as I love My spiritually begotten sons. I will, because of their rejection from the brothers, often meet them and do greater things for them than for their rejectors.

One of My children has said, "A seeking soul and a seeking Saviour will always meet."

This is true. Did I not search out and find the man I healed at the Pool of Bethesda (John 5:14) and the young man who was blind from birth (John 9:35-38)? Yea, I even found the woman of Samaria alone and rejected by society, and revealed My Sonship to her. (John 4:25,26)

When they sought to seize Me, or I was surrounded by the great multitude of overly excited people, I many times conveyed Myself away from their midst. (John 5:13)

Even as I knew how and when to leave a place, I knew how and when to appear suddenly at the right time, at a certain place. I am always on schedule for all My appointments and I never stay too long. All My children who are true sons need to walk in this truth. They would be much wiser and waste less of their time.

I came to Martha and Mary by this Divine schedule. ("Lord, by this time he stinketh:"): That is when it is time for Me to work wonders; to save, to heal, to raise from the dead, to cleanse, to supply the need: when "it stinketh," when a soul is so fallen in sin that "he stinketh," a financial situation is so embarrassing that "it stinketh." Then I am right on schedule. Only believe. "Said I not unto thee, that, if thou wouldest believe, thou shouldest see the glory of God?" (John 11:40)

February 23

LET THE GLORY OF GOD CHANGE YOU

Scripture Reading — John 12:23-50; Isaiah 6:1-3

"These things said Esaias, when he saw his glory, and spake of him." (John 12:41)

Glory is a wonderful thing. The same glory which Isaiah saw, even 600 years before I came to earth, blinded the Pharisees in My day. Glory is judgment. When man touches the glory, he will either enter a new dimension of revelation, or he will begin to wither up and die. Because glory kills the flesh, and if one does not have the truth of eternal life then one cannot survive in the presence of glory. It will blind him spiritually.

The one thing that kept some of the chief rulers from confessing Me was their fear of losing the support of the Pharisees. They compromised with death to hold their positions of power, and this they did because they loved the praise and honour that man gave more than the honour which comes from God.

It was to these that I spoke the immortal words, "Except a corn of wheat fall into the ground and die, it abideth alone: but if it die, it bringeth forth much fruit. He that loveth his life shall lose it; and he that hateth his life in this world shall keep it unto life eternal....If any man serve me, him will my Father honour." (John 12:24-26)

They loved their life in the world of man's praises and they could not give it up. Many are lost because they prefer their way of life rather than God's way of life.

Isaiah saw My glory with the eye of revelation and lived. These Pharisees saw it by the evidence of the miracles performed and the words that I spoke (which My Father had given Me), but they rejected My glory and the curse of death came upon them and this only because they wanted to steal My glory for themselves.

They loved their position of power, the praise of men, the chief seats in the synagogue, their influence with the Roman leaders, and the adulation of the crowd. How could they hate their life in this religious world when they had striven all their life to attain unto it? And even if a glimmer of truth leaked through the crack of their understanding to lighten their spirit, they denied the truth of glory and kept it secret so that they would not lose their "life" in this world.

My child, always be true to truth. Be honest with reality. Never compromise with the darkness of the religious life, the highest object of devotion, such as another mortal in a "chief seat."

Always seek to see My glory like Moses did and Isaiah did, and even My disciples did, for then you shall not speak of man, but of the Creator of man. You shall not follow man, but the Creator of man. And you shall not see man, but the Creator of man, and you shall become what you see, what you follow and what you speak about.

February 24

WHEN YOU KNOW YOURSELF YOU AREN'T AFRAID TO SERVE

Scripture Reading – John 13:1-17, 33-38

"Jesus knowing that the Father had given all things into his hands, and that he was come from God, and went to God; He riseth from supper, and laid aside his garments; and took a towel, and girded himself. After that he poureth water into a bason, and began to wash the disciples' feet, and to wipe them with the towel wherewith he was girded." (John 13:3-5)

My child, if you know who you are in Me, your destiny and calling, then you have found yourself in the Spirit and you need have no search for identity.

You will have confidence in yourself, your ability to attain unto all that I have planned for you. Fears will vanish. There are many fears: fears of failure, of criticism, of danger, of rejection, of embarrassment, shame, disgrace and being looked down on as someone to be humiliated.

But when you know who you are, you can afford to take the most difficult rebuke, do the most menial task, attempt the most dangerous deed. What others will say or think about you won't even faze you. You know who you are.

If you are an ambassador, carrying a suitcase will not make a redcap out of you. If you are a queen, rinsing a tea cup won't make a scrubbing maid out of you. If you are a bishop, rinsing out a shirt won't make a butler out of you. You know who you are and what you are, so you can afford to serve, to deviate from what your regular assignments and positions call for. It does not humiliate you to be different, because you know that you know who you are.

That is why I could gird Myself with the towel of a servant and do the work of a slave. Humility is a grace which only those have who know who they are, and by doing a humble task they do not lower their station in life.

It is the man or woman who is always trying to climb some ladder of success and who is insecure in himself, who is afraid that people will think less of him, or that he will mar his public image, just because he performs some menial task.

Public image is just that, "public" image. If you have the God image and know you are giving to God, as I did, and that your calling is a God-given calling, you can let down your hair, roll up the carpet and be you yourself.

Gird your apron on and serve My children. You will still get to where you are destined, even though you wash a lot of stinky feet.

February 25

CHRIST IS THE WAY TO GOD

Scripture Reading — John 14:1-31, John 13:33

"And whither I go ye know, and the way ye know...I am the

way, the truth, and the life: no man cometh unto the Father, but by me." (John 14:4,6)

Yes, My child, even as I knew where I was going, you too can know where you are going because you know Me and to know Me is to know the truth, because I am the truth. To know Me, is to know eternal life, because I am the life.

I told My disciples I was going to the Father, and you, because you know Me, also know the way to the Father, for I am the way into His presence.

The reason that the Pharisees could not go where I was going was because they could not come into the Father's presence, except through Me. My Father sent Me to earth as His ambassador of love, that I might take them (My mortals) by the "God-hand" and lead them into God, the Father's, presence.

Although I told My disciples earlier that "whither I go, ye cannot come" (John 13:33), I was not referring to heaven then, but to the coming hour of My death, the grave and sheol. They were forbidden from following Me into hell, where I had to go to preach to those held in captivity since the days of Noah (I Peter 3:17-20; 4:6) and to open the gates of death for all the righteous who had died in the Lord, that they might come with Me into the Father's House.

On My way up, I stopped in the garden to talk to Mary. I could not delay, as I was delivering multitudes of souls into the presence of the Father. That was when many were seen walking about the city. For they came out of their graves after My resurrection, and went into the Holy City, and appeared unto many. (Matthew 27:53)

I not only am the **way** to the Father, but My **words** are the words of the Father. (John 14:10) I also did the Father's **works**.

You are in Me, as I was in the Father. Now you are My ambassador sent here to do My works (vs. 12), speak My words, and show mortals the way by reaching the God-hand (which is the hand of love), to them, even as I did.

That is why I gave you the key in the new commandment I gave you. "That ye love one another; as I have loved you, that ye also love one another." (John 13:34)

This is the sign that you are My disciple. And besides this there is no sign. All other signs and wonders and miracles can be imitated by the evil one. But the sign of love is the true sign of the Father who is **love**.

February 26

LOVE PRODUCES SPIRITUAL FRUIT

Scripture Reading — John 15:1-27

"Herein is my Father glorified, that ye bear much fruit; so shall ye be my disciples. As the Father hath loved me, so have I loved you: continue ye in my love. If ye keep my commandments, ye shall abide in my love; even as I have kept my Father's commandments, and abide in his love. These things have I spoken unto you, that my joy might remain in you, and that your joy might be full. This is my commandment, That ye love one another, as I have loved you. Greater love hath no man than this, that a man lay down his life for his friends." (John 15:8-13)

I love you, My beloved, with the same love with which My Father loved Me. He loves Me with His great, eternal, protective, Divine love, and that is the way I love you.

Because you are begotten of Me, even as I am begotten of the Father, you will continue to love others even with this same love that I have for you, and in loving them, they will be begotten of you.

The Divine order of birthing is that the seed is planted through an act of love when the bridegroom abides in the bride. It is an intimate act of coming together, and without it the seed cannot fuse with the egg, and there can be no fruit of the womb.

When you and I are abiding in love and intimate relationship, it will result in much spiritual fruit in your life. Without it there will be no fruit. Fruit is a result of love.

I have given you the Holy Spirit that He may dwell inside of your being. He overshadowed Mary, but He shall dwell within you. (John 14:17)

My one and only commandment to you is for you to continue in that intimate relationship of love with Me. As you love Me, you will be enabled to love others. For the fruit of love is the result of loving Me. My Spirit will come upon you and reproduce My love from your innermost being.

You never need to work at "loving people." Your love for others will be the result of your relationship with Me.

In this loving is joy. It is hard to love when you have no joy. A miserable, unhappy person is a self-centred person. But when you have My love, you have joy, for love and joy cannot be separated. Love gives birth to joy.

All fruit of the Spirit result from abiding in love.

A tree does not bear fruit till it reaches maturity, neither does a maid. So even when you abide in Me, you will, as a mature Christian, produce all the fruit of the Spirit.

February 27

MANY ARE UNABLE TO BE TAUGHT DEEPER TRUTHS

Scripture Reading – John 16:1-33

"I have yet many things to say unto you, but ye cannot bear them now." (John 16:12)

My children are living in different stages of growth. Some are more advanced in their knowledge of truth and more able to receive instruction than others. It has always been so.

Because some of My children are spiritually retarded, they are not able to receive advanced spiritual revelation. It is even dangerous to give to these the deeper truths of the Father for they will use them ignorantly and to their destruction. That is why I warned you about where to give your pearls. For the ignorant will trample your pearls of truth and then destroy you. And this they will do because they will think they are doing God's service. (John 16:2)

It was God's children, men of the family of Israel, who distorted the few grains of truth I sowed in Jerusalem and condemned Me to Pilate. "We have a law, and by our law he ought to die, because he made himself the Son of God." (John 19:7)

A little truth in the hands of a fool becomes a dangerous thing. He will kill because of his lack of balance, for it will turn a normal man into a fanatic.

This is why many cannot grow in the knowledge of the Lord's truths. They cannot hear it. Truth is very heavy. My messenger to the Hebrews rebuked My children for their infant stage of development: "Of whom we have many things to say, and hard to be uttered, seeing ye are dull of hearing. For when for the time ye ought to be teachers, ye have need that one teach you again which be the first principles of the oracles of God; and are become such as have need of milk, and not of strong meat. For every one that useth milk is unskilful in the word of righteousness: for he is a babe. But strong meat belongeth to them that are of full age, even those who by reason of use have their senses exercised to discern both good and evil." (Hebrews 5:11-14)

They stayed only at the base of the principles of the doctrine. The foundation is good and important, but it is upon the foundation that the structure is built and no children of Mine are fully developed unless they have completed the structure.

It is the office work of the Spirit of truth to guide you into all truth. He will show you the truths of today and also things to come. (John 16:13) And if you let Him truly teach you, then you shall grow into the wisdom and knowledge of a fully developed and enlightened son. And when I return, ye shall ask Me nothing, for you shall have been taught by the Holy Spirit, the Divine teacher who is able to teach all men, if they will listen, and if they desire to know truth, and if they are humble enough to receive it without destroying others with it. Ask Me to give you a teachable spirit.

February 28

MISSION ACCOMPLISHED

Scripture Reading – John 17:1-26

"Father, the hour is come;" (John 17:1)

It is important to know My timing. My Father has a schedule for you, just like He had for Me. There will be no lingering around after a job is done. Like Me, you will be able to say, "I have finished the work which thou gavest me to do." (John 17:4)

There is tremendous relief in knowing that you have finished what God the Father has called you to do. "Mission Accomplished!" is the triumphant cry of the victor.

Great tasks unfulfilled break the heart of the Father and small ones accomplished give the Father's heart great joy.

Do not strive for that which I have not given you to do. Sometimes the task I call you to do is simply to "give them the words that the Father gives you to give them." (vs. 8)

One of My great truths was to keep My children united in one. It is only as they are one as I and My Father are one, that they are perfect and that they can be a true witness to the world. (vs. 21,23) Make this a part of your mission, to unite people of all faiths in one.

Some of My last words on the cross were "It is finished." That was My greatest shout of triumph and victory. My voice was not loud, but it echoed throughout this sin-cursed world into the farthest reaches of the heavens and down into the deepest pits of hell. It is finished! Satan was defeated. The final victory has been won!

Even so, My child, when you finish your life's work and look into My eyes and report to Me that your mission is accomplished, and I crown your years of service with the victor's crown, you will enter My glory, even as I entered My Father's glory.

Glory comes with fulfilling the thing I have called you to do and becoming the one I have called you to be.

February 29

PUT YOUR SWORD INTO THE SHEATH

Scripture Reading — John 18:1-40

"Then said Jesus unto Peter, Put up thy sword into the sheath: the cup which my Father hath given me, shall I not drink it?" (John 18:11)

My beloved child, I would counsel you with these words of long-suffering and patience. There are many times when you could easily escape the pain and discomfort, even the trial and test. But the easy way may not be the right way.

Many man-pleasers are simply only pleasing those who will protect and bless the flesh.

The human who has not caught a glimpse of the rewards of those who suffer for My sake will always seek to spare the flesh. The flesh is the gateway to glory only if it can endure the rending which it must suffer, in order to make open a way. Otherwise, the flesh is the terrible hindrance and wall between God and man's soul.

When My servant Peter used the sword, he was attempting to spare his flesh, even more than Mine, for he too feared arrest. But it only endangered him still more, because it was this act of cutting off the ear which truly endangered him.

Later, in the garden of Caiaphas the high priest, one of the servants of the high priest, who was a relative of the man whose ear Peter had cut off, said, "Did I not see thee in the garden with him (Jesus)?" (John 18:26)

It was this witness against Peter which made Peter deny the Lord the third time.

If you try to defend yourself or seek for revenge, it will put you in a dangerous place, a place where you may spare the flesh, but destroy the soul.

Therefore you must follow My example in the garden. I am with you. You need fear nothing. Don't fight for yourself. Put your sword back in the sheath where it can harm no one. Remember that I said, "He who taketh the sword shall perish by the sword."

In surrender to the school of suffering and drinking the cup which the Father has given you to drink, you will find quick release from the bondage and entanglement of the flesh.

Reach out to My provision of grace. For My grace is sufficient for you, that you may be able to win the greatest battle of all, not the battle over your enemy on the outside, but the one on the inside: yourself. Drink your cup, and self will die.

March 1

THE "PILATES" IN YOUR LIFE

Scripture Reading — John 19:1-42

"Jesus answered, Thou couldest have no power at all against me, except it were given thee from above: therefore he that delivered me unto thee hath the greater sin." (John 19:11)

No man has any power to harm you at any time. Neither do they have authority to pass sentence on you, unless I authorize it, Myself.

I take full responsibility for everything that happens to you, both good and evil, if you will continue to stay in submission to My perfect will at all times.

Never fear the "Pilates" in your life who seem to be in some position of authority over you and who presume to pass sentence on you or your ministry. They are nobody. They have only the authority I give them, and in your case, that is NONE. I will only use their position to allow you to pass through the valley of suffering, the seat of judgment and the cross of rejection. If it were not one "Pilate," it would be another. They are simply vessels of My wrath that I use to temper you and form you, blow by blow, so that you can become the saint I want to make out of you.

I am the one who has delivered you into their hands to do this work on you. I take responsibility. I will stand by you through it all and enable you to be perfected into My likeness and beauty. Rest your case in My righteous judgment.

March 2

LOVE AND GRIEF ENABLE YOU TO SEE MY GLORY

Scripture Reading — John 20:1-31

"Then the disciples went away again unto their own home. But Mary stood without at the sepulchre weeping:" (John 20:10,11)

Mary came first and stayed the longest. Her great love and grief slowed her down so that she was able to keep things in the right priority.

The two disciples also loved Me greatly. But one was impetuous (Peter) and because he was really afraid of meeting Me after his denial, he also wanted to hurry away from the grave.

The other disciple knew I loved him and he felt a great longing in his heart to see Me and talk to Me, but he was influenced by Peter. When Peter went into the grave, he followed him. When Peter decided to leave, he left also.

But Mary stayed still. Her great grief helped her to be uninfluenced by the others who came and went. Love and grief will separate you from the crowd. It will enable you to have the strength and courage to be different from others. It will give you grace to linger until you can see the glory of God. It will take fear away. Great grief knows no fear. Great love and great grief are twin sisters. Without great love, there can be no grief.

It will slow your pace, so you will not be part of that mad race, that coming and going and dashing about without accomplishing anything. It will set you apart, so that you can see the Lord.

March 3

DIE TO SELF

Scripture Reading — John 21:1-25

"Verily, verily, I say unto thee, When thou wast young, thou girdedst thyself, and walkedst whither thou wouldest: but when thou shalt be old, thou shalt stretch forth thy hands, and another shall gird thee, and carry thee whither thou wouldest not." (John 21:18)

A sign of maturity and spiritual sainthood is to die to self, stretch forth your hands to the will of God and let Me lead you.

My disciple, Peter, was always impetuous and self-willed. He did what "Peter wanted to do." He not only was harmful for his own soul, but he led others astray also.

Who but Peter would go fishing and be naked in the cold morning air? Who but he would jump in the lake when he knew it was I standing there? Who but Peter would be more interested in what would happen to John than himself? My beloved Peter. That is why I loved him so much. I saw the struggle he had with himself and I knew he had a great task to do for Me; only by loving Me with more than a double portion love could he do it. That's why I asked him three times "Simon, son of Jonas, lovest thou Me?" I also saw in that moment his complete surrender unto Me and finally his triumphant death to self. That is why I told him about his final victory. "Peter, when you were young, you wore what you wanted to wear, you dressed yourself to your own taste and will, you girded yourself to work and you were ready to work and did only the thing you wanted to do." He was typical of all young men today and all people who do not know the joy of surrender to My will.

"But when thou shalt be old..." Peter had many years of service ahead of him then. Years of breaking and discipline.

"Thou shalt stretch forth thy hands..." That speaks of surrender and yieldedness and acceptance of all that came to him. It also was a revelation that he would one day stretch forth his hands and be nailed to a cross.

"Another shall gird thee,...." Someone else would one day put a robe of mockery and filth on him, even as they had with Me, his Master.

"And carry thee whither thou wouldest not..." Even I prayed, "If it be possible, let this cup pass from me." The flesh always seeks to flee from pain and suffering, and old flesh would spare itself more than young flesh. Life becomes precious with old age.

At that time Peter hardly listened to what I told him, but later he remembered these words and they gave him the strength to go through great suffering and to lay his life down for Me. He was able to suffer and leave mankind a glorious thesis on suffering. (I Peter 4:12-19) It was Peter who qualified to leave My children their glorious truth, "Forasmuch then as Christ hath suffered for us in the flesh, arm yourselves likewise with the same mind: for he that hath suffered in the flesh hath ceased from sin; That he no longer should live the rest of his time in the flesh to the lusts of men, but to the will of God." (I Peter 4:1,2)

He had armed himself with a mind to accept suffering, for he knew that suffering would deliver him from flesh-rule and put him in the place where he could live only to the will of God and say like My servant Paul, "For me to live is Christ."

March 4

THE DANGER OF ANGER AND HATE

Scripture Reading — Amos 1:1-15

"Thus saith the Lord; For three transgressions of Edom, and for four, I will not turn away the punishment thereof; because he did pursue his brother with the sword, and did cast off all pity, and his anger did tear perpetually, and he kept his wrath for ever: But I will send a fire upon Teman, which shall devour the palaces of Bozrah." (Amos 1:11,12)

My child, anger and hate are horrible and terrible feelings which you should never allow to possess your heart. Edom still hates his brother today. So long can hatred and anger last. It is fired by the fires of hell. That very fire that burns in his heart to destroy his brother will also destroy his very own soul. I warn you, My precious child, never allow the darkness of hell to burn its hate in your heart. It is not good. It is **not** good. It will destroy you.

Anger causes you to spend your time and energy pursuing your brother or sister with the sword. You will waste precious hours talking against him or her. Lay down all arguments and disagreements. Do not pursue your brother with the sword of your tongue. Remember Isaiah 30:27 says, "the tongue is a devouring fire." Fire fights fire, and all who use their tongues as a destroying fire shall be awarded when I come against them with the breath of My mouth.

Neither cast off pity. Always try to have pity in your heart for every person, every situation. Don't be ashamed to pity even those who seem to be undeserving of it. I have pity on the unrighteous and you should do the same.

It sometimes is almost impossible for you, in your humanity, to keep from feeling anger, but I warn you to cast it off as soon as it comes. Put your mind under My Blood. The Blood will guard you and protect you from strong, wrong emotions and it will keep your soul pure.

March 5

GOD EXPECTS US TO BE FAITHFUL TO HIM

Scripture Reading — Amos 2:1-16

"Yet destroyed I the Amorite before them, whose height was like the height of the cedars, and he was strong as the oaks; yet I destroyed his fruit from above, and his roots from beneath. Also I brought you up from the land of Egypt, and led you forty years through the wilderness, to possess the land of the Amorite." (Amos 2:9-11)

My very own, precious and beloved children are constantly breaking My heart. I had done such great things for Israel. I had destroyed the Amorite from before them, that race of giants (who were also My creation). I brought them up from Egypt to possess the land of giants. I raised up their sons to be My holy prophets and their young men to be My Nazarenes. They were My holy and beautiful people. Upon the face of the earth were none who had known My love and power to deliver and conquer like they did. They were My example to the heathen nations. I set them apart and separated them from all of the other peoples on the face of the earth to show My glory to the other nations.

But they turned to the sins of the other nations. They turned to whoredom, first spiritual, then physical, for spiritual and physical whoredom go together. When a man covets power, position, possessions, he will soon pant after flesh (the dust of the earth).

I will judge My beloved, chosen ones in the same way as I will judge the heathen, unless they turn away from their evil ways. Do not think that I will spare any nation who has forgotten Me, their God. I will send the fire on Jew and Gentile, bond and free, male and female, young and old, rich and poor, swift and slow. My eye will not spare sin. I call for the prophets to prophesy truth and warn My people, but My people do not want truth. They want lies. They want softness and the sweetness of honey in the day of battle and blood. There shall be no softness and sweetness in this day of the end-time. There shall be only fire, fire, fire.

Sound the alarm. Prepare for battle in the day of battle!

March 6

THE WARNING OF JUDGMENT

Scripture Reading — Amos 3:1-15

"Shall a trumpet be blown in the city, and the people not be afraid? shall there be evil in a city, and the Lord hath not done it? Surely the Lord God will do nothing, but he revealeth his secret unto his servants the prophets. The lion hath roared, who will not fear? the Lord God hath spoken, who can but prophesy?" (Amos 3:6-8)

There is coming great judgment upon the nation and the whole world. It has already begun. I have spoken and revealed it to My servants, the prophets. They have prophesied it to the people; you have prophesied it, but people do not want to listen to it because it is a discomforting message. It puts fear in the hearts.

There is no evil or tragic thing that can take place without My permitting it. I know it will happen, because the perpetrator of the evil must get permission from Me before it can take place. I am still in control of the devil, and his activity. When I give permission to him to send trial and testing, I tell My prophets what is going to take place at that same time, so that they can begin to pray and fast and go to battle against the forces of evil. There is no evil or good upon the earth or in the future which I will permit to happen without revealing it to My prophets. And they will not be able to be still, for it will be the roaring of a lion when I speak into their ears.

But I do not have many true prophets, for the prophet is hated and rejected because he tells the people what they do not want to hear.

With every judgment that I have pronounced and decreed there is a way of escape, and that is through repentance. Even Israel was promised a remnant who would escape. (vs. 12)

In the judgment that has now begun on the earth, there will be also those who shall escape, one in a city, two in the field, for the greater wrath shall fall on the cities, because of their evil. The greater the evil, the greater the judgment.

I am raising up handmaidens and servants who shall hear My voice and prophesy truth to the cities of this nation. They shall not be loved or accepted by those whose hearts are closed to truth. The only ones who will receive the message of judgment are those who shall escape it, for in their heart is already a work of grace that has been wrought because of their gentle, teachable and humble spirit.

The ones who will not receive My warning message are those who are doomed, and they are doomed because, long before I spoke through you, I spoke in their hearts. They rejected the whisper of the Holy Spirit; they shall also reject the roaring of the lion. Nevertheless, the lion must roar, that God be not accused of not warning the unrighteous. Go forth My watchmen and roar.

March 7

PREPARE TO MEET YOUR GOD

Scripture Reading — Amos 4:1-13

"Therefore thus will I do unto thee, O Israel: and because I will do this unto thee, prepare to meet thy God, O Israel." (Amos 4:12)

To meet Me is not always a good thing. It can be the end of a person's existence. It can be death, destruction, torment, judgment and hell.

Many are afraid of meeting Me, because they do not love Me. If you love Me, then it will be only glory. It will be the climax of all joys, the ending of all sorrows, the fulfilment of all dreams.

But this is only for those who love Me. I was angry with sinful Israel. They had forsaken Me for the "kine of Bashan," the golden calves and the Baal of Jezebel, a deceitful form of worship and idolatry which brought suffering on the poor and sinfulness upon the nation.

They still held a form of tithing to their idolatrous system, for even the priests of Baal taught the people to tithe so **they** could eat. Their sacrifice of thanksgiving was mingled with the leaven of corruption, and they made great publication of those who gave above their tithes, for they loved the praises of men. (vs. 4,5)

I sent famine (vs. 6), withheld rain (vs. 7), sent mildew and palmerworm on their fields and gardens (vs 9), pestilence like the plagues of Egypt, war that slew their young men, and much death (vs. 10), but still they did not repent.

Therefore I told them they should now get ready for the worst. That was to meet Me face to face as the mighty God above all gods, the judge of the whole earth. The one who formed the mountains, who created the wind, who can read the thoughts of a man, who can turn the morning into darkness, who walks on the Alps, the Andes and the Himalayas.

I am no golden calf that has been formed by the hands of sinful men. Neither am I a spirit demon, nor a beast of the field, nor a being from outer space. I am the Lord God Almighty who created all things, even the things which are often mistakenly worshipped by man in his ignorance and foolishness.

I am the "unknown" God. The God that made the world and all things therein, the Lord of heaven and earth. I dwell not in temples made with hands. The times of ignorance, I, your God, winked at, but now I command men everywhere to repent and get ready to meet Me, for they have an appointment with death and judgment, and multitudes are not ready. Read Acts 17:23-31.

March 8

SEEK THE LORD AND LIVE

Scripture Reading — Amos 5:1-27

"For thus saith the Lord unto the house of Israel, Seek ye me, and ye shall live:" (Amos 5:4)

"Seek the Lord, and ye shall live;" (vs. 6)

"Seek him that maketh the seven stars and Orion, and turneth the shadow of death into the morning, and maketh the day dark with night: that calleth for the waters of the sea, and poureth them out upon the face of the earth: The Lord is his name: That strengtheneth the spoiled against the strong, so that the spoiled shall come against the fortress." (vs. 8,9)

"But let judgment run down as waters, and righteousness as a mighty stream." (vs. 24)

It was the "end-time" for Israel, even for the House when I spoke through the mouth of My servant, the prophet.

The virgin of Israel was as a "fallen woman." There was no more hope for her. (vs. 2) Out of 1000, only a hundred were left in the city, and out of 100 only 10. (vs. 3) I had preserved for Myself ten percent (a tithe) of the people.

When the end-time judgment passes over the earth and the great tribulation has passed by, there will remain only a tithe of the earth's population.

And yet, though the riders of Revelation (6:1-8) destroy with utter destruction the multitudes, still those who seek Me in that time shall be spared. For I am the ALMIGHTY who created the seven stars (known as the seven sisters) and Orion; I alone can turn the night into morning, pour rain upon the earth and strengthen the "spoiled" against their enemy with his forces.

My people's sins were:

1. They hated the prophets and the righteous ones whom I sent to rebuke them of their sins.

2. They trod upon (threshed out) the poor and took from them their wheat, their food, even the food stamps.

3. There was corruption through dishonest gain and a false prosperity of building and planting.

4. It was a time when the prudent had to keep his mouth shout, for there was defamation and spies were all about to report everything man said.

I called upon My people to:
1. seek good, not evil (that they might live),
2. hate evil, love goodness,
3. establish righteous judgment in the gates, so that I, the Lord could still save the remnant of Joseph.

Terrible things had happened and more was yet to come:
1. wailing in the streets,
2. the fields and vineyards destroyed by fire,
3. it would be like fleeing from a lion and meeting a bear.

...eration has the same thing happened as the ...e tried to be freed from their British sovereignty ...d have been swallowed up by Russia (even the

...r into the U.N. and it is a place of serpents. I hate their ... assemblies, even that of the U.N., for it is a mockery unto Me.

I call for you to let judgments run down as waters, and righteousness as a mighty stream. Let purity of the heart be your goal, not religious acts.

March 9

AWAKEN MY PEOPLE WHO SLEEP!

Scripture Reading — Amos 6:1-14

"Woe to them that are at ease in Zion, and trust in the mountain of Samaria, which are named chief of the nations, to whom the house of Israel came!" (Amos 6:1)

Yea, it is a day when many will try to escape the reality of the judgment. They play while multitudes perish. They feast while multitudes starve. They revel and are consumed by pleasures while multitudes are suffering in anguish. They lie on their beds of "ivory" while multitudes are slain in battle.

This is the day of the beginning of judgments, but many in Zion are still at ease. They refuse to hear the sounding of the alarm. They spend their days in pleasing and comforting the flesh, not realizing that by closing their eyes to the coming judgment and refusing to see it, they are hastening its approach. (vs. 3)

On the eve before the tribulation and affliction of Joseph they party and anoint themselves with the most costly of cosmetics. Their hearts are not grieved for the breach of the house of Joseph. Instead of weeping, their house is filled with the sound of music and celebration (vs. 5,6).

I send you to the sleeping house of Jacob to warn them that are at ease in Zion. They will not hear your words gladly, for they do not want to be disturbed from their ease and pleasure. Therefore be prepared to suffer at their hand.

March 10

YOU ARE GOD'S PLUMBLINE

Scripture Reading — Amos 7:1-17

"Thus he shewed me: and, behold, the Lord stood upon a wall made by a plumbline, with a plumbline in his hand. And the Lord said unto me, Amos, what seest thou? And I said, A plumbline. Then said the Lord, Behold I will set a plumbline in the midst of my people Israel: I will not again pass by them any more:" (Amos 7:7,8)

I have set a plumbline on the wall of this house of America. This is true of many nations. I am even today standing on the wall and I am reckoning with this wall of America.

This is the last time I will measure it and pass by it. For I am grieved with this nation like I was grieved with Israel and Judah.

I am sending a plumbline of end-time prophets, both men and women, who shall bear a faithful witness of truth before all that they see.

The plumbline "cries out" against the imperfections of the wall and reveals all of its faults, for the plumbline tells the truth. It **cannot** compromise with a crooked wall. I have called you to be a plumbline in My hand. Even as I called out Amos, who was neither a prophet nor the son of a prophet but a humble herdsman and gardener on the hills of Judea, to stand before priests and kings (Amaziah and Jeroboam) and to bear a faithful witness of the coming judgment, so have I called you even though you were not trained by the church to stand before these people of this generation and warn them concerning these end-time judgments that are coming upon the land, and to pray and intercede on their behalf.

Through his prayers, Amos twice spared and saved Israel from judgment; once from the grasshopper plague (vs. 1-3), which speaks of demonic invasion, and from a terrible judgment of fire (vs. 4), which speaks of judgments of nuclear warfare.

As I called Amos to prophesy, I also called him to travail and intercede on behalf of the nation.

I call all My prophets to be intercessors. For a prophet who does not pray and weep and intercede for the people which he judges, will become hard and cruel, for the calling of an end-time prophet is a hard and difficult calling, and the prophet must rise above the people and not be identified with them when he prophesies hard things. He will live a lonely life, for he will be rejected and hated by the people to whom he prophesies.

If he does not travail for them, he can easily turn to hate them, and then he will lose his balance and effectiveness. Never preach judgment without a broken heart!

March 11

A FAMINE FOR GOD'S WORD HAS BEGUN

Scripture Reading — Amos 8:1-14

"Behold, the days come, saith the Lord God, that I will send a famine in the land, not a famine of bread, nor a thirst for water, but of hearing the words of the Lord: And they shall wander from sea to sea, and from the north even to the east, they shall run to and fro to seek the word of the Lord, and shall not find it. In that day shall the fair virgins and young men faint for thirst." (Amos 8:11-13)

My child, this day is this scripture fulfilled in your ears.

Never before has there been such a famine for My Word. Nation after nation has forbidden the preaching of the pure Gospel and the distribution of My Holy Word.

You, yourself, have been involved in taking God's Word to vast famine-stricken areas of the world. Famine is when people have not and hunger, and it is always caused by drought. For decades, these famine areas have not had the "rain" of heaven upon their land because of the ungodliness of their leaders. They have rejected Me and My Holy Word. I have closed up the heavens so that the spiritual clouds cannot yield rain. Where there is no rain, there is no wheat, no harvest, no joy, no life and no blessing.

That is why there is no Word of God. My Word falls like the rain and with the rain. Revelations and truths of heaven always accompany the moving of My Holy Spirit. And My Spirit moves where people love Me and receive Me.

The cry for My Word shall become greater and greater. Requests shall come from nation after nation. You must prepare to give portions of My Word to the multitudes. Do not say you cannot. With five loaves and two fishes I fed the multitudes. I will use the End-Time Handmaidens like I used the lad to feed the multitudes. Yea, they shall have bread (My Word), and fish, even the delicate, delicious, hard to find fish and honey, secrets of the ages. Many shall come to be taught the truths of heaven and shall go on their way refreshed. I will make you a house of bread and a sea of fish.

Yea, there shall be both natural bread and fish and spiritual bread and fish. And though the multitudes will follow you for the loaves and fishes, I will have a remnant who will remain to accompany Me through My hours of passion and suffering while the crowd passes through its hours of crucifixion.

Prepare bread and fish for that day, saith the Lord. For many fair virgins and young sons of the church shall faint in the land, for there shall be no bread in their houses of worship. The songs of the temple shall be like a howling in that day, and many shall backslide and fall away of the younger generation as the Fathers of faith who had My truths and My Word are removed from the scene. Prepare ye therefore My Word for that day. Enlarge your tents! Stretch forth the curtains of thy habitation.

March 12

GOD'S PROMISE TO ISRAEL

Scripture Reading — Amos 9:1-15

"In that day will I raise up the tabernacle of David that is fallen, and close up the breaches thereof; and I will raise up his ruins, and I will build it as in the days of old: That they may possess the remnant of Edom, and of all the heathen, which are called by my name, saith the Lord that doeth this. Behold, the days come, saith the Lord, that the plowman shall overtake the reaper, and the treader of grapes him that soweth seed; and the mountains shall drop sweet wine, and all the hills shall melt. And I will bring again the captivity of my people of Israel, and they shall build the waste cities, and inhabit them; and they shall plant vineyards, and drink the wine thereof; they shall also make gardens, and eat the fruit of them. And I will plant them upon their land, and they shall no more be pulled up out of their land which I have given them, saith the Lord thy God." (Amos 9:11-15)

Amos, my servant, was a prophet, a seer, and hence he was not limited in vision and understanding. He saw not only the immediate judgment, but also the distant restoration, even this day which your eyes see.

It is important that the prophet see not only the soon coming judgment, but the eternal plan of God, which includes the raising up of the fallen tabernacle of David, the restoration, the reaping of the harvest and the drinking of the new wine. My people, Israel, have been brought back by Me, their God. They have been raised up by Me. I will continue to bless them, in spite of all their enemies.

I will bless their crops and give them an abundant harvest. Yea, is not this even now fulfilled in the grapes of Eshcol, the citrus of Jaffa? (vs 14)

I will give them the hearts of the Gentiles (heathen) who are called by My name. (vs. 12) They shall continue to build up the cities of former times. Even out of the ruins shall come again the design of buildings which stood there centuries ago, for I will restore what I have destroyed in My wrath.

Man has not planted Israel. I have! No one shall uproot My people out of My land which I have given them.

There aren't enough powers of all the nations united to pull down this nation, for it is not erected by man, but by Me, the Lord.

As sure as the temple of Herod was destroyed, the tabernacle of David shall stand there in its same place on the day appointed.

> All that's scattered I will gather;
> All that's injured, I will heal;
> All that's broken, I will mend it;
> To prove to Israel, I am real.

March 13

IN THE LIGHT IS FELLOWSHIP AND CLEANSING

Scripture Reading — I John 1:1-10

"But if we walk in the light, as he is in the light, we have fellowship one with another, and the blood of Jesus Christ his Son cleanseth us from all sin." (I John 1:7)

Fellowship! One of the most precious treasures in the world is fellowship with other humans. Cleansing from all sin! The one great essential to enter into the presence of God and have fellowship with God is the cleansing from all sin. How does one reach that beautiful and important state of relationship where one has fellowship with God and man?

My child, it is by walking in the light. Not the light which another human's life shines upon your pathway, but the light which comes from following the Lord of Glory. Only through the light do you have full revelation and full enlightenment, and this brings about perfect fellowship with others who are walking in the same light. It brings about a harmony in working together and flowing together with one heart and vision.

It keeps man from the sin of arguing, divisions, strife, competition, and quarrelling with each other. For this walking in the light is really walking in the love of the Lord.

My child, My purifying blood is in the light, and as you walk in that light, you are walking on the crimson pathway of My precious blood, living in harmony with Me, working together and flowing together with the same heart and vision as I, your Lord.

March 14

THE ANOINTING KEEPS YOU IN THE TRUTH

Scripture Reading — I John 2:1-29

"But the anointing which ye have received of him abideth in you, and ye need not that any man teach you: but as the same anointing teacheth you of all things, and is truth, and is no lie, and even as it hath taught you, ye shall abide in him." (I John 2:27)

My child, the only way that you can abide in Me, and not be ashamed before Me at My coming, is through the anointing.

It is the anointing which comes from Me that all Christians need. The anointing will teach you all the truths pertaining to My Kingdom. It will not only reveal the deep secrets of God to you, but it will keep you in the way of truth and preserve you from false teachers and the corrupters of truth. It is when men fall away from the anointing that they fall away from pure truth and begin to teach a lie. You will never believe these lies because My anointing upon you keeps you safe from the lie, for My anointing is the anointing of truth and revelation of truth. It is the key to the mind of the Father.

Even as I was anointed to know the mind of My Father, so are you anointed to know Him and His pure truth, and to know Him and His pure truth is the great protection from all false teachings.

It is also the only key to righteousness, and only through this purity will you be pure and ready at My coming. Without the anointing no one is pure, no one is ready.

March 15

THE SONS OF GOD ARE PURE

Scripture Reading — I John 3:1-24

"Beloved, now are we the sons of God, and it doth not yet appear what we shall be: but we know that, when he shall appear, we shall be like him; for we shall see him as he is. And every man that hath this hope in him purifieth himself, even as he is pure." (I John 3:2,3)

The great goal of all of My children should be purity—not fame, greatness, power over devils, gifts of healing, workings of miracles, ability to preach or teach, nor accomplishing great deeds. All these things are good, but they do not make the doer of them perfect. Neither are they essential to the Christ-nature. I am coming for a people who are like Me in purity. I ask you, dear one, to daily check your heart. Make sure that the motives for all that you do are perfect.

Never do anything for selfish gain. All your works must pass through the fires of testing. Everything that is not done out of a pure motive will be burnt up! There will be no reward for all the works that are not motivated out of a pure heart. Not only that, but judgment will even fall on some who have seemingly done many great works and made great sacrifices, because it will reveal the sins of pride, self-esteem, desire for praises of men, hunger for recognition and greed for Mammon.

You are My child; in love I call you a son of God, making you My brother. You must strive to live up to this high calling by purifying yourself through honest self-examination and the grace to see what is wrong in your life, and then come to Me for deliverance and cleansing.

March 16

TO KNOW GOD IS TO BE ABLE TO KNOW TRUTH

Scripture Reading — I John 4:1-21

"We are of God: he that knoweth God heareth us; he that is not of God heareth not us. Hereby know we the spirit of truth, and the spirit of error." (I John 4:6)

My child, don't expect the world to hear what you have to say, or to read what you have to write.

John knew he was of Me. He knew that he was "right on." He had no doubts or misgivings about whether or not he was of the truth. You too can know, by your intimate relationship with Me and the sense of My nearness, who you are.

Those who know Me like you know Me, know who they are also. Those who are not My intimates are afraid of you because they naturally are suspicious of the unfamiliar. They suspect you because you are different to them and they can feel that difference. They will drop a wall down between you and them. Nothing that you can say or do will remove that wall. You also live on two different elevations. Remove the wall and the elevation still remains.

What is the spirit of truth? It is the Holy Spirit within you who bears witness to Me, for I am the Truth and Life and the true Way to the Father.

What is the spirit of error? It is the opposite of the Spirit of Truth, the Holy Spirit. It is the anti-Christ spirit of self, which is unholy because it cannot bear witness to Me as Lord, for it does not reveal truth and life, but manifests a lie and death. Not all who walk in the lower plane of self-worshippers are sinners. Some are simply blind, and their evil is that they cannot be taught truth. They "know it all!"

March 17

ANYTHING ACCORDING TO HIS WILL HE ANSWERS

Scripture Reading — I John 5:1-21

"And this is the confidence that we have in him, that, if we ask any thing according to his will, he heareth us: And if we know that he hear us, whatsoever we ask, we know that we have the petitions that we desired of him." (I John 5:14,15)

The big thing is to know My will, not My permissive will, but My perfect will. There are many who do not know what My perfect will is, nor can they, because it is too painful for them to face the facts, and so they stumble on blindly, often after quoting scriptures to prove to themselves that a certain thing is My will, when it may not be My will at all.

There are certain laws which I cannot break. One is the law of freedom which I have given mankind. Every person is a free moral agent. I cannot manipulate man, nor do I handle him as though he were a puppet. I do not force anyone to love or hate, not even to love Me, Myself. I can direct the Holy Spirit to work on a heart and reason with it; however, I cannot force it to love or worship Me.

All this you must take into consideration when you pray. Certain things you pray for are My will, but they are conditional. I cannot transgress My own laws and neither can you. If you can see this law and understand it and know that your request does not contradict this high law, and you know that what you request is My highest will, then you know you have the petition. My promise stands firm: I will do for you that which you ask of Me.

March 18

BEWARE OF THOSE WHO DO NOT HAVE TRUE LOVE

Scripture Reading — II John 1-13

"The elder unto the elect lady and her children, whom I love in the truth; and not I only, but also all they that have known the truth;" (II John 1:1)

"And now I beseech thee, lady, not as though I wrote a new commandment unto thee, but that which we had from the beginning, that we love one another. And this is love, that we walk after his commandments. This is the commandment, That, as ye have heard from the beginning, ye should walk in it....Look to yourselves, that we lose not those things which we have wrought, but that we receive a full reward. Whosoever transgresseth, and abideth not in the doctrine of Christ, hath not God. He that abideth in the doctrine of Christ, he hath both the Father and the Son." (vs. 5,6, 8,9)

My child, even as John, the elder, wrote to his spiritual sister in the Lord to remind her of the way of truth and righteousness, so I would remind you that the one great thing that you must adhere to, that you must teach, that you must look for in others, is the truth of love.

This is the doctrine of Christ, "If there come any unto you, and bring not this doctrine (of love), receive him not into your house, neither bid him God speed:" (vs. 10)

The doctrine of Christ is the doctrine of love. It is seeing others through the eyes of love. It does not look for separations and divisions. It does not promote schism. It looks for oneness and unity. Love is the key to heaven. It is the message of heaven. It is the theme of heaven. It is the beauty of heaven.

I came to earth to bring men this one doctrine. They have rejected it, and in order to cover up their lack of love they have written volumes of books on doctrines and commandments.

But the one great doctrine, the commandment of Christ, even My command to love, they have rejected.

If they come unto you and bring not THIS doctrine, do not receive them. They will contaminate your life with the spirit of hate, separation and division.

Even as love is contagious, so hate and the seed of bitterness will also spread quickly among you. It will divide the flock. It will cause havoc in the family of God.

The spirit of the anti-Christ is the opposite of pure love. It disrupts the unity, the singleness of vision, the flowing together in one spirit.

Receive not these "teachers" in your midst, for they are "kingdom of self" builders and will cause much hurt and harm.

March 19

RECEIVE THOSE WHO WALK IN LOVE

Scripture Reading — III John 1-14

"Beloved, thou doest faithfully whatsoever thou doest to the brethren, and to strangers; Which have borne witness of thy charity before the church: whom if thou bring forward on their journey after a godly sort, thou shalt do well: Because that for his name's sake they went forth, taking nothing of the Gentiles. We therefore ought to receive such, that we might be fellowhelpers to the truth." (III John 5-8)

John wrote to the elect lady whose open heart and hospitable spirit put her in a position where she received and entertained the false teachers who did not have the doctrine of Christ. He warned her not to receive them unto her home or to bless them, because if she did, she would become a partaker of their evil deeds. (II John 10,11).

To Gaius he wrote a completely different letter. He congratulated him on his spirit of hospitality on receiving the brethren and the strangers who were witnesses of the Lord among the Gentiles (heathen). They had worked for the Lord for nothing, and John said he was so happy to hear about the report of Gaius' love for these "missionaries," and that by helping them he had a part in their ministry and was a fellow helper to the truth.

John told Gaius that he was grieved with Diotrephes who loved to have the pre-eminence and had made himself the "shepherd" of the church. Because of Diotrephes' jealousy against John, he had talked against John with malicious words. Not only that, he had refused to accept the true servants of Jesus Christ and had thrown them out of the church. (III John 10) He also had forbidden others to receive them.

John was sending Demetrius with both of these letters, one for the elect lady and the other for Gaius. (III John 12-14)

Many of My children, like the elect lady, are being influenced by "Diotrepheses" to take into their home the teachers and ones that belong to particular doctrines of divisions and strife, and they fall under their control and influence. John warned her not to receive them because they were messengers of strife and not of love. For if she did, she was helping them and therefore sinning because they did not preach love (i.e. the Doctrine of Christ.)

On the other hand, John complimented Gaius who received the ones Diotrephes rejected, the two messengers of Christ who were "faith workers," preachers of the truth among the heathen. They were the faith missionaries of that day, rejected by the "big-time Diotrephes pastors" who had set themselves up to rule over My flock with a controlling spirit because they loved the pre-eminence. They hated the Johns, the apostles of love and closed the door to them. But Gaius had opened his heart and home to them because he had a true spirit of love, even as John the Beloved did.

Learn from these two letters and be wise. Satan will send many who will seem righteous but who will be agents of his to cause division and strife. Always close your heart's door to those who are evil, and open it to the true apostles of love who come in humility and love.

March 20

FAULTLESS IN AN EVIL DAY

Scripture Reading – Jude 1-25

"But ye, beloved, building up yourselves on your most holy faith, praying in the Holy Ghost, Keep yourself in the love of God, looking for the mercy of our Lord Jesus Christ unto eternal life." (Jude 20,21)

There are four vital steps which you must take care to walk in, for you are living in an evil day, yea it is even a more evil day than the evil days mentioned by Jude.

He spoke to those who fell away from a great and royal estate:
1. the children of Israel coming out of Egypt;
2. the angels who lost their first estate;
3. Sodom and Gomorrah who lived in a land like the Garden of Eden.

Many fell away because they were led away by three spirits:
1. the spirit of Cain, who hated his brother and was jealous of his place in God;
2. the spirit of Balaam, who hated his brother and also "sold" Israel for lucrative gain;
3. the spirit of Korah, who was jealous of his brother's (Moses) ministry.

Hatred and jealousy of another's ministry is the root of many who fall from My grace and who come under the terrible judgment of My wrath. These people become like:

1. spots of darkness in your fellowship meetings;
2. clouds with no latter rain in them;
3. withered up, plucked out, fruitless, dead trees;
4. roaring, moving, dangerous and treacherous waves of the sea;
5. stars that wander out of their courses. (vs. 12,13)

They want only the graces of man, they cultivate only the relationships that are to their personal advantage and prestige. (vs. 16)

My beloved, I call you to another life, another walk, one of purity and righteousness, even a holy walk. You must build yourself up in the holy walk, not in the prestige which man can give you.

You must never seek popularity or the praises of man. They are empty and mean nothing in the light of eternity.

Seek only the elevation that comes in the Spirit realm by
1. praying in the Holy Ghost;
2. keeping your heart filled with the love of God;
3. trusting in the mercy of our Lord Jesus Christ alone for eternal life.

These alone will enable you to keep from falling and to present you faultless before Me and the Father in our glory with exceeding joy. (vs. 24)

March 21

GOD LOVES ALL NATIONS

Scripture Reading – Zechariah 1:1-21

"So the angel that communed with me said unto me, Cry thou, saying, Thus saith the Lord of hosts; I am jealous for Jerusalem and for Zion with a great jealousy. And I am very sore displeased with the heathen that are at ease: for I was but a little displeased, and they helped forward the affliction. Therefore thus saith the Lord; I am returned to Jerusalem with mercies: my house shall be built in it, saith the Lord of hosts, and a line shall be stretched forth upon Jerusalem." (Zechariah 1:14-16)

When I choose to save and spare a city or a nation, it shall be saved and spared. Nothing can reverse My decision. I am displeased with the heathen who are at ease, be they black, yellow, red or white. It is not the colour of man that I am angry with, it is the heart and spirit. I care not for a country or a people to be at peace if there is no peace with Me in their hearts. The great peace is not national peace, but the peace of God which passeth all understanding.

One must reach the hearts of the natives of every nation with the peace of Jesus Christ. One must find the soul of the one who is lost and bring it to salvation or there will be no peace. War comes from a warring soul and a disturbed spirit.

The war in every nation did not begin in the heart of the terrorists. It began when My people, who should have been nursemaids to these despised, rejected and hindered ones, exploited them, sold them as slaves and stole their land. Now there is a spirit of retaliation and anger risen in the heart of many nations which will only be quenched when a Jesus-company arises in these lands in the power and might of the Holy Spirit to bring His people back to redemption and reconciliation with the ones whom they hate.

I love all nations. I want to return to Jerusalem with mercies;

mercy for them in their fear, their suffering, their hurt, their losses; I want to build My house again in this Jerusalem. It shall be called after My name. If My people will humble themselves and pray and seek My face and turn from their wicked ways, then will I hear from heaven and forgive their sin and HEAL their land, saith the Lord of hosts.

March 22

GOD "SEES" THROUGH MY EYES

Scripture Reading — Zechariah 2:1-13

"For thus saith the Lord of hosts; After the glory hath he sent me unto the nations which spoiled you: for he that toucheth you toucheth the apple of his eye." (Zechariah 2:8)

My beloved, you are the apple of My eye. The very pupil through which I see.

Not only must you see others through My vision and My understanding, but what is even more wonderful, I see through your eyes.

That is why you must be so careful in all that you do and all that you look upon. You must always live in My glory.

According to the glory that is within you will I send you out. After you have been filled with My glory I will send you to the nations. I will even send you to the nations which have robbed you of your treasures and persecuted you. There I will be with you and use you for My glory. My presence shall be seen upon you. And whoever toucheth you to do evil or harm unto you is touching a part of My body, even My precious pupil of My eye.

As you serve Me in the nations whithersoever I send you, I will give you the protection of My glory and My Divine presence.

You must bring the nations to Me, for I will visit them through you. I will look upon them again through your life. What your eyes see, My eyes see. What you weep for, I weep for, for you are the pupil of My eye. Only stay full of My glory, so I can visit these many nations through you.

March 23

THE STONE WITH SEVEN EYES

Scripture Reading — Zechariah 3:1-10

"For behold the stone that I have laid before Joshua; upon one stone shall be seven eyes: behold, I will engrave the graving thereof, saith the Lord of hosts, and I will remove the iniquity of that land in one day. In that day, saith the Lord of hosts, shall ye call every man his neighbour under the vine and under the fig tree." (Zechariah 3:9,10)

This Stone which was laid before Joshua, the high priest, was not given without much difficulty. Satan stood at the priest's right hand trying to interfere and to keep him from receiving what the Lord had for him.

Joshua was elected in filthy garments. He needed a change of raiment and a fair mitre for his bare head. For I cannot work in the life of those who are My priests unless their life is holy, sanctified and separated unto Me. Upon their heads must be the sign of the true covering, even the new mind, the mind of Christ.

To My Joshuas I gave a charge to "walk in Mine own ways and to keep My courts." If they do this, then they shall be chosen to judge My house and have a special place among My anointed who stand by (Zechariah 4:14), even the sons of oil.

The Stone I gave Joshua I give you. This is the Stone which the builders rejected (Luke 20:17, Acts 4:11, I Peter 2:7) and which Daniel saw cut out of the mountain without hands which smote the image, and became a great mountain, filling all the earth. (Daniel 2:35,44,45) It is the Shepherd, the Stone of Israel from the loins of Jacob, the shepherd (Genesis 49:24), the precious, true Stone of Zion (Isaiah 28:16). It is the covering glory of the bride (Revelation 21:11), the possession of the overcomers (Revelation 2:17), the Stone that possesses the seven eyes which are the seven-fold Spirit of God (Revelation 1:4) and which are related by Isaiah 11:2. Even the Spirit of the Lord of wisdom, understanding, counsel, might, knowledge, and the fear of the Lord. Without this you are nothing, and with it you can do all things. It is your qualification for greatness. It is your strength, your wisdom, your guidance, your counsel, your understanding in a situation and the fear of the Lord!

March 24

BY MY SPIRIT

Scripture Reading — Zechariah 4:1-14

"Then he answered and spake unto me, saying, This is the word of the Lord unto Zerubbabel, saying, Not by might, nor by power, but by my spirit, saith the Lord of hosts." (Zechariah 4:6)

"Who art thou, O great mountain? before Zerubbabel thou shalt become a plain: and he shall bring forth the headstone thereof with shoutings, crying, Grace, grace unto it. Moreover the word of the Lord came unto me, saying, The hands of Zerubbabel have laid the foundation of this house; his hands shall also finish it; and thou shalt know that the Lord of hosts hath sent me unto you." (vs. 7-9)

My child, hide yourself under My anointing. It is the anointing, that golden oil of the Holy Spirit, which is your help for every one of your needs.

Man may seem to be very powerful, even like the enemies of Zerubbabel. They may use every method conceivable to hinder God's plan. Do not lift one hand to fight back with these flesh and blood enemies. Rather, cry to the Lord for a mighty deliverance through the power of the Holy Spirit.

My Holy Spirit will work mightily to remove every mountain of hindrance. Your own might and power is nothing compared to My might and power. Put Me on your case and watch Me work for you. Great mountains shall become plains as you rest in Me.

Have you, like Zerubbabel begun to build a great building for Me? My child, you shall, through the power of My Holy Spirit, also complete this building. My Spirit is striving, speaking, dealing, working with many disobedient, faithless, and greedy hearts to bring in the finances for the completion of this building. I will not give them peace till they obey, and if they never obey, they will never have My peace, for it is My building they are building. By My Spirit I will complete all that I have begun to do.

March 25

RETURN TO PARADISE

Scripture Reading – Zechariah 5:1-11

"Then I turned, and lifted up mine eyes, and looked, and behold a flying roll. And he said unto me, What seest thou? And I answered, I see a flying roll; the length thereof is twenty cubits, and the breadth thereof ten cubits. Then said he unto me, This is the curse that goeth forth over the face of the whole earth: for every one that stealeth shall be cut off as on this side according to it; and every one that sweareth shall be cut off as on that side according to it. I will bring it forth, saith the Lord of hosts, and it shall enter into the house of the thief, and into the house of him that sweareth falsely by my name: and it shall remain in the midst of his house, and shall consume it with the timber thereof and the stones thereof." (Zechariah 5:1-4)

The word of judgment for this generation has already been decreed. Yea, it is written within and without, because of the overabundance of judgments that are determined upon this generation.

Neither is there a nation where the curse shall not come, for there is sin and iniquity in every nation. This great judgment of the end-time shall be upon those who steal and those who swear falsely by My name.

Many who think they are honest, steal from God, taking the tithe which belongs to the Lord and keeping it for themselves. It does not belong to them, yet they steal it from the Lord as Malachi, My prophet, said in Malachi 3:8,9.

They swear falsely by My name. Oh, the words, words, words, that come out of man! There never is a Sunday or a Sabbath when My name is not profaned by the false prophets of My people, who promise prosperity and good in the hour of judgment. Their mouth is full of untruth and lies which they preach to My people. For then My judgment shall enter even My house until they be consumed.

This is a day when there is a curse on the finance. The ephah is the symbol of justice, the symbol of true weight and judgment on commerce.

I will judge all nations and people in regard to their handlings and dealings of finance and commerce. I, the Lord, shall bring forth a talent of lead before the people, which is the symbol of a woman. She shall sit in the midst of the symbol of justice. (This talent of lead shall be cast into the symbol of justice.)

This symbol of justice, together with the weight of lead (which is the woman), shall be lifted up by two women with wings who shall fly as a stork to the land of Shinar, taking with them the symbol of justice. They shall return it there upon its original base.

(Women shall take the ephah [symbol of justice] back to the original site of the Garden of Eden, even the land of Shinar). It was My daughter Eve who led My sons out of paradise, and it shall be her daughters who shall be used by My Holy Spirit to restore My sons back to their lost paradise.

March 26

GOD WILL QUIET THE NORTH SO HE CAN BLESS THE SOUTH

Scripture Reading — Zechariah 6:1-15

"Then cried he upon me, and spake unto me, saying, Behold, these that go toward the north country have quieted my spirit in the north country." (Zechariah 6:8)

It was a time of turmoil and confusion, treachery and intrigues, and there was no way to build My house in the midst of these interruptions. So I sent out My chariots, driven by the horses of heaven from between the mountains of brass, the heavenly Mt. Gerizim and Mt. Ebal. They quieted the spirit of turmoil and anger and revenge and gave a time of peace in the land so that the chosen ones could be anointed and the House of God completed.

So today I send you to the nations of the south. There is much turmoil and preparation of warfare in the nations north of her. But I send you as horsemen in the heat of the spirit, even to their southern nation, even the "South country." (vs. 6)

I will use you as My horsemen from the heavenly Mount Zion. There, you will anoint My Josiahs to be a kingdom of priests unto Me. There is a holy branch in the nations whom I will anoint through you to build the "temple of the Lord" even in the south country.

Many will be anointed and crowns of anointing will be given to the elders (after the Spirit), and they shall grow over the wall (go up out of his place, vs. 12), as missionaries to the nations about them. And many shall come from afar to build My temple in the south country.

March 27

DO NOT IMAGINE EVIL AGAINST YOUR BROTHER

Scripture Reading — Zechariah 7:1-14

"...and let none of you imagine evil against his brother in your heart." (Zechariah 7:10)

My child, be very careful about your imagination. Imagination is very powerful. It comes from the verb "to image-in." It has the ability to create a thing through the power of the mind. It can be used in a good and positive way and also in a negative way.

The power of positive thinking is no myth. It delves into the hidden mysteries of man's creative powers. As such, it can be misused by misguided people. Even My children, who are ambitious for self and not wholly yielded to My highest will, can create through their mind things and situations which they feel I have given them, whereas it is not I who have given them what they have, but their own ability to bring it to pass by the power of the mind which has caused these things to be. My child, I am putting great power at your disposal. Be careful what you do with it.

Do not confuse your imagination with My word of knowledge or revelation of the Holy Spirit. Enlightenment concerning a person or situation is **not** imagination. Many imagine evil concerning you. This is because they do not have the true spirit of enlightenment in their hearts.

Many of My dearest and most precious children are misunderstood because someone has thought an evil thought and has spread a rumour of imagination which is a lie, and has destroyed My child's life. If you are not sure, do not imagine a thing in your heart.

March 28

MY PEOPLE SHALL POSSESS ALL THINGS

Scripture Reading — Zechariah 8:1-23

"For the seed shall be prosperous; the vine shall give her fruit, and the ground shall give her increase, and the heavens shall give their dew; and I will cause the remnant of this people to possess all these things." (Zechariah 8:12)

I am now, in this time, surely fulfilling Zechariah 8. I am bringing My people together from the nations of the world, and I am giving back to them My Holy City, for it was theirs since the day their Father Abraham ascended Mount Moriah to offer his son Isaac unto Me. And lest there be a doubt as to who the true possessor be, let it be remembered that Jerusalem, the city of peace, is truly the city of David. In these days I am giving it to My people to dwell therein in peace and truth. (vs. 16) If there be no truth, then there shall be no peace.

I will give you, who are blessed of My hand, a portion in the Holy City. Prepare your heart to receive it, for a portion, even a small but blessed portion, shall be yours. I shall cause My people to possess all these things. There I shall make you fruitful. Your vine shall give her fruit.

Yea, it is of Me that you return again. Did you not speak the word which caused it to break forth into fruitfulness? I have blessed and I will bless. But I will use you in a greater way in the Holy City and the Holy Land. You have not even begun to do in My City all that I shall yet put in your hands to do, but do **not** stop what you are doing! Continue to ascend My Holy Hill. Continue and possess the ground. It is decreed, it is yours.

March 29

THE LORD SHALL VISIT THE SOUTH LANDS

Scripture Reading — Zechariah 9:1-17

"And the Lord shall be seen over them, and his arrow shall go forth as the lightning: and the Lord God shall blow the trumpet, and shall go with whirlwinds of the south." (Zechariah 9:14)

This is the day when I am moving in the great south lands. Even in the southern hemisphere of this universe. I am visiting these nations in the same way as I did Indonesia. I will work in the same way with signs and wonders in the countries of South America.

But first I am calling for an army of intercessors who shall pray through. Did Indonesia's revival not begin because of their prayers? Have I not saved Korea and sent revival there because of their prayers with fasting? Have I not always visited a people or a nation because they prayed?

Yea, I say unto you that prayer changes things, and I will change the temperature of this nation as you call out the prayer warriors and intercessors. Did I not even save most of the white population from annihilation in Rhodesia because of the men and women who prayed and interceded?

Prayer is the arrow of the Lord. It is the artillery of saints. It flies from one continent to the next faster than the speed of sound! While you are yet praying I will hear.

As you pray, new life will come to the nation of South Africa. I will defend it, (vs. 15) and it shall shall become the strong nation which shall devour and subdue. It shall be as people drunk with new wine. I, the Lord, their God shall save them in the day of battle (vs. 16) for they shall be as the jewels of a crown, held up on My hand as an ensign to the holy land. And a great awakening shall come on South Africa (vs. 17).

March 30

RAIN IN THE TIME OF LATTER RAIN

Scripture Reading — Zechariah 10:1-12

"Ask ye of the Lord rain in the time of latter rain; so the Lord shall make bright clouds, and give them showers of rain, to every one grass in the field." (Zechariah 10:1)

I have promised My people that in the last days I will do great and mighty things. I will also visit you and use you and you shall be as clouds bringing the rain to the dry nations of the world and to pour My blessings out upon My people all over the world.

The time has come to gather the house of Joseph together with the house of Judah, and nothing but the rain of the Holy Spirit can unite them and make them one. I will do it now! (vs. 6)

I will also greatly strengthen the house of Judah, and I will bless the house of Joseph and they shall be as though I had not cast them off. And I will pour the rain of My Holy Spirit upon them. (Psalm 72:6) This is the time for the outpouring of the latter rain. It is time to fill out the corn and prepare the wine and the oil. (Deuteronomy 11:14,15)

This rain will not miss anyone. It will fall on every single blade of grass in the field. My people will be shaken to the core by this rain. But you must ask for it. Cry unto Me for the rain, believing the time has come for Me to send it and that the rain of the Spirit is for all nations, all churches, all peoples, all flesh. As the sun comes out the grass will sparkle as diamonds glittering in the sunlight. The rain will adorn the people for the coming of the Sun of righteousness.

March 31

THE LORD'S COVENANT WITH US

Scripture Reading —Zechariah 11:1-17

"And I will feed the flock of slaughter, even you, O poor of the flock. And I took unto me two staves; the one I called Beauty, and the other I called Bands; and I fed the flock." (Zechariah 11:7)

I, the Lord, have made a covenant with My beloved, even a double covenant of grace (beauty) and fellowship (bands). I will feed My flock, I will love them and care for them. I will never forsake them as long as they love Me.

You must be faithful to Me, My child, and I will keep My covenant of grace and unity with you. We are one. Only give Me what I desire of you: your faith, obedience, your love, your very life. And nothing shall at any time be able to break these staves which are the tokens of our covenant.

With Israel this was not so. They abhorred Me. Instead of them feeling that I was worthy of their love and faithfulness, they weighed for Me (sold Me for) 30 pieces of silver. So I broke My covenant of grace and oneness (in fellowship) with the house of Israel, and handed them over to many evil shepherds, whom also I have judged and shall continue to judge. Learn from Israel, that this may not happen to you. Give Me your love and loyalty, and My covenant with you will stand for eternity and never be broken, for I am faithful.

April 1

GOD'S PROTECTION OF JERUSALEM

Scripture Reading — Zechariah 12:1-14

"And in that day will I make Jerusalem a burdensome stone for all people: all that burden themselves with it shall be cut in pieces, though all the people of the earth be gathered together against it." (Zechariah 12:3)

I have made you so great and strong in Me, that all who try to "mess around" with you shall be cut to pieces. This is what I have promised Jerusalem. Jerusalem is My chosen city, the apple of My eye, the beloved. And you are as Jerusalem to Me.

Be not fearful what man may try to do with you. He cannot hurt or harm you, for My hand is upon you, and I will surely give you Divine and supernatural defences.

Your defence is invincible. Though **all** the nations (people of the earth) be gathered against it, still it cannot be overcome. All who come against her shall be smitten with blindness. (vs. 4) Yes, it is only because they are spiritually blind that they even attempt to come against My beloved, chosen one.

I will make My leaders as a hearth of fire. (vs. 5-7) You are My burning fire. All who come against you shall be burned by this fire. As My children abide in this fire, they are invincible. I have promised to save the tents of Judah, as I did long ago. There is special glory upon the house of David, My beloved ones and the inhabitants of Jerusalem, My people who dwell in peace, (vs. 7) and who walk humbly before Me.

April 2

THE FOUNTAIN OF CLEANSING

Scripture Reading — Zechariah 13:1-9

"In that day there shall be a fountain opened to the house of David and to the inhabitants of Jerusalem for sin and for uncleanness." (Zechariah 13:1)

There is a fountain filled with blood
Drawn from Emmanuel's veins
And sinners plunged beneath that flood
Lose all their guilty stains.

Yes, My child, I have become a fountain for sinners. I am the source of cleansing. There is no more need for the blood of bulls and goats. I am the cleansing fountain for the world, and even for the house of David for all sin and all uncleanness.

This fountain has been opened to Jewry. You must get this message of My Blood to the Jewish people, for, besides it, there is no cleansing, there is no deliverance from sin. The Blood has never lost its power to redeem the fallen and sinful man.

This Blood cuts off the idols and rids My church of the "false prophets." Neither will they be able to deceive My people by wearing the "cloth" of the clergy, for the marks of the Messiah of Israel are the wounds in His hands which He received in the house of His friends.

April 3

THE LORD SHALL BE KING OVER ALL THE WORLD

Scripture Reading — Zechariah 14:1-21

"And the Lord shall be king over all the earth: in that day shall there be one Lord, and his name one." (Zechariah 14:9)

Yes, that day is not far off. The final take-over will take place when the multitudes of nations join forces as one army to come against My Holy City and My holy people. (vs. 2) When the armies of many nations unite against My city, and come up against the city, there shall be much suffering for those who remain of both men and women; others shall flee into the Judean hills. (vs. 2)

In the last hour I will return, and I come not alone (vs. 3,4), but the armies of heaven come with Me to fight those nations. My landing field is the one from which I took off, even the Mount of Olives. In that moment the Mount of Olives shall cleave in half, and a fountain shall break forth in the Holy City which will flow east and west. The enemy shall be destroyed and the wealth of their armies shall belong to My people. (vs. 12-15)

The remnant of the nations shall come up to My Holy City yearly for the Feast of Tabernacles (vs. 17), and they shall rejoice together with My people at the fulfilment of God's plan, the great ingathering of the elect. I will rule over this world in peace and holiness (vs. 20), for when there shall be peace in Jerusalem, there will be peace in all the world. (vs. 11)

April 4

ANOINTED WITH THE OIL OF GLADNESS

Scripture Reading — Hebrews 1:1-14

"Thou hast loved righteousness, and hated iniquity; therefore God, even thy God, hath anointed thee with the oil of gladness above thy fellows." (Hebrews 1:9)

My beloved child, what is more to be desired than the oil of gladness? It will give you strength for your life's journey, for truly the joy of the Lord is your strength.

It was this joy which carried Me through the greatest trials of My life, for even when I faced the cross, it was the joy which I saw on the other side of the cross that gave Me the strength to go through My hours of rejection, betrayal and suffering. "Looking unto Jesus the author and finisher of our faith; who for the joy that was set before him endured the cross, despising the shame, and is set down at the right hand of the throne of God." (Hebrews 12:2)

But this joy was only the result of My pure life. Only those who love righteousness and hate iniquity have the right to this anointing of gladness. You must always be careful, My child, to love that which is right in the eyes of your God. Not what man says is right will bring gladness, but what I, your God, show you is right. As you turn away from all iniquity and are pure in heart, even as I was, the anointing of gladness shall come into your innermost soul, and you shall walk in My joy.

April 5

PERFECTED THROUGH SUFFERING

Scripture Reading — Hebrews 2:1-18

"But we see Jesus, who was made a little lower than the angels for the suffering of death, crowned with glory and honour; that he by the grace of God should taste death for every man. For it became him, for whom are all things, and by whom are all things, in bringing many sons unto glory, to make the captain of their salvation perfect through sufferings." (Hebrews 2:9,10)

"For in that he himself hath suffered being tempted, he is able to succour them that are tempted." (vs. 18)

My child, let no one ever try to tell you that suffering is invalid. It is in the hour when body, soul and spirit is in deep agony that you are being perfected into the likeness and image of the "Man of Sorrows."

There is a crown of glory awaiting all who suffer for My sake. In no way can this crown of glory be given to you if you do not qualify for it. It is a very costly reward, and what greater price can one pay than that of suffering?

I, Myself, was made perfect through suffering. (vs. 10) You and I, the "sanctified and the sanctifier" are one. What is Mine is yours. That is why I can call you brethren, because we are one in suffering the same way, the same hurts, and the same rejections.

Even as I suffered and was tempted so that now I am able to succour, comfort all who are tempted, so you too can comfort and understand what others suffer, only because you too have suffered.

The trials you have gone through are your crown of glory to give you understanding to help and succour others.

Never despise the crown of glory, even though the price tag is suffering!

April 6

BE FAITHFUL TO OBEY HIM IN EVERYTHING

Scripture Reading — Hebrews 3:1-19

"Wherefore, holy brethren, partakers of the heavenly calling, consider the Apostle and High Priest of our profession, Christ Jesus; Who was faithful to him that appointed him, as also Moses was faithful in all his house." (Hebrews 3:1,2)

Yes, My child, consider Me! Think about My faithfulness to My Father under whose appointment I came to earth. You too are here under Divine appointment. You are here because I sent you and I appointed you to be My ambassador.

I have a work, a calling, for you to fulfil. You must strive, at all costs, to be faithful to fulfil this calling. Remember, you are not on your own. You are under My Divine appointment. I will lead you, I will open doors and channels for you to flow into. I will send you here and there. I will also stop you from doing certain things which are not My perfect will.

Be faithful to the One who appoints you; be obedient, be loyal, be happy to do all that I ask you to do.

I ask no more of you than I, Myself, gave. The key to greatness is simply to be faithful to all that I ask of you, all that is required of you, all that I appoint you to, little or much.

April 7

GOD PLANNED YOUR LIFE FROM THE BEGINNING OF TIME

Scripture Reading — Hebrews 4:1-16

"For we which have believed do enter into rest, as he said, As

I have sworn in my wrath, if they shall enter into my rest: although the works were finished from the foundation of the world." (Hebrews 4:3)

All your needs, all that is right, has been secured for you from the foundations of the world. But you will never obtain these great and precious promises if you do not mix My promise with **your** faith.

Before a miracle can happen, you must believe that My promise to you is true and that I **am** faithful to you and true to My Word. Call Me faithful, call Me true, and it will build faith in your heart.

My child, I have separated you to a special, holy and high calling. What you have done this last while you will not be permitted to do again. You must prepare your heart for separation, for a change. You can cling to no-one, not even your dearest and nearest. Ask of Me a long life, for there is so much yet which I need you to do. Don't give up. It is time for a new anointing, even a new visitation. Be careful, now especially, to get My will for all you do, for you will have many calls in different directions. You have learned some very important lessons, which will change you. Do nothing except by My appointment. Your life, your calling, is too precious to waste. It is even My life.

Never fear anything but to fail to enter into the promises of God and to possess that which is destined for you.

My promise, plus your faith in Me, makes a miracle.

April 8

COMPASSION ON THE IGNORANT

Scripture Reading — Hebrews 5:1-14

"Who can have compassion on the ignorant, and on them that are out of the way; for that he himself also is compassed with infirmity. And by reason hereof he ought, as for the people, so also for himself, to offer for sins." (Hebrews 5:2,3)

My child, always remember where you came from and what you really are. You are nothing without My grace in your life. Have compassion on those who are ignorant, knowing always that in comparison with the knowledge of the eternities you are ignorant too. There is so much you do not yet know, things which will take an eternity for you to learn. I have much strong meat to teach you, but it only belongs to those that are "full of age," those who are matured in wisdom and in spirit, even those who by reason of using God's Word in much study and meditation have their senses exercised to discern both good and evil. (vs. 14) My child, you need to exercise your senses more in My Word. I cannot do it for you. You alone can do it for yourself with the help of the Holy Spirit who will teach you the knowledge of the eternities. Have compassion therefore on those who seem to you to be ignorant, knowing you are ignorant too when compared with the eternal Wisdom of Ages.

Also, have compassion (love with understanding) on those who are "out of the way." There are many who are not living in the centre of My will. They are out of the way. Nevertheless, I have compassion on them. I love them, I am patient with them. I am long-suffering with them. I pity them.

You can never be a shepherd over My flock if you will be critical of the failures of your sheep. Demand perfection, but expect them to fail, knowing you also are compassed with infirmity and need to constantly go to God to ask for forgiveness of your sins.

You are My shepherd, not by any choosing of your own, but because you are called of God, as was Aaron. You cannot make yourself the shepherd of a people. It is I who call you to it. Therefore, prepare your heart to accept every calling which I give you.

April 9

OFFER UP TO GOD YOUR WORKS

Scripture Reading — Hebrews 6:1-20

"For God is not unrighteous to forget your work and labour of love, which ye have shewed toward his name, in that ye have ministered to the saints, and do minister...That ye be not slothful, but followers of them who through faith and patience inherit the promises. For when God made promise to Abraham, because he could swear by no greater, he sware by himself, Saying, Surely blessing I will bless thee, and multiplying I will multiply thee. And so, after he had patiently endured, he obtained the promise." (Hebrews 6:10, 12-15)

My child, what you do for self I have not remembered, but what you have done for Me will have a great reward from Me. Offer up to Me all your ministry. Remember that I am your reward. Even though you do not have the praises and acclaim of others, if you do it all as unto Me you will surely have a great reward of Me.

I would encourage you to have faith and patience, for faith must also be mixed with patience. I will do wonders for you. What I have done in the past is nothing in comparison with what I will do for you in the future.

I am multiplying your life and I will multiply it an hundredfold. But you must have faith and patience. I am not unjust; I am not unfair. Rest in Me. Keep believing. Let your hope be as an anchor of your soul. Never lose that anchor or you will be shipwrecked on the sands of time. Keep in your heart the anticipation of something wonderfully good happening to you.

April 10

MAKING A VOW TO GOD

Scripture Reading — Hebrews 7:1-28

"For the law made nothing perfect, but the bringing in of a better hope did; by the which we draw nigh unto God. And inasmuch as not without an oath he was made priest: (For those priests were made without an oath; but this with an oath by him that said unto him, The Lord sware and will not repent, Thou art a priest for ever after the order of Melchisedec:) By so much was Jesus made a surety of a better testament." (Hebrews 7:19-22)

My child, I have, Myself, made a covenant and spoken (through My Son, My Word and My prophets) concerning the vow which I have made with all who will enter into the covenant relationship with Me.

A vow is only an offence to the weak and to those who want to look at their own limitations. I called My chosen Bride of all ages to enter into covenant relationship with Me. Abraham (I Chronicles

16:16), Isaac (I Chronicles 16:16), Jacob (I Chronicles 16:17, Genesis 28:20, 31:13), Joseph (Genesis 37:5-11), Moses (Exodus 3:7-10), Israel (I Chronicles 16:17, Numbers 21:2), Joshua and Caleb (Joshua 14:9), Elkanah (I Samuel 1:21), Hannah (I Samuel 1:11), David (Psalm 56:12), Simeon (Luke 2:25-29), Jesus Christ (Matthew 26:28, Hebrews 8:8), and many others were faithful to Me in this covenant relationship, even as I am faithful to them. These are My elect, and many of whom you know not are My chosen elect.

A covenant relationship brings both partners into a position of responsibility. Many do not want to accept responsibility of any kind these days. So they say it is wrong to make a vow. Yet, they did the same when they married. The entered into a covenant relationship with their spouse by giving and accepting of vows, one to the other, in the presence of their Lord and others. They did this because the laws of the land demanded it to make legal their relationship. So today I am calling My servants and handmaidens into a covenant relationship of love and responsibility to My end-time vision to the nations.

April 11

THE LAW IN OUR HEARTS

Scripture Reading – Hebrews 8:1-13

"For this is the covenant that I will make with the house of Israel after those days, saith the Lord; I will put my laws into their mind, and write them in their hearts: and I will be to them a God, and they shall be to me a people:" (Hebrews 8:10)

This is perfection, that you may have My laws in your mind and written on your heart, for then alone can you be perfect.

These are not the laws of man, or the laws of the church, but My very own laws, which are the laws of the fruit of the Spirit, even love, grace, patience, longsuffering, tenderness, meekness, joy, gentleness, goodness, faith, temperance, understanding and compassion, hope and forgiveness.

When these attributes are written in your heart, you become so identified with them that you become loving, joyful, gentle, good, meek, faithful, temperate, full of understanding and compassion, patient and longsuffering, forgiving.

But first you must have these truths put in your mind, that you may know and understand that this higher law is My perfect law and is the law of heaven.

As your mind dwells on these truths your heart will be strengthened to accept these truths, and your very life will live out these truths, that you might become Christ-like, perfect in My law of love, purity and truth. (Proverbs 23:7)

April 12

A LIFE OF DEDICATION ONLY THROUGH HIS HELP

Scripture Reading — Hebrews 9:1-28

"How much more shall the blood of Christ, who through the eternal Spirit offered himself without spot to God, purge your conscience from dead works to serve the living God?" (Hebrews 9:14)

It was through the power of the Holy Spirit alone that I could become the offering for sin. My life was indwelt by the mighty power of the Holy Spirit, even from the moment that Gabriel decreed it to My fleshly mother, Mary. "And the angel answered and said unto her, The Holy Ghost shall come upon thee, and the power of the Highest shall overshadow thee: therefore also that holy thing which shall be born of thee shall be called the Son of God." (Luke 1:35)

Even as the Holy Spirit of God rested upon the earthly tabernacle and the cherubims of glory shadowed the mercy seat (Hebrews 9:5), so My life, from the moment of Gabriel's appearance, was overshadowed by the exact same mighty power of the Holy Spirit.

Even as in the Ark of the Covenant were three things:

1. the manna in the golden pot,
2. Aaron's rod that budded,
3. the tables of the Covenant,

so these three things were in Mary's womb:

1. I am the bread come down from heaven, (John 6:51)

2. I am the undisputed, chosen High Priest, (Numbers 17:10, Hebrews 7:21),
3. I am the Word become flesh, (John 1:14).

Even as the high priest could enter the holy place only once in a year (Hebrews 9:7), and anyone presumptuous enough to try to enter in would be smitten dead, so Mary's womb became My holy dwelling place, and My Father commanded Joseph not to know her until after I was born. (Matthew 1:25) So I was conceived, developed, birthed, grew up, lived My life in perfection, died and was resurrected and ascended through the power of the Holy Spirit. He is your key to this Christ-life also. Only through the Holy Spirit can you peacefully fulfil your destiny.

April 13

A COMPANION OF THE PERSECUTED

Scripture Reading — Hebrews 10:1-39

"But call to remembrance the former days, in which, after ye were illuminated, ye endured a great fight of afflictions; Partly, whilst ye were made a gazingstock both by reproaches and afflictions; and partly, whilst ye became companions of them that were so used." (Hebrews 10:32,33)

Not all are willing to identify themselves with those who are a gazingstock. Most people are willing to be the friend of the one who is popular and well received, but when persecution comes, they deny any relationship with the persecuted one.

I want you to always remember how you, yourself, have been rejected by My children and how, after your illumination, you have been misunderstood and become a gazingstock.

Remember, I too was a gazingstock. As I hung on the cross, naked, bleeding, beaten and rejected, I was not there for any reason of My own, but only for your sake, and the sake of the whole world.

Now, you have become My companion in suffering. You have hazarded yourself for Me, because you love Me.

Every time you identify yourself with the persecuted, you are going to be persecuted. But always be faithful. Have compassion on those in their bonds, taking joyfully the spoiling of your goods, knowing you have an enduring reward in heaven.

April 14

FAITH IS THE KEY TO UNDERSTANDING

Scripture Reading — Hebrews 11:1-40

"Through faith we understand that the worlds were framed by the word of God, so that things which are seen were not made of things which do appear." (Hebrews 11:3)

Yes, My child, it is by faith that you understand the works of My hands. In fact, without faith you have no understanding. You go into error.

It is because men like Darwin had no faith, and therefore no understanding, that the world was led into error, because at that time there was no faith in the heads of many on the earth. It was the age of reasoning. Reasoning is blind because it makes no allowance for "the act of God," and therefore it leads the reasoner into error, unless the reasoner takes Me, the Almighty, into consideration.

When faith operates in your heart, you begin to have understanding. This understanding has creative power in your life to conceive what I am capable of doing and cause it to come to pass in your life. When you see that My "Words," My expression of thought, caused the worlds to come into existence, you can begin to see how powerful your expressions of thought, i.e. your words, are. You can speak into existence all things when you understand this faith-formula.

Neither do you need any evidence beforehand of any possibility that the miraculous can be achieved, for the things which are seen were not made of things which do appear, but out of seeming nothingness. There needs be no visible reason upon which you can base your faith. Faith has only one ingredient to make it operative and holy. It must be birthed out of knowing Me, the Faithful and True.

April 15

YOU HAVE NOT SUFFERED AS MUCH AS JESUS

Scripture Reading — Hebrews 12:1-29

"Ye have not yet resisted unto blood, striving against sin." (Hebrews 12:4)

My child, My beloved, it is in suffering that I made you great. I gave you enlargement of soul for others through the sword that pierced your heart.

Only you and I know how you have bled on the inside and I know that the greatest suffering is not that of the body, but of the soul and spirit. But how else can you be lifted into that high and holy realm of the company of the saints?

You have wept because you had nothing more to give. So now you have something: I come to ask you to release your dearest treasure unto Me and even your great friendship, which really was only a gift from Me, for without Me you would not have had it.

Your suffering is great, but not as great as that of many of My children. I endured the contradiction of sinners on My back as two different Roman soldiers beat and whipped My back, sadistically possessed of demons, both in their own particular way (vs. 3). That is what I ask you to endure, the contradiction of these sinners who call themselves My children. They have separated you by mocking you as an offscouring, but if you accept even this through My hands, then will I give you grace to rise above it and it shall not overcome you, but give you honour in the sight of the holy witnesses of the company of angels, the general assembly of the church of the firstborn, the spirits of holy men made perfect, My Father, your Father and Me, Myself. I am your mediator. I made a covenant with you. You shall receive a kingdom which none can take away from you (vs. 28), because it is not between you and mortals but between you and Me. I cannot lie, I am truth.

So My child, keep running. I command you to keep on running, for in your running, you will be healed. (vs. 13)

April 16

SUFFER WITHOUT THE GATE

Scripture Reading — Hebrews 13:1-25

"Wherefore Jesus also, that he might sanctify the people with his own blood, suffered without the gate. Let us go forth therefore unto him without the camp, bearing his reproach. For here have we no continuing city, but we seek one to come." (Hebrews 13:12-14)

My beloved, who told you that serving Me was a popularity contest? What makes you think that the one before the earthly multitudes is more honourable than the one before the heavenly cloud of witnesses?

Look at Me! Who accepted Me? The stragglers, the rejects, the humble, the women and the poorest of the poor, the harlots and sinners.

Who went out to David at the cave of Adullam? Everyone that was in distress, and everyone that was in debt and everyone that was discontent. (I Samuel 22:1,2) It is not what people make you to be that counts for anything, but what you are.

I suffered. Why do you think you should not know suffering? I accepted this path of suffering because I knew how far-reaching its power would be. Suffering for a nation will do more for it than preaching to it will. If preaching were so important, I would have preached from the cross.

I suffered outside the gate. They threw Me out from their midst. I wasn't fit to be a member of their society. I was unloved, unwanted and unappreciated. Since when can you, My disciple, expect any different treatment than your Master?

I call to you. Yea, I even command you! Come out with Me, even outside of their camp. Bear My reproach. It is My reproach you bear! No city on earth is your eternal habitation. You are only camping temporarily. You must keep seeking for the eternal city.

So with praise in your heart and thanksgiving on your lips follow Me on the Via Dolorosa. Die daily! Tomorrow you will live with Me in Paradise!

April 17

PRAYING THROUGH FOR A NATION AHEAD OF TIME

Scripture Reading – Romans 1:1-32

"For God is my witness, whom I serve with my spirit in the gospel of his Son, that without ceasing I make mention of you always in my prayers;" (Romans 1:9)

The key to a great missionary is his life of prayer for the nation to which he was called. Even long before he went there his prayers opened the door for him to go there and to be used, for they went before him to conquer demons and bind up the works of Satan, so that the Gospel would be preached in power.

Paul served Me with his spirit. It is not enough to worship Me in spirit and in truth. One must also strive in this pure way to be a blessing to the nations.

"Making request, if by any means now at length I might have a prosperous journey by the will of God to come unto you." (vs. 10)

Paul had a true missionary heart. He knocked and knocked on the door of Rome in prayer, that he might be able to go to them. Prayer will open the door to any nation for you.

"That is, that I may be comforted together with you by the mutual faith both of you and me." (vs. 12)

His purpose for going was not only to preach to the heathen and save his soul, but to establish the believer, comfort him, and be a blessing to him.

"Now I would not have you ignorant, brethren, that oftentimes I purposed to come unto you, (but was let hitherto,) that I might have some fruit among you also, even as among other Gentiles." (vs. 13)

My child, remember how you prayed for a certain nation, asking Me to give you a part of that great harvest? Remember how you travailed and how I sent you in the power of the Holy Spirit? So today, never cease to ask Me for the nations. I want to give them to you because you are My missionary, My apostle to the nations. Never cease asking. If your feet do not stand upon them, then the feet of your children and children's children shall.

"I am debtor both to the Greeks, and to the Barbarians; both to the wise, and to the unwise. So, as much as in me is, I am ready to preach the gospel to you that are at Rome also." (vs. 14,15) You are a debtor, because of My grace in your life, to take the message of saving grace to the nations.

"For I am not ashamed of the gospel of Christ: for it is the power of God unto salvation to every one that believeth; to the Jew first, and also to the Greek." (vs. 16) Take it to ALL.

April 18

THE IMMORTAL GLORY

Scripture Reading — Romans 2:1-29

"To them who by patient continuance in well doing seek for glory and honour and immortality, eternal life:...But glory, honour, and peace, to every man that worketh good, to the Jew first, and also to the Gentile:" (Romans 2:7,10)

Yes, My child, there are great and wonderful rewards further up the road. If My children could see for a minute the glory, the honour, the immortality which awaits them if they are faithful and patiently endure their trials and tests, continuing to do good for evil, they would completely change their attitudes. They would try so much harder to please Me. They would permit nothing to interfere with My great plan for their eternal destiny.

The glory and honour and the peace that you have today on this earth is nothing compared to that of eternity. All earth's glory is limited by the carnality of the flesh, for the full impact of glory would dissolve you immediately. The honour of earth is mixed with criticism, contempt and rejection.

There are different degrees of immortality. Some are of much higher order than others. Do not strive only to escape the damnation of the lost, but rather strive for the higher degrees of celestial attainment, that you may spend eternity in the highest realm of glory and honour. It is here that you determine what you shall be there.

April 19

THE ORACLES OF GOD ARE COMMITTED TO US

Scripture Reading — Romans 3:1-31

"Much every way: chiefly, because that unto them were committed the oracles of God." (Romans 3:2)

It is a great honour for My people to have received the very oracles of God.

The world searches for words of wisdom. But the greatest wisdom, the wisdom of the ages is stored up for the righteous.

It is only as the soul is attuned with the infinite Spirit of God, who is the source of all revealed Divine wisdom, that true enlightenment can be given to mortal man.

Even as a man can speak extemporaneously, relying on My anointing to give him the words, so can he also write guided by the Spirit of God who teaches the truths of heaven to the most simple soul, even the one whose faith is able to release the flow of wisdom which is stored up for the righteous.

"Prophecy came not in old time by the will of man: but holy men of God spake as they were moved by the Holy Ghost." (II Peter 1:21)

It is only through the Holy Spirit that the truth of heaven is revealed.

Paul, My servant truly said, "But as it is written, Eye hath not seen, nor ear heard, neither have entered into the heart of man, the things which God hath prepared for them that love him. But God hath revealed them unto us by his Spirit: for the Spirit searcheth all things, yea, the deep things of God...Now we have received, not the spirit of the world, but the spirit which is of God; that we might know the things that are freely given to us of God. Which things also we speak, not in the words which man's wisdom teacheth, but which the Holy Ghost teacheth; comparing spiritual things with spiritual. But the natural man receiveth not the things of the Spirit of God: for they are foolishness unto him: neither can he know them, because they are spiritually discerned." (I Corinthians 2:9-14)

April 20

SEEING THROUGH THE EYE OF FAITH

Scripture Reading — Romans 4:1-25

"...even God, who quickeneth the dead, and calleth those things which be not as though they were. Who against hope believed in hope, (hoped when there was no hope)." (Romans 4:17b,18a)

Yes, when I determine a thing shall be done, I see it as accomplished. This is what you must do by the eyes of faith.

When I begin to do a thing, I move heaven and earth to fulfil My plan. I see the finished product, and not the ingredients out of which that product is made.

When you ask your cook to make a chocolate cake, you see in your mind the chocolate cake. You do not see the flour, eggs, sugar, etc.. You see the finished product. Flour and eggs are tasteless, but combined with the cocoa and sugar and vanilla, and the other ingredients, you produce, under heat, a tasty morsel.

The flour and sugar, etc., are the ingredients of faith, patience, hope, trust, all of which seem "tasteless" and useless. But when combined together under the heat of My promises, the "cake" will materialize and it shall be good.

When I declare a thing, it is surely going to come to pass, for all the hosts of heaven are there to bring it to pass. My Word has creative power.

Remember, Abraham is your spiritual father. He had faith. He hoped when there was no hope. You are his spiritual child, even his faith-child. You have the characteristics of your earthly father. You also have the characteristics of your spiritual father, Abraham. You have inherited his faith.

Even as he did not take into consideration his own "dead" body, so you must not regard the "dead" members of your spiritual body, but believe only in My eternal promises, which cannot fail, that which I have promised, I will surely perform. In fact, in My eyes it is already done.

Do not look at the "dead" womb which shall produce the "promised child." But look at the finished product of your faith. See it with the eyes of faith. You will not stagger at My promise through unbelief, but you will be strong in faith as you see your promise as though fulfilled and give "glory to God" for the finished work of God. (vs. 19,20)

April 21

TRIALS MAKE YOU TOUGH

Scripture Reading — Romans 5:1-21

"By whom also we have access by faith into this grace wherein we stand, and rejoice in hope of the glory of God. And not only so, but we glory in tribulations also: knowing that tribulation worketh patience; And patience, experience; and experience, hope:" (Romans 5:2-4)

You can rejoice in the midst of tribulation, My beloved child, because through the faith which I have given you, which has matured through years of experience, you know that only good can result from all these trials and heartaches through which you pass.

Yea, My beloved child, even in the midst of your trials and heartaches you can rejoice in hope of the glory of God which shall be imputed to you because of the grace which is given to you in this hour of fiery trials. Yes, even in tribulation you take glory because you know that this tribulation works patience in your life.

Patience is that quality in a good person that enables him to endure difficulties, trials and testings, so that he can gain experience through the school of suffering, knowing by experience that only good can result, because the heart is filled with hope.

You need these trials. They do not make you hard, they make you strong. The people who are going to take the Kingdom are going to be tough.

Patience is the toughness that comes to a metal that is tempered by heat. "For ye have need of patience, that, after ye have done the will of God, ye might receive the promise." (Hebrews 10:36)

April 22

RESURRECTION LIFE THROUGH DEATH

Scripture Reading — Romans 6:1-23

"For if we have been planted together in the likeness of his death, we shall be also in the likeness of his resurrection:" (Romans 6:5)

You have not yet entered into the fulness of My resurrected life, only because you have not completely entered into My death. There remains yet a death to self which My children find hard to yield to. They want the glory of the resurrection life without the tomb. But without the tomb there is only a stinking body exposed to onlookers, naked, ravaged by sin and marred by the scars of disobedience.

In ancient times slaves could only be freed by:

1. their master giving them freedom,
2. escape,
3. someone redeeming them with a ransom price,
4. death.

You were a slave to sin. Your master, Satan, would never free you. For to do so is an act of love. Neither could you escape. You did not have the strength for it. But I redeemed you with the Blood of My Son. You have accepted His Blood for the price of your atonement. Accept it also as your release from all weakness and sins. Die to self through the power of the Blood.

Neither your works nor strength will release you from the sins of your mortal self-pride, personal ambition, fears, unbelief, criticism, lack of love. All these links of the chain that holds you in bondage to mortality can only be broken by the power of My Son's Blood, as you die to self through the Blood's efficaciousness and thereby enter into the resurrected life which sets you free from the former rulers of your life.

What master wants a dead slave? If you are dead to sin, surely Satan will cast you out and you shall be alive in Me.

April 23

MARRIED TO CHRIST

Scripture Reading — Romans 7:1-25

"Wherefore, my brethren, ye also are become dead to the law by the body of Christ; that ye should be married to another, even to him who is raised from the dead, that we should bring forth fruit unto God." (Romans 7:4)

Yes, My beloved child, My beloved bride, you are married to Me. I am your husband.

I killed your first husband, even "the laws" that declared you dead in trespasses and sin. I gave My life to kill the old authority that declared you to be a sinner in bondage and destined to the judgment fires of hell. I destroyed the law of condemnation by giving My life for you to win you as My bride. You are now My bride. You belong to Me. I am your husband. I have given you a new set of laws to live by.

When you were married to your former husband, the law, you produced children of transgression. Your life was failure after failure.

But now you are married to Me. I am love. You obey your new husband who died to win you by freeing you from the tyrant of the laws and ordinances that held you in bondage and slavery, making you always feel like a failure.

By My authority and grace you live in a higher realm. You have moved out of the old house; you now live in a new house. I am your Lord and Master. I will protect you. In this house we live by the law of love and not by the laws and traditions that bring condemnation and death. You are married to a "Lover." My law is love.

> Hephzibah is what I call you,
> For the Lord delights in thee;
> No more shalt thou be forsaken,
> Forever more, married to Me.
> I have seen your pain and longings,
> No more will you lonely be,
> Soon My face you too shall see.

April 24

ALL MIRACLES WROUGHT BY THE HOLY SPIRIT

Scripture Reading – Romans 8:1-16

"But if the Spirit of him that raised up Jesus from the dead dwell in you, he that raised up Christ from the dead shall also quicken your mortal bodies by his Spirit that dwelleth in you." (Romans 8:11)

My child, it is that very same life that raised Me up from the dead that accompanied Me in all My earthly life. It was there when the "power of the Highest" overshadowed Mary of Nazareth, enabled her womb to receive the seedling of My body as I left My heavenly body and took on Myself the form of a fœtus.

It was there as I was born and angels sang. It was there as I was carried to Egypt. It was there as I disputed, at the age of 12, with the theologians of the temple. It was there as I was manifested to Israel by John the Baptist. It was there when I did the signs and wonders and miracles, when I walked on the water, multiplied the loaves and fishes, raised the dead and cleansed the lepers. It was there in the garden, when I hung from the cross, and it was there in the tomb, waiting to raise Me up from the dead on the third day.

It dwelt in Me and it dwells in you at all times. It enables you to supercede the norm. Rely not on your own strength or ability, but in the strength and ability of this same Spirit, even the Spirit of the Father in the person of the Holy Ghost. It is there with you today and will be tomorrow.

April 25

THE SLAIN LAMB SEES THE GLORY

Scripture Reading – Romans 8:17-25

"For I reckon that the sufferings of this present time are not worthy to be compared with the glory which shall be revealed in us." (Romans 8:18)

Yes, My beloved child, you have long known the path of suffering. Tears have often been your companion, but you have always accepted your broken heart as a very special gift of great value coming directly from Me.

And My child, it is only with a broken heart that you can submit to all the difficulties, trials and tests. For in brokenness you are deeper into the holy of holies.

It was only as the high priest carried the blood of the slain lamb that he was permitted to approach into My Divine and holy presence.

Sometimes you weary of having a broken and a contrite heart, but remember, you only come into the royal chambers as a slain lamb.

The high priest only came into this high and holy secret habitation once a year. There will be times when you will go about as if nothing has happened, your heart released of all hurt and suffering and the pain of yesterday will recede into the past. But when you long again for the intimacy of that close relationship with Me, then circumstances will again come into your life. The lamb within shall be slain, the blood shall flow, the heart will break, and you will find yourself entering once again into My glory.

And this will continue all your life till the day when you will not only enter into My glory, but My glory shall enter you.

April 26

ALL THINGS WORK FOR GOOD

Scripture Reading – Romans 8:26-33

"And we know that all things work together for good to them that love God, to them who are the called according to his purpose." (Romans 8:28)

Only the Holy Spirit could reveal such a glorious truth to man as this one. If ever you have trouble with the writings of My servant Paul, remember that he also gave this wonderful truth to My children.

Paul said "we know." But many of My children do not know that all things, even the hurts and tragedies of their lives, work together for good to them who are called to be My elect.

I will use every circumstance of your temporal life to bring about a good thing for your eternal life. I allow many things to come into your life which you cannot understand but which are painful, only because I know you so well. I will not allow you to suffer more than you are able to bear.

With every trial and test I will make a way of escape for you. But if you refuse to accept the easy way out, you shall be perfected into My eternal plan for you that much more quickly.

I love you too much to destroy you. I love you more than all My other created work; I will only do you good because you are My dearest treasure. If you let Me, I will take even the ruins of your life and make you a better person because of them.

April 27

NO ONE HAS THE AUTHORITY TO CONDEMN YOU

Scripture Reading – Romans 8:34

"Who is he that condemneth? It is Christ that died, yea rather, that is risen again, who is even at the right hand of God, who also maketh intercession for us." (Romans 8:34)

Yea, My beloved child, there are many who would seek to condemn you, but their condemnation cannot harm your soul if you refuse to retaliate.

I call you to My rest. Let Me avenge your adversary. Rest in Me. I do not call you to silent anger, but to the sweetness of resting in Me. My understanding in the matter is all that you need.

I am your final and only judge. I am the one you need to fear displeasing. It is before Me you stand or fall. I give the only verdict of validity. All others are chatter.

And I am not only your judge, but also your defence lawyer. I plead your case. I am not your prosecuting lawyer. Let others persecute you. You must only be honest with Me. Tell Me all, so I can defend your case. I cannot defend hidden, unconfessed sins. For your hidden sins themselves will condemn you and deliver you up to an eternal prison. I am even now standing before the judgment bar of eternity, making intercession for you to the Father, your Father and mine.

Unconfessed sins will be judged. Unrepentant attitudes will be judged. But all things confessed shall be forgiven. I am a merciful God.

April 28

NOTHING CAN SEPARATE YOU FROM GOD

Scripture Reading — Romans 8:35-39

"Who shall separate us from the love of Christ? shall tribulation, or distress, or persecution, or famine, or nakedness, or peril, or sword?" (Romans 8:35)

"Nor height, nor depth, nor any other creature, shall be able to separate us from the love of God, which is in Christ Jesus our Lord." (vs. 39)

My child, where there is love, there is no separation. There are not enough evil powers of the universe in existence to separate you from My great love for you.

Nothing can make Me stop loving you. You will always feel My presence. I will always be near you. No matter what terrible things may happen in your life, these things will only serve to draw you closer to Me.

It is in tribulation, distress, persecution, famine, nakedness, peril and sword (war) that you will feel My closeness to you more than ever. My angels are always near to you, and as the veil of flesh is rubbed thinner through the friction of suffering, you will have many peeks into My glory.

Yes, even as, for My sake, you lay your head on the slaughterblock, I am there, holding your hand. I'm never closer to you than when you are "dying."

In all these adversities, these pains, hurts and distresses you are more than a conqueror through My love in you. You can never conquer in your own strength, only in My love.

And **nothing** can come between you and Me, My child. Things often come between My children. And often those who were the dearest friends yesterday become separated. But you and I will never, ever, be separated. I am the inspiration of your life, and death will only serve to bring you into My immediate presence.

Good angels are there with you to bring comfort and aid. Principalities and powers are the demon forces which only serve to make you wiser and stronger in My love and power. They have come into your midst, but love will "sizzle" them, and **only** love. Hurt feelings, silent treatment, rebukes, whisperings, accusations, critical advice, confidences will only add to their power to divide and conquer. For they too have a façade of love and goodness. They only cannot exist where true, pure "Jesus-love" is turned on them.

Neither the happenings of yesterday, today or tomorrow can separate you from My love.

Neither heights of fame and acclaim, depths of shame and slander, sin and sorrow, or any creature in existence shall be able to separate you from My love.

You were there when I was crucified. Your sins sent Me to the cross. And I am with you when you are crucified.

I have raised you up to show My love to the world, and nothing shall succeed in keeping you from fulfilling this high and holy calling. NOTHING!

Go and show My great love to all mankind! And they will see God.

April 29

YOUR CONSCIENCE BEARS WITNESS

Scripture Reading — Romans 9:1-16

"I say the truth in Christ, I lie not, my conscience also bearing me witness in the Holy Ghost," (Romans 9:1)

My child, your greatest witness, for or against you, is your conscience. I have given you this silent, powerful witness, through Him that dwelleth in you, even the Holy Spirit.

The indwelling presence of the Holy Spirit is the conscience of the Godhead. I have given Him to dwell in you that you may live a life well-pleasing to Me.

He bears witness of Me to you and makes you to feel My presence with you and My love towards you. He is in you to gently nudge you when you have done that which is not pure.

If you constantly ignore His witness against you, you will become callous to His gentle admonition and ultimately you will not feel His touch or hear His rebuke in your innermost being.

Know this: you can never lie to others or to yourself without bearing terrible damage to the conscience I have given you by the Holy Spirit. Stop listening to the counsel of your advisers. I am in you to counsel you. Walk gently before Me. It is before **Me** you must give account of all you do.

April 30

GOD HAS CHOSEN YOU TO BE A VESSEL OF GLORY

Scripture Reading — Romans 9:17-33

"And that he might make known the riches of his glory on the vessels of mercy, which he had afore prepared unto glory," (Romans 9:23)

My child, if I have ordained to choose you as a vessel of mercy, what have you to fear? Do you not want **My** glory more than anything else?

The glory this world gives is here today and lost tomorrow, but the glory which I give you is eternal. I will manifest, through eternity, the riches of My glory upon the vessels which I have chosen aforetime and am preparing for this event.

It is not of your own works that you have been chosen. Have mercy and compassion on the vessels that are fitted for destruction. (vs. 22)

Be humble and grateful that you are a life I have chosen, that through you I might make known the riches of My glory. For surely, you are a vessel upon which I have extended My mercy. Even from before the foundations of the world, I have planned you into My plan.

Walk carefully, My child, that you do not miss this glory, for truly it is a great and a precious gift which I have given unto you, that you should know My glory and walk in My presence, and be a vessel to the glory of God.

May 1

STRETCH OUT YOUR HAND

Scripture Reading — Romans 10:1-21

"But to Israel he saith, All day long I have stretched forth my hands unto a disobedient and gainsaying people." (Romans 10:21)

My love knows no limitation. This is the kind of love that I want you to have. Stretch out your hands to a disobedient and gainsaying (contradictory) church.

Many times you will be shocked and deeply grieved as you see the hearts of those who have been close to you become cold and hard towards you. You will not begin to understand what has happened to cause it.

But you must continue to stretch your hand out towards them. Reach out in love. Your love must make up for their lack.

"All the day long..." Can you not see My longsuffering and patience? Go back to Me as your model of love. You will find it in everything I do.

Many whom My children have rejected as being hopeless are safely with Me here.

I brought you here to stretch out your hands. So **love, love, love.** Do not even listen to that which is prejudiced. First **approach** every problem with love. Only then can you stretch out your hands. Find every person in the Spirit. And then deal with them accordingly. Do not wait till they are perfected in love before you stretch your hand out to them.

May 2

GOD WILL GRAFT IN THE DEAD BRANCHES

Scripture Reading — Romans 11:1-32

"And if some of the branches be broken off, and thou, being a wild olive tree, wert graffed in among them, and with them partakest of the root and fatness of the olive tree;" (Romans 11:17)

"And they also, if they abide not still in unbelief, shall be graffed in: for God is able to graff them in again." (vs. 23)

"Even so have these also now not believed, that through your mercy they also may obtain mercy." (vs. 31)

My power is unlimited, but I need your mercy. Do not give up. Do not stop caring. Do not stop having compassion. Do not stop feeling mercy. Do not stop praying. There is always hope, if you will still have mercy and pray, love, hope and try one more time to forgive. Then you, My child, give Me authority and an open door to work.

Many branches have been broken off the tree of life. But the case is not hopeless. If I made Aaron's dead rod to bud, can I not bring life back into a broken-off, dead branch, that is dried up and cast aside? Yea, I can even make it to be fruitful.

I am able to graft them back in. But I need you to be merciful. You **must** forgive, you **must** have mercy, you **must** have hope, faith and love so that you remove the hindrances.

Never be fearful of bringing your dead rods before the tabernacle. During the night season of your life, as you have mercy and pray for them and wait before Me, I will graft in your loved ones again and restore them to life in their place in the family tree. Only have mercy.

May 3

GOD'S GREATNESS AND WISDOM

Scripture Reading — Romans 11:33-36

"O the depth of the riches both of the wisdom and knowledge of God! how unsearchable are his judgments, and his ways past finding out!" (Romans 11:33)

Don't think for one minute that you know Me, or that you can predict what I will do in a certain situation.

My children have missed Me because they thought they knew Me. When I came to them in the person of Jesus of Nazareth, they were not able to receive Me because of their limited understanding of Me.

Even today, many miss Me because they know Me only after the limitations of their forefathers and teachers. They have an idea of what I am, after the understanding of their progenitors, and they know Me only after their teachers and not from their own personal experiences with Me.

No one knows My mind. No one counsels Me, or tells Me what to do. No one has taught Me anything. No one has made Me what I am. No one has promoted Me to My position. I am not dependent on anyone's helping or honouring Me, or promoting Me to My position.

Everything that exists, that happens, is because of Me. I am the source of everything in existence, seen and unseen. Not one thing happens without My allowing it. I permit much evil only because I do not choose to destroy the evil-doer.

People misunderstand Me because they do not make allowances for Me to act as the need of today arises. If you know Me only as your forefathers knew Me, you will miss Me today. Make allowances in your understanding of Me, to do a new thing. My ways are past your finding out, past your understanding of Me. The first thing about knowing Me is that you can never know what I will do. I will do today what I didn't do yesterday. And tomorrow I will do what I didn't do today.

May 4

THE SACRIFICIAL LIFE IS A LIFE ON FIRE

Scripture Reading — Romans 12:1-8

"I beseech you therefore, brethren, by the mercies of God, that ye present your bodies a living sacrifice, holy, acceptable unto God, which is your reasonable service. And be not conformed to this world: but be ye transformed by the renewing of your mind, that ye may prove what is that good, and acceptable, and perfect, will of God." (Romans 12:1,2)

My child, this is one of the greatest truths of consecration and dedication in the entire scriptures. It is open and simple, easy to be understood and true. But many miss it completely. Let Me explain it to you again.

It is the Holy Spirit crying through Paul to My people that, through the power of My mercy upon them, they may make themselves available for the Levitical priesthood, even a life of service unto Me.

The Levites were My firstfruits tribe. They had no inheritance simply because they were a type of the true sacrificial life. I was their inheritance. They were to find fulfilment, not in houses, land and wealth or possession, but only in Me. On one hand it was a terrible sacrifice, for they could never be like anyone else, but on the other, was glorious, a foretaste and symbol of the heavenly life, which finds its source and contentment in Me. Their awards would only be eternal rewards.

Their bodies were the fulfilment of the symbol of the very sacrifices which they laid upon the altar day after day. Even as the sacrifice was to be perfect and without blemish, so they too were to live a life perfect and without blemish.

Even as the sacrifice on the altar no longer belonged to the man or woman who brought it, but was now totally Mine, so the believer who could pay the price of total commitment was to live a life totally separated unto Me and divorced from his former life. The sacrifice no longer belonged to its former owner. Now it was Mine, and as the fire entered it, it was transfigured. So it is when you are totally offered unto Me as a living sacrifice. The fire of the Holy Spirit will totally enter you, and you will be transformed.

May 5

DO NOT SEEK TO BE IMPORTANT

Scripture Reading — Romans 12:9-21

"Be of the same mind one toward another. Mind not high things, but condescend to men of low estate. Be not wise in your own conceits." (Romans 12:16)

My children often do not understand that greatness does not lie in fame, name, riches nor powerful position. The people of the world go after the wrong kind of greatness. This inner drive to be a cohort with famous people is the same as what was in the heart of Lucifer when he said, "I will ascend into heaven, I will exalt my throne above the stars of God: I will sit also upon the mount of the congregation, in the sides of the north." (Isaiah 14:13,14)

When I was upon earth, walking among men, I never cultivated the favour of the elite of Israel or Rome. I received those whom the Holy Spirit sent to Me and went to those whom He sent Me to. I could have won the favour of Caiaphas, Ananias, Pilate or Herod by one sentence. But I was not a social-climber.

Do not be bewitched by popularity, power or praises of men. Never, for one minute, think it great to be great in the eyes of the religious world. Do not seek to cultivate the friendship of the so-called important people.

Treat the beggar on the street with the same respect as you would a governor. Take time to spend time with an unwanted child as you would with the pastor of a church. Stand in your neighbour's shoes. Put yourself in his position and you will understand him and find him in the Spirit and in so doing, you may find yourself too and realize more clearly how others see you. This may shock you as you may, to your amazement, find yourself "wise in your own conceits."

> Come, and walk earth's dusty highways
> Where the mortals pass you by,
> There is where you'll find earth's treasures,
> Not in lofty castles, high;
> Talk with those to whom I bring you,
> Maybe thus, you'll talk with Me.

May 6

OWE NO MAN ANYTHING BUT LOVE

Scripture Reading — Romans 13:1-14

"Owe no man any thing, but to love one another: for he that loveth another hath fulfilled the law." (Romans 13:8)

Every problem that develops between people is caused by lack of love. When there is love, there is understanding. It is love which enables you to find one another in the Spirit.

Look back into your past, and there you will see many shipwrecked lives, destroyed families, broken hearts, suicides and murders, all because someone could not love.

Love is the one thing which anyone can give, be he king or beggar. Yet, so few have true love. They have passion, lust, attraction for, appreciation of, but not love. Because of this, their hearts become hard and cruel. It is almost as though men think it weak to love, and women think it dangerous.

You need to remember to teach love to My people. They are a hurting, suffering, disappointed flock. Even their own shepherds have shorn them and left them bleeding. Many are weeping in the night. Give them love, love, love. It is the one big, important, eternal thing you have to give.

Strengthen the things which remain. Love remains, so strengthen love. You can do this by talking about it.

Talk about demons and you feel their presence. Talk about love, and you feel love.

May 7

EDIFY ONE ANOTHER

Scripture Reading — Romans 14:7-23

"Let us therefore follow after the things which make for peace, and things wherewith one may edify another." (Romans 14:19)

There are so few of My children who truly are peacemakers. They have forgotten that I said on the mount, "Blessed are the peacemakers, for they shall be called the children of God." (Matthew 5:9)

I am grieved because most of My children, who call themselves children of God, are indeed trouble-makers. They are easily aggravated, quickly angry, self-righteously critical, pass judgment without understanding, and are malicious gossips. These precious ones cannot begin to realize how they grieve Me, for in spreading gossip and rumours and in creating friction in the body they are talking against My children whom I love as much as I love them. They have forgotten that they are putting dirt in their own nest.

I have called you to live peaceably with all men. Do not be critical of the sister who is in bondage to her church or family or friends, or the brother who thinks he needs an elder's permission to buy a new car. Neither be critical of that child of Mine who is a vegetarian or health-food adherent. Also stop criticizing the child of Mine who still is bound by the habit of smoking or chewing tobacco and who is held captive by the sickness of alcoholism.

My children are too critical. They lack love and understanding. They look for faults in each other. They need to stop pulling one another down and start edifying each other, for in so doing, they edify themselves and Me, their God.

May 8

BEAR THE INIQUITIES OF THE WEAK

Scripture Reading — Romans 15:1-7

"We then that are strong ought to bear the infirmities of the weak, and not to please ourselves." (Romans 15:1)

The great laws of heaven can be summed up in this one small scripture, or in one small word: caring. I have so few who have the true spirit of heaven. If they did, they would have reached the lost long ago.

My people are self-centred, caring much only about their own needs and pleasures.

My angels live only to serve and to bring comfort and pleasure to Me and to My world.

I want you to begin to live by the laws of heaven. As you begin to give of your strength, I will add to your strength.

It is not always easy to **bear** the infirmities of the weak. To wait to walk with a weaker vessel, to help someone by taking care to see they have what they need without their asking, to assist in whatever way would bless them, or simply to **bear** their peculiar personality without complaining.

But if you are strong, then the eccentricity of the weak will not aggravate you and cause much friction to your spirit. For your strength will have the capacity to make allowances for others' weaknesses, both in body, in temperament and in spiritual things.

Do not live to please yourself. That is not the law of the Kingdom. It is the law of self.

May 9

SING UNTO THE LORD

Scripture Reading — Romans 15:8-20

"And that the Gentiles might glorify God for his mercy; as it is written, For this cause I will confess to thee among the Gentiles, and sing unto thy name." (Romans 15:9)

"And again, Praise the Lord, all ye Gentiles; and laud him, all ye people. And again Esaias saith, There shall be a root of Jesse, and he that shall rise to reign over the Gentiles; in him shall the Gentiles trust." (vs. 11,12)

"For I will not dare to speak of any of those things which Christ hath not wrought by me, to make the Gentiles obedient, by word and deed." (vs. 18)

When the time comes for Me to reach a nation I will send My singers to it. When the time comes for Me to reach an individual I will sing to that one.

I send you forth to sing My song to the world. Sometimes your voice will be tired and worn, but still they will hear My call to them through the song you sing to them. And as you sing, My Holy Spirit will fall upon them and begin to meet their hearts.

Although all will not understand the words you sing, yet, when they hear you sing, they will be blessed because they will hear My call to them in your song.

Your song will bring revival. Your song will open doors. Sing in the huts, on boats, in great temples, in high places, in desert places, in great buildings, before atheists and believers in nation after nation. Sing a song, My beloved.

May 10

GO IN THE FULLNESS OF THE BLESSING

Scripture Reading — Romans 15:21-32

"And I am sure that, when I come unto you, I shall come in the fulness of the blessing of the gospel of Christ." (Romans 15:29)

Paul's plan was to finish ministering to the Gentiles, accept their offerings for the poor saints who lived in Jerusalem, deliver it to them and then begin a journey to Spain, stopping to minister in Rome.

Paul had a vision, an eternal vision for the distant nations of the world. If I had not permitted him to be My prisoner, so he could pen these immortal letters from Me to you, he would have gone, and gone, he would have run, and run, until there were no nations left that had not heard the Gospel.

But he was My prisoner, and he knew it and accepted it, longing only to go and yet never complaining. So there will be times when you feel like a prisoner, longing only to go, but you will not be able to do so. Do not complain, for I will use you wherever I desire and I will refurbish you even in your prison. I will strengthen and prepare you for the work I have for you to do, and when I send you forth it will be in the fullness of the blessing of the Gospel of Christ.

How can I send you out with an empty cup? Your cup must be full, so that you can give others to drink. They await you in Rome, in

Spain, in France, in all of Europe, Asia, Africa, America, the Arctic and Australia, unto the uttermost isles of the sea. Go, at My command, in the fullness of the blessing of the Gospel of Christ.

May 11

PHEBE, MY DEACONESS

Scripture Reading — Romans 16:1-16

"I commend unto you Phebe our sister, which is a servant of the church which is at Cenchrea: That ye receive her in the Lord, as becometh saints, and that ye assist her in whatsoever business she hath need of you: for she hath been a succourer of many, and of myself also." (Romans 16:1,2)

Phebe, the "shining one," was My special handmaiden whom Paul could trust to take his message to the church at Rome. She came from the port of Corinth and she brought the greatest of Paul's writings those thousands of miles.

Paul calls her a "servant." The word in Greek is *diakonas*. She was a deaconess of the church of Cenchrea (harbour of Corinth). She was a perfect handmaiden, ready to serve in any way, whether to run an errand like this one of carrying a letter from Corinth to Rome, or being the pastor and teacher of the church, for the word *diakonas* means "pastor and teacher," as well as "menial errand girl."

You need to realize that in My sight, in order to be a good pastor, you need to be a good errand runner.

Paul honoured her, asking God's people to help her in any way she might need it, and commended her for the many times she had helped him and others. This is the way I see My daughters who serve Me.

May 12

AVOID TROUBLE MAKERS

Scripture Reading — Romans 16:17-27

"Now I beseech you, brethren, mark them which cause divisions and offences contrary to the doctrine which ye have learned; and avoid them. For they that are such serve not our Lord Jesus Christ, but their own belly; and by good words and fair speeches deceive the hearts of the simple." (Romans 16:17,18)

These words of My servant Paul seem to sound cruel, heartless, and lacking in love, but they are words of truth and wisdom.

The body of Christ is made up of all kinds of people. Some do not have a true, pure motive. Because their past is full of much evil, they live by the law of self-preservation. They will destroy anything they touch. Every life they come in contact with, they will cause divisions and offences. If they come into a ministry, they will bring division in the camp. They will cause people to be offended and hurt and grieved. They are emissaries of Satan and are used by him to destroy ministries. They will not look evil, they will not be idol worshippers, thieves, adulterers as such. But they will cause more trouble than all of these. And though they may come in as friends of a ministry, sooner or later they will destroy it.

My people would save themselves much heartache if they would avoid these trouble makers. Their purpose in life is to make themselves great, to gain positions of power. They will pretend to love, and say the right words to gain the affection of those who have no discernment, whose hearts are simple. You must be careful not to let these gain a foothold in the camp. I say "Avoid them!"

When you have a check in your Spirit, know it is a warning from Me. Do not ignore it. Do not go around asking others for advice, but set your face to pray to be shown what truly is in the heart of those who come to you. For many will come in these days, only for their own belly's sake and not because they have your burden and want to help you carry it. They will only add to your burden.

Let My Spirit help you to know what is right. Watch for their good words and fair speeches. A true saint does not need to flatter you to gain your confidence. Be not deceived by flattery, praise and ego-building manipulation.

Pride has made great ministers to fall. And many are those who are sent by Satan into the churches and organizations to cause havoc by causing divisions and offences. First, Satan divides the camp, then he causes offences. Beware, keep your camp clean!

May 13

WRITE MY MESSAGE AND SEND IT TO THE WORLD

Scripture Reading – Revelation 1:1-20

"...What thou seest, write in a book, and send it unto the seven churches which are in Asia; unto Ephesus, and unto Smyrna, and unto Pergamos, and unto Thyatira, and unto Sardis, and unto Philadelphia, and unto Laodicea." (Revelation 1:11)

The message I have given to you is for the world. Get it out. It will change lives. Get it to the nations of the world. The message must reach the seven churches.

Seven is the perfect number. You need to reach the perfect number. It is time for the message to reach out to all.

Do not be content with what you have accomplished. Seek to accomplish more. You must get the message of fasting into Red China and Russia. You must get the message of the Blood into those nations. Germany needs to hear the message of love. No one will love it more than Germany.

It is important that you write the message down and get it out. If others had not been obedient, many would be lost. But because they wrote out the message I gave them, and started giving and sending it, multitudes of souls have come to My saving knowledge. You do not need to wait for someone to hire you. Write My message, make it plain and send it out.

May 14

GOD SEES YOUR FAITHFUL SERVICE

Scripture Reading – Revelation 2:1-7

"And hast borne, and hast patience, and for my name's sake hast laboured, and hast not fainted." (Revelation 2:3)

My child, if there is any verse that describes your service to Me, it is this verse.

For the last years of your life, ever since you totally surrendered yourself to Me, you have laboured untiringly for Me. You have borne the heavy load of the ministry, the burden of the call, the pain of the lost, the rejection, the heat, the cold, the long hours of labour, the separation from home and loved ones, the pain of slander and the humility of abuse.

You have laboured long hours in uncomfortable situations, and you have not fainted nor given up. Your eyes have always been on Me. You have never sought reward from man nor honour from the so-called great people of the world.

Your patience and endurance has been noticed by the heavenly recorder. But all these things are not as important as your love. You must be careful not to do these things because you get into the habit of it, but only because of your love for Me. You started serving Me like this only because of your great love, and you must never lose this great fire of love. It is the heat that generates your strength to continue a few more miles.

May 15

YOU ARE RICH

Scripture Reading – Revelation 2:9-11

"I know thy works, and tribulation, and poverty, (but thou art rich) and I know the blasphemy of them which say they are Jews, and are not, but are the synagogue of Satan." (Revelation 2:9)

My child, there is not a thing about you that I do not know. You are the "apple of My eye," therefore I look at everything through your eyes. I observe all of your ways. There is nothing that you do or say or think that is hidden from Me.

I see the diligent, long hours of sacrificial labour, the tribulation you have endured from others who are My children. Though sad to say, they are of the synagogue of Satan. They do not have the true Spirit. It is only a close imitation, a façade that deceives.

I see how you have given everything to Me. You have made a total commitment of all possessions, inheritance, children, family, dearest friends to Me. It will be easy for you to say good-bye and leave it all behind.

In your ability to be poor towards yourself and rich towards others, you have been given the power to get wealth and to lay up for yourself eternal riches, for you have proven to Me to be a faithful steward of My Kingdom's finances and possessions.

I see the tribulation you have suffered and still suffer from those who think they are My Jews (people of praise). They are not true people of praise. Because of them I am evil spoken of. For with every word they say against you, they are also denouncing the work of righteousness and perfection which I have done through you. They are religious but not holy, and full of self-righteousness. Leave them to Me. See only that you continue to glorify Me.

May 16

THE WHITE STONE AND THE NEW NAME

Scripture Reading — Revelation 2:12-17

"He that hath an ear, let him hear what the Spirit saith unto the churches; To him that overcometh will I give to eat of the hidden manna, and will give him a white stone, and in the stone a new name written, which no man knoweth saving he that receiveth it." (Revelation 2:17)

My child, there are such rewards laid up for the righteous that if people knew the greatness of them, the honour and eternal praise, they would strive to be righteous only for the rewards. But I have hidden the true interpretation of these words, that your heart be not drawn after the gifts, but rather after the Giver. Keep your eyes on Me, My child; I am your exceeding, great reward.

The manna of My truth have I already given to you, but there remaineth still much truth and many mysteries in My Word which have yet to be revealed in these last days. As you press into My bosom, My heart will commune with your heart and reveal these truths to you.

The white stone is the seal of authority, the earnest of the inheritance, that touch of eternal glory, that sense of My indwelling. You can have the white stone in part now, but when you come through the gate, that stone will give you eternal status, eternal rewards, eternal position, recognized by the authorities of heaven.

Man does not recognize the "white stone," but heaven does. What more do you need?

The new name is your eternal high calling, your heavenly office, your place of leadership. Heaven will not be a place of many chiefs and no Indians. The chiefs (i.e. the overcomers) will be few. Strive to attain. This fiery trial of your life can give you great perfecting and stature, but only if you overcome all your adversaries of self.

May 17

THE ROD OF IRON AND THE MORNING STAR

Scripture Reading — Revelation 2:18-29

"And he that overcometh, and keepeth my works unto the end, to him will I give power over the nations: And he shall rule them with a rod of iron; as the vessels of a potter shall they be broken to shivers: even as I received of my Father. And I will give him the morning star." (Revelation 2:26-28)

To overcome does not mean to win the victory in battle over an outside adversary, but over one on the inside.

Most of man's most deadly, deceitful enemies are in the **inside** of his garden. These enemies are called pride, jealousy, anger, deceit, unforgiveness, greed, self-pity, fears, lust, love of self, and many others.

Some of My children have all of these enemies and all have some of them. You cannot be called to be a ruler of the nations until you have defeated your own enemies on the inside of your kingdom. For you truly are a kingdom within yourself.

How can you break into pieces and slivers the outside evil forces, if you cannot break them on the inside?

I received this high commission of the Father. And I need My soldiers to fight with the same purity within themselves. There is grace from the Father for this, and there is grace for you. Even as I received this grace from the Father, so you too can receive it from Him.

After complete inner victory, I will elevate you to rulership over nations, over demon spirits, and in the millenium, nations of continents.

I will give you the morning star. This is the outbreaking of My glory after the night of struggle and doom. It declares that morning is coming and the glory of the day shall overtake the darkness of the night. It speaks of hope in dark and troubled times. It is the one who has been overcome by sin who loses his hope. Seek therefore to overcome and you will be lifted into a place of rulership and authority.

One of the first signs of overcoming is your love for the nations.

May 18

THE WHITE RAIMENT

Scripture Reading — Revelation 3:1-6

"Thou hast a few names even in Sardis which have not defiled their garments; and they shall walk with me in white: for they are worthy. He that overcometh, the same shall be clothed in white raiment; and I will not blot out his name out of the book of life, but I will confess his name before my Father, and before his angels." (Revelation 3:4,5)

My child, you know that one does not readily dress a child in pure white to go out to play, for within a few minutes the child will soil itself. When you travel on dirty trains, ride horses, or do menial tasks where there is danger of soiling your garments, you seek to wear a colour that will not show the soil.

I see My children, many who are walking about in soiled garments. They are still playing, grovelling and occupied with the spiritually unclean things of this earth life. It is not until they leave their old ways, which defile the soul, that I can give them that pure white garment which is a mark of identification of their heavenly status.

This white garment gives you the authority to rule in My Kingdom. It is the mark of a ruler and overcomer, for no one can be ruler until he is an overcomer. The Father and your angel see your garment which you are wearing today. Look at it. Is it white and pure? Or is it flecked with marks of self and sin?

Come to Me and be washed in My blood. It was shed, not only for the sinner, but for the transgressor, that child of Mine who loves Me, but transgresses the laws of My covenant which I have made with them.

My children in Sardis had very few overcomers and so the church fell to dissimulation, arguing and splits. The overcomers in white will never fall away from the true calling in Christ, the holy unity of the Spirit. For they walk with Me in white, and I walk in the midst of the overcomers.

May 19

THE OPEN DOOR

Scripture Reading — Revelation 3:7-14

"I know thy works: behold I have set before thee an open door, and no man can shut it: for thou hast a little strength, and hast kept my word, and hast not denied my name." (Revelation 3:8)

My beloved child, the door is open because you heart is open. Many do not know that the key to the open door lies within their own hearts. I wait for them to unlock their heart's doors to Me and to be released from certain wrong feelings in their hearts; and sometimes I wait a life-time.

It is as a man who has a beautiful castle on a hill, furnished and ready for him to move into, but there are fears which are like invisible chains which keep him bound, (not locked, but bound) to the hovel in the valley. Every day he looks up the hill at his castle and longs to be there, but he is afraid that if he moves up there he will leave the scene of his memories forever, and never be able to return. He cannot stand that cutting off of the past attachment. And so he passes his life, missing out on what good things are prepared for him.

So it is, many hang on to their dead churches, their employment without a future, their dwelling place, and some hang on to their clothes closets, knowing that if they should go out to the mission field life would bring simplicity of styles. But the castle has a full wardrobe. I have promised to dress you, as I clothed Solomon.

If you will begin to go, you will find that the door is open. What I open, no one can shut. That is because you have obeyed the word which I put into your heart, which is to **go**. Untangle yourself therefore from every yoke of bondage and go forward fearlessly. The future is better than you think.

May 20

PURE GOLD, WHITE RAIMENT AND EYE SALVE

Scripture Reading — Revelation 3:14-22

"I counsel thee to buy of me gold tried in the fire, that thou mayest be rich; and white raiment, that thou mayest be clothed, and that the shame of thy nakedness do not appear; and anoint thine eyes with eyesalve, that thou mayest see." (Revelation 3:18)

There are three things I counsel you to buy, My child. To buy means that you must pay a price for them. They are not free like My precious blood was free. Some of My thoughtless children think everything is free. No, indeed! Either I or you must pay a price. The price of your salvation was so great, you were unable to pay for it, so I did. Now, in order for you to progress, you too must pay a great price.

The **first** of these is **gold**. You need to be rich in the Kingdom, though not towards yourself, for I said, blessed are the poor in spirit, for theirs is the Kingdom of God. Gold has always and will always be the basis of earth's monetary system. The only thing which defiles it is the image stamped upon it. The value of gold increases, and its purity increases, and this only after it is melted down the second time. So I would refine you and melt you down and make out of you pure and precious gold, tried and true, but you must invest your whole life into trusting Me to make pure gold out of you. Do not be afraid to make a total commitment of your life unto Me. In the end you will be rich. It is a life investment. It pays off.

The **second** valuable, priceless thing you need to strive to obtain by great acts of self-sacrifice is **white raiment**. There is only one garment accepted in the Kingdom, and that is the heavenly robe of purity. But in the ruling company of great saints, there is a robe of identity, earth's robe of purple turns to heaven's royal robe of white. This is the saints' mark of identity in the overcomer's celestial parliament.

But this garment is only procured through tests of faithfulness and loyalty here on earth. "His lord said unto him, Well done, good and faithful servant: thou hast been faithful over a few things, I will make thee ruler over many things: enter thou into the joy of thy lord." (Matthew 25:23)

The **third** thing you must seek for is **eye salve**. There is a salve which gives deep, spiritual insight into situations. Most of My children do not have it because they do not pay the price.

The lack of this insight makes it difficult for them to make the correct decision regarding essential things in their life. They make rash and foolish decisions, often missing My best for them. The lack of this insight makes them prejudiced and resentful of My dealings in the lives of My saints who walk in a higher realm. The result of this is spiritual blindness. Because of their spiritual blindness they become cruel to those of My children who are enlightened, cruel, even unto death. For it was My children who tortured My children to death because their eyes had not been anointed with eye salve.

May 21

THE DOOR TO HEAVEN IS OPEN

Scripture Reading – Revelation 4:1-11

"After this I looked, and, behold, a door was opened in heaven: and the first voice which I heard was as it were of a trumpet talking with me; which said, Come up hither, and I will shew thee things which must be hereafter. And immediately I was in the spirit: and, behold, a throne was set in heaven, and one sat on the throne. And he that sat was to look upon like a jasper and a sardine stone: and there was a rainbow round about the throne, in sight like unto an emerald." (Revelation 4:1-3)

My child, the door to heaven is always open. If you will only look you will see.

But the invitation is not only for you to look, but there is a sounding of the trumpet calling you to come up hither into My presence. I want to show you things, even things which **must** be hereafter, that you may do warfare against Satan and prevent his works by your spiritual warfare ahead of time. But you cannot come with your natural thinking. It is only as you come in the Spirit that you can enter into the secrets of the heavenlies. John was "in the Spirit." The natural man receiveth not the things of the Spirit of God. Read again the words of My servant Paul. (I Corinthians 2:9-16)

It was only after John saw "one" sitting on the throne, that his mind was quickened to look into the hidden future. Many desire to know the secrets of the book of Revelation, but they do not come the right way. They are not in the Spirit, and neither have they seen the "one" who can give them the key into the future.

May 22

ALL WILL GIVE GLORY TO GOD

Scripture Reading – Revelation 5:1-14

"And every creature which is in heaven, and on the earth, and under the earth, and such as are in the sea, and all that are in them, heard I saying, Blessing, and honour, and glory, and power, be unto him that sitteth upon the throne, and unto the Lamb for ever and ever." (Revelation 5:13)

This is the grand finale. The conclusion of My mighty works of grace, when all the heaven and earth and sea shall give glory to the Lord above.

Always keep your eyes on that goal. You are living in a time when many shall only give glory to themselves and to each other. But the time is coming when everyone will lose sight of everyone and no one will see anyone, save the Lord of Glory.

You do not need to wait for that great day of acclaim and recognition. Begin to give glory to Me now. Glorify Me while you still are on this earth, in this body, in this life. Let your whole life be one that glorifies Me and brings praises and honour to Me.

Self-love, self-worship, self-praise, self-honour, self-power, all will end in the presence of the Lord of Glory.

The closer one comes to Me, the more the old self-life dies out. It must die. Flesh never can abide in the day of My coming, for no man can see God and live.

The worst blasphemer, atheist, agnostic, mocker, yea even those who crucified Me will give honour to Me, and the Father, on that day when every knee shall bow.

May 23

THE RIDER WHO TAKES PEACE FROM THE EARTH

Scripture Reading – Revelation 6:1-17

"And there went out another horse that was red: and power was given to him that sat thereon to take peace from the earth, and that they should kill one another: and there was given unto him a great sword." (Revelation 6:4)

My child, you are living in that time which John saw coming upon the earth as he looked down upon the earth from heaven's open door.

The rider on the red horse is riding. His name is "hate," for everyone who hates his brother is a murderer. (I John 3:15)

There is a terrible spirit of hate let loose upon the earth from the pit of hell and the caves of darkness to try everyone dwelling on this earth, whether Christian, Moslem, Jew, Hindu, Buddhist, or any religion. It is working its hate between those of the same belief, those of the same family, same persuasion. Even the atheists and communists shall hate each other.

It is the first of the terrible judgments when every man's love for his neighbour, his family, country and calling will be tested.

With the freeing of this spirit, peace is being taken from the hearts of men, for peace comes through love, and where there is no love, there is no peace.

Today people are killing one another savagely in some places; in other circles they are killing one another with the tongue of slander just as cruelly.

Neither will this change until **I** take the sword out of a family, a ministry, a nation, or a heart. Only **one** thing can overcome the rider on the red horse, and that is the Spirit of **My** love!

May 24

THE ANGELS ARE SEALING THE OVERCOMERS

Scripture Reading — Revelation 7:1-17

"And I saw another angel ascending from the east, having the seal of the living God: and he cried with a loud voice to the four angels, to whom it was given to hurt the earth and the sea, Saying, Hurt not the earth, neither the sea, nor the trees, till we have sealed the servants of our God in their foreheads." (Revelation 7:2,3)

My child, the angels have everything in control. There is nothing that will be permitted to happen without them participating in it or approving of it. They carry the seal. And they are even now marking My servants who dwell on this earth.

It is important that they know you and recognize you so that you receive the official, heavenly stamp of approval, for everyone who does not have it will be left to the mercy of the heartless multitudes over which the beast has control.

The angels will recognize you by your pedigree. Do you have the sign of an overcomer in your life? Are you walking in victory over your fleshly weaknesses and inherited sins?

There is **nothing** in this world worth the price of your soul. Pride, honour, position, wealth, all are but foolishness and dung which must be cast off that you may attain the goal of getting the angels' end-time marking for My protection in this hour.

May 25

PRAYERS MUST PRECEDE THE JUDGMENT

Scripture Reading — Revelation 8:1-13

"And another angel came and stood at the altar, having a golden censer; and there was given unto him much incense, that he should offer it with the prayers of all saints upon the golden altar which was before the throne. And the smoke of the incense, which came with the prayers of the saints, ascended up before God out of the angel's hand. And the angel took the censer, and filled it with fire of the altar, and cast it into the earth: and there were voices, and thunderings, and lightnings, and an earthquake. And the seven angels which had the seven trumpets prepared themselves to sound." (Revelation 8:3-6)

Before judgment begins, heaven's throne must be filled with the fragrance of the incense of the praise and prayers of the saints.

The angel who releases these precious prayers before Me is given a golden censer to contain all the prayers of the saints. As he stands before Me holding the golden censer, its fragrance reaches up to My throne and to Me.

Then the angel fills this same censer with My heavenly fire from off the altar. It is the same fire that was used to cleanse the lips of My prophet Isaiah. (Isaiah 6:6) It is the fire that fell on the burning bush (Exodus 3:2), the sacrifice of the tabernacle (Exodus 40:38; Leviticus 9:24), Elijah (I Kings 18:38), David (I Chronicles 21:26), Solomon (II Chronicles 7:1), the temple (II Chronicles 7:1), the upper room (Acts 2:3), and Gog and Magog (Revelation 20:9).

I am going to pour this fire out in measured quantity upon all the earth just before the seven trumpets of terrible judgment will sound. According to the amount of prayers, so will the amount of fire be. The same censer will hold both. The whole earth will reel under the impact of this fire. It will be another Mount Sinai visitation. My fear will fill all the earth. It is coming! Keep praying! Call the people to pray to fill up the censer, that My glory may fill all the earth one more time.

May 26

GOD PROTECTS THE GRASS

Scripture Reading — Revelation 9:1-21

"And it was commanded them that they should not hurt the grass of the earth, neither any green thing, neither any tree; but only those men which have not the seal of God in their foreheads. And to them it was given that they should not kill them, but that they should be tormented five months: and their torment was as the torment of a scorpion, when he striketh a man." (Revelation 9:4,5)

My child, even when it seems like hell itself has broken loose, I am in control. I control all demon activity. Not one devil is free to move a finger without My Divine permission.

If I protect the green growth upon the cursed earth, shall I not protect the "greening" of the ministry to which I have called you?

I suffered **not** the destroyer to enter the house of My children in Egypt where the blood mark of a slain lamb was placed on the door. Today again I am, Myself, as head of My household, putting My mark upon My righteous. It is **My** seal. Only I have the authority to mark My righteous.

Satan has orders to keep his hands off those who have My seal mark. Yea, is he not even Apollyon, the destroyer, (verse 11), the same one who journeyed through Egypt on the first passover night?

Yes, I am in control, for even with the unrighteous the destroyer Apollyon shall be given a limited time of 5 months. Fear not, nothing can happen which I do NOT permit. I test the love and purity of all men.

May 27

THE SWEETNESS AND BITTERNESS
OF THE END-TIME MESSAGE

Scripture Reading — Revelation 10:1-11

"And I went unto the angel, and said unto him, Give me the little book. And he said unto me, Take it, and eat it up; and it shall make thy belly bitter, but it shall be in thy mouth sweet as honey. And I took the little book out of the angel's hand, and ate it up; and it was in my mouth sweet as honey: and as soon as I had eaten it, my belly was bitter. And he said unto me, Thou must prophesy again before many peoples, and nations, and tongues, and kings." (Revelation 10:9,10,11)

The end-time message is one of sweetness and bitterness. It is sweet for those whose hearts are ready, but bitterness will follow as the price gets greater and greater.

If you "water down" the message you will not need to pay so great a price, but if you tell it as it is, you will know, see and preach a message of bitterness. What shall be joy and blessing for some shall be bitterness and judgment for others, and even you, as you give it out, shall know both sweetness and bitterness.

I send those out to prophesy who have eaten from the Word themselves. Unless you have become a partaker, how can you give out My Word?

Many do not have the true end-time message because they have not eaten the Word which the end-time messenger is holding in his hand. Therefore they have not the truth of this day. It is a new day, a day of finishing up, a very important day, a day with a hard and bitter message which must be given in the sweetness of a fresh anointing.

But as you eat, I will send you to many peoples, tongues and nations. It is a message for the nations. Go and preach this message to all the world.

May 28

MEASURE THE TEMPLE OF GOD!

Scripture Reading — Revelation 11:1-14

"And there was given me a reed like unto a rod: and the angel stood, saying, Rise, and measure the temple of God, and the altar, and them that worship therein. But the court which is without the temple leave out, and measure it not; for it is given unto the Gentiles: and the holy city shall they tread under foot forty and two months." (Revelation 11:1,2)

My child, the time has come when My end-time overcomers who have eaten the book of judgments and glory shall be given the rod of judgment and glory.

This is even as the rod of Moses, which, when lifted up, brought victory to Israel and judgment on Israel's and My enemies. (Exodus 17:9-11) Always remember that the happenings of the end-times are two-fold. For the righteous they are glory; for the wicked they are judgment.

The time has come for judgment to begin in My house. The righteous among My people see the sins in My house. I command you to point out these sins. I command you to measure them and judge them. Do not compromise with those who sin against Me. Do not agree to sin in My house. I am measuring My house and I am measuring those who serve Me in My house and who worship Me.

This is not yet the time to judge the Gentiles. They are without. I have anointed you to judge My house and to show them their sins. Fear them not! They cannot destroy you, nor can they stop you until your work is finished. Be faithful to your anointed calling.

May 29

THE KINGDOMS OF THIS WORLD BELONG TO GOD

Scripture Reading — Revelation 11:15-19

"And the seventh angel sounded; and there were great voices in heaven, saying, The kingdoms of this world are become the kingdoms of our Lord, and of his Christ; and he shall reign for ever and ever." (Revelation 11:15)

There is no way that Satan can take control over My universe. His dominion is doomed. All spirits of men and hearts who work for him are doomed. The nations that obeyed him faithfully shall not be governed by him eternally. His time is very short. He knows this. That is why he goes around like a roaring lion, because he knows his time is short. You have just read his sentence and judgment. It is now zero-hour for Satan. It is time to take the kingdom. The nations are Mine. The nations and the peoples therein belong to Me. I will soon manifest Myself in such a way that they will immediately leave off following the deceiver, and follow Me.

In your own life and your own work remember you are not in control. I am. Do everything that I say. Do not run ahead of Me. Be not fearful of others getting the upper hand, as long as I have the upper hand in your life. Every subtle, undermining, controlling, spirit in man and demon shall be judged and destroyed as you let Me control you and guide you in every decision.

Even the acts of rebellion you see in others have already been judged by Me and shall shortly reap the harvest of My wrath. The kingdom of your ministry is in My hands. Fear not! I am in full control.

May 30

SATAN IN FLESH — THE ANTI-CHRIST

Scripture Reading — Revelation 12:1-17

"And there was war in heaven: Michael and his angels fought against the dragon; and the dragon fought and his angels, And prevailed not; neither was their place found any more in heaven. And the great dragon was cast out, that old serpent, called the Devil, and Satan, which deceiveth the whole world: he was cast out into the earth, and his angels were cast out with him." (Revelation 12:7-9)

"Therefore rejoice, ye heavens, and ye that dwell in them. Woe to the inhabiters of the earth and of the sea! for the devil is come down unto you, having great wrath, because he knoweth that he hath but a short time." (verse 12)

Wars have been raging all over the world since ancient times, but never has there been a war of such significance as this war of the heavens. It is a revolutionary war in the heavens for the power of the throne. Lucifer wanted throne-rights. He desired to be My firstborn son. He wanted the kingdoms of this earth. He was not willing to be prince over this earth under My command. He wanted full authority and power. He rejected the laws of Divine leadership.

Michael had to contest him and he was defeated in his plot and cast to this earth. He is now planning to enter the body of a human, just as My Son inhabited human flesh and through his life in earth obtained Kingdom rights.

Lucifer will shortly fully possess a human form, a zombie. He will take up the form of one whose spirit has departed his body and will live through that body. He is seeking to copy Emmanuel, God in man. It shall be Satan in man. As the powerful anti-Christ, he will have almost unlimited powers, both natural and psychic. He will use witchcraft, sorcery, demon spirits and natural warfare methods. His time is short. His wrath is great. He will turn his wrath and anger, which he holds against the Godhead and Michael, towards God's people. He will persecute the Lord's people and seek to utterly annihilate them.

But they shall be given a hiding place during the time of his reign of terror. And I will command the earth to protect them. Nature's elements shall protect them, while fighting against the evil inhabitants of the earth.

There will be a time of world chaos. The only ones to receive any protection are those who are hidden by the Lamb.

They will overcome all forces of Satan and evil by the blood of My Son and the word of their testimony, only because they are ready to lay down their lives for Me.

The stage for the anti-Christ to take over has been set. Prepare your people! Prepare your heart! Prepare the children!

May 31

THE ANTI-CHRIST'S POWER IS LIMITED

Scripture Reading — Revelation 13:1-18

"And there was given unto him a mouth speaking great things and blasphemies; and power was given unto him to continue forty and two months. And he opened his mouth in blasphemy against God, to blaspheme his name, and his tabernacle, and them that dwell in heaven. And it was given unto him to make war with the saints, and to overcome them: and power was given him over all kindreds, and tongues, and nations." (Revelation 13:5-7)

No one has any power except it is given to him. I have the full control of every living person and every devil and angel.

You need to have no fear. Did I not say to Pilate, "Thou couldest have no power at all against me, except it were given thee from above:"? (John 19:11)

David knew the great truth when Shimei came out against him and cursed him, casting stones at him and calling him evil names, accusing and condemning him. David refused to let anyone touch Shimei. He said, "...so let him curse, because the Lord hath said unto him, Curse David, Who shall then say, Wherefore hast thou done so?...let him alone, and let him curse; for the Lord hath bidden him. It may be that the Lord will look on mine affliction, and that the Lord will requite me good for his cursing this day." (II Samuel 16:10-12)

Total commitment of all the hurts and pains, misunderstandings, and misgivings in your life is one of the great qualifications of a leader. Neither Jesus nor David sought to avenge themselves of their adversaries. They accept all this as coming from My hand. No one has power to do anything without My permission, not even the Anti-Christ.

June 1

THE FIRST-FRUITS COMPANY

Scripture Reading — Revelation 14:1-20

"These are they which were not defiled with women; for they are virgins. These are they which follow the Lamb whithersoever he goeth. These were redeemed from among men, being the firstfruits unto God and to the Lamb. And in their mouth was found no guile: for they are without fault before the throne of God." (Revelation 14:4,5)

I have always had My holy company of intimate ones. Even in tribulation times, past, present and future, I have My beloved, who are "the excellency of Jacob," whom I love. (Psalm 47:4)

These are they who let Me choose their inheritance for them. I love them because their only desire is towards Me, their Lamb. They follow Me whithersoever, never seeking their own way, or to do their own will. They are not conniving or manipulating. Their hearts are like the hearts of children before Me.

They are the choicest of My creatures. The first-ripe, most perfect, precious fruits of the earth. They are My pride and joy and comfort. They are My companions.

Their life is holy, pure and undefiled in a wicked and abominable world of lust, perversion, hate and murder. They are sanctified through and through. Their mouths are clean before Me, their Judge, for they themselves are without guile. Their innocence is their protection for purity. They are children of love and sincerity, trust and honesty, and they walk with Me as Enoch did. They shall be translated as Enoch was, before the earth is reaped, even as Enoch was before the flood.

June 2

THE ANGEL THAT ACCOMPANIES THE MISSIONARIES

Scripture Reading — Revelation 14:6

"And I saw another angel fly in the midst of heaven, having the everlasting gospel to preach unto them that dwell on the earth, and to every nation, and kindred and tongue, and people," (Revelation 14:6)

This time has come. The Gospel must be preached in all the world for a sign and then shall the end be. This is the hour for reaching the nations of the world. There is no time to wait.

You have a very special message to bring, even a message of warning of the coming anti-Christ system and the terrible judgment that will follow as the angels go forth with the sickles to reap the earth. Millions upon millions will perish. The population of the nations will be decimated. All who hear My call and go to the nations shall be working under the command of this end-time angel who shall go with them and help them in their work of spreading the Gospel.

Even as My angel accompanied My people on their journey through the wilderness, so shall the angel of the Gospel missionary ministry of the end-times go with you on all your journeys.

June 3

THE SONG THAT BRINGS VICTORY

Scripture Reading — Revelation 15:1-8

"And they sing the song of Moses the servant of God, and the song of the Lamb, saying, Great and marvellous are thy works, Lord God Almighty; just and true are thy ways, thou King of saints. Who shall not fear thee, O Lord, and glorify thy name? for thou only art holy: for all nations shall come and worship before thee; for thy judgments are made manifest." (Revelation 15:3,4)

The song of praise is the song that secures the victory. It is wrong to assume that the victory must first be won before the song of praise can be sung.

Begin today to rejoice and sing My praises. As you praise, the Satanic hosts of hindrance and confusion shall flee. The song of praise will open the way for Me to work. It will also give rest and peace in the midst of turmoil.

Heaven is full of victory and peace because it is full of the song of praise. You can have heaven in your soul. It will lift you up above the turmoil of life.

Do not allow your soul to be dragged into the hell of confusion that surrounds even My people who cannot praise Me. Much discussion is weariness to the bones. Much praise is the lifting up of the Spirit. It is healing to body, soul and spirit.

Ask Me to waken you with a song. Ask Me to give you a new song in your spirit day by day and all through the day, no matter how dark the way, and you shall have the key to a higher way.

June 4

LET NO ONE STEAL YOUR GARMENT

Scripture Reading — Revelation 16:1-21

"Behold, I come as a thief. Blessed is he that watcheth, and keepeth his garments, lest he walk naked, and they see his shame." (Revelation 16:15)

I am there, watching, observing, taking note of all you do. The thief often comes in broad daylight, acting as a friendly person, to spy out the situation before he commits the crime.

Although I do not reveal who I am, I walk as a silent oberver in your midst. I observe your activities, listen to your conversations, and take note of all that you do, where you keep that which is precious to you.

Then, when you least suspect it, I will come as a thief in the night and snatch away the precious valuables. These are the things you prize the most of all.

In Bible times, and times of great poverty a man's dearest possessions were not his jewels; he had none. They were his clothes. The thief often came to steal a man's garment, with the result that he found himself naked when he awoke to find his garments stolen by the thief.

Some of My children are asleep. They do not realize that they have already lost their garment. I gave it to them and took it away. And they walk in your midst as naked. Their self-appointed garments cannot cover them. Everyone sees their nakedness and shame.

So keep your garment of glory and beauty about you. Cherish the covering I have given you.

> Behold, I come as a thief in the night;
> Be watching, and waiting for Me;
> For many, their garments have already been "stolen,"
> And naked, they walk before Me.

June 5

THE MIND OF CHRIST

Scripture Reading — Revelation 17:1-18

"For God hath put in their hearts to fulfil his will, and to agree, and give their kingdom unto the beast, until the words of God shall be fulfilled." (Revelation 17:17)

Be careful of the mind that is in you. Be sure that it is the mind of Christ and not the mind of a reprobate. I will give the end-time nations over to a reprobate mind, and they shall have the mind of the beast, even the world ruling system which shall control them.

The woman is the harlot riding the false Christ spirit. The false Christ spirit is not only in Rome; it is where every rebellious spirit lifts itself against anointed leadership. It was in Korah, Levi, Dathan and Abiram of Reuben (Numbers 26:8), Zimri of Simeon (Numbers 25:14), Saul of Benjamin (I Samuel 15:26), Adonijah of Judah (I Kings 1:5) and Judas Iscariot.

My child, the purpose of the "one-mind" of the evil one is to make war with Me, the Lamb. But I will overcome this confederation of evil, for I am the ruling monarch of this universe. I **alone** am the Lord of lords and King of kings, and there be those who are not deceived by the "one mind" system of the evil one, and those are they who are CALLED and CHOSEN and FAITHFUL.

Satan's key personnel shall have limited time to work havoc. Only until the Word of God be fulfilled. I have already decreed the final hour of the count-down.

As sure as the sun rises and sets on schedule, the moon waxes and wanes to the exact second and the stars shine in their courses, so the time schedule for the rise and fall of every evil system of Satan in the end-times is pre-determined and controlled by Me. Only see that you be among the **called, chosen and faithful.**

June 6

COME OUT OF THE HARLOT CHURCH

Scripture Reading – Revelation 18:1-24

"And I heard another voice from heaven, saying, Come out of her, my people, that ye be not partakers of her sins, and that ye receive not of her plagues." (Revelation 18:4)

I hate the religious façade of the world's Babylonian system. "Having a form of godliness, but denying the power thereof" is what I see as I pass through your Sunday morning congregations.

To the world's observer it appears to be a gathering of dedicated, sincere, God-loving people who have come to worship Me. But, sad to say, this is not the case. Instead, My house has become a habitation of devils, the hold of every foul spirit, the cage of every unclean and hateful bird.

In all nations, where My church has spread, carried by My dedicated missionaries, I have seen the corrupting of My bride, My church, the salt of the earth, into a house of thieves, a habitation of devils, a lurking place for every foul spirit, and a cage for every hateful bird.

There is no way, when it has become that corrupt, to convert or change her. The only thing left is to come out of her, separate yourself from her. A split is better than the defilement of the lot, the cutting off of a right arm is better than the poisoning of the blood stream. Cry mightily unto Me for cleansing in My house. For judgment is surely coming. The angel is come down from heaven, having great power, and as the earth is being lightened with His glory, every evil shall be detected. Nothing shall be hidden. Nothing shall be made to appear what it isn't.

Do not cling to that which I will destroy. For the judgment shall be sudden and it shall be great and it shall be swift, even in "one hour."

June 7

MY BRIDE HAS MADE HERSELF READY

Scripture Reading — Revelation 19:1-21

"Let us be glad and rejoice, and give honour to him: for the marriage of the Lamb is come, and his wife hath made herself ready." (Revelation 19:7)

My beloved, it is not always easy to make yourself ready for any great event. Sometimes it is harder than other times. There are always many interruptions, many unexpected things which happen, things you did not anticipate. But still you must not give up, you must keep working at it.

Let Me help you. I know what you need the most. I know what will be useful. I have a plan for good for you, and not for evil.

The greatest event of your life is before you. This is your wedding to the Lamb. You need to make yourself ready for this great event. All of heaven is awaiting this great wedding. Angels and saints are anticipating it momentarily. It has already been announced, invitations have gone out. But the bride is not ready. She is unprepared for the greatest event of her life. Heaven's citizens cannot understand why she delays in purifying and perfecting herself. The wedding music is already playing, 'The Hallelujah Chorus' has begun, but the bride, where is she? Where is she? Where is she?

June 8

ANGELS HAVE POWER OVER SATAN

Scripture Reading — Revelation 20:1-15

"And he laid hold on the dragon, that old serpent, which is the Devil, and Satan, and bound him a thousand years," (Revelation 20:2)

There is not an angel in heaven who cannot handle the dragon, for they have My power and My authority.

But I have given My children this same kind of power. Have I not promised you power over unclean spirits to cast them out, to heal all manner of sickness, all manner of disease, to cleanse the leper, raise the dead, to tread on serpents and scorpions and over all power of the enemy, to cast out devils and to do My works and even greater works than I have done?

This is the same power and authority I have given the angels. Why then do you seem to have less power than the angels? Is it not because:

1. They come from My presence. You are not in My presence enough in prayer and communion.

2. They are pure. Your mind sins and your tongue transgresses and the devil knows it, so you have no power against him.

3. You haven't the perfect faith.

So, My child, you know the conditions. Blessed shall you be if you obey them.

June 9

THE WONDERFUL NEW JERUSALEM

Scripture Reading — Revelation 21:1-27

"And I heard a great voice out of heaven saying, Behold, the tabernacle of God is with men, and he will dwell with them, and they shall be his people, and God himself shall be with them, and be their God. And God shall wipe away all tears from their eyes; and there shall be no more death, neither sorrow, nor crying, neither shall there be any more pain: for the former things are passed away." (Revelation 21:3,4)

My beloved child, always keep looking forward to this glorious day when I will move out of the heavens, down here to this world, bringing My glory with Me.

The change will be so great that the very foundation of this earth will shake. All evil shall be removed. There shall be righteousness.

The ruling city of the New Jerusalem shall be the jewel of the new earth. The prophets and apostles and saints shall be in full authority. The saints shall serve as administrators. Under them it shall be a just and righteous rule. There shall be no more suffering, no tears or physical pain. And death shall be no more. For life shall be so glorious that death will no longer be a necessary messenger that releases the righteous from the chain of flesh with all its weaknesses, and the wicked from their controlling influence.

And the tribes shall be there, all 12, Manasseh and Ephraim united as one. It shall be a glorious thing to behold. And you shall be there, My child, and walk on those streets, singing and serving. And you too shall be new, to fit with the New Jerusalem.

June 10

AND WE SHALL SEE HIS FACE

Scripture Reading — Revelation 22:1-21

"And they shall see his face; and his name shall be in their foreheads." (Revelation 22:4)

Can you picture, My child, just what it will mean just to look upon Me, Jesus? I will talk with you, visit with you and reveal the secrets of the ages to you. We will have time to spend together. For all of eternity lies before us.

There will be no rush for time, no deadlines to meet, no grief of parting or saying good-bye. You will travel at the speed of light, making the farthest distances as close as the nearest.

There will be no more fear, worries, dangers, influence by evil forces, darkness, financial strain, injustice, impurity, or religious façade.

Zebulun shall rejoice and be at home in the purity of the new world, coming and going out of her southern gate and dwelling with the righteous seed of all nations and all dispensations. The day comes, it is not far hence. Think on that day. Anticipate it and rejoice over it.

June 11

WE ARE CALLED TO BE HOLY AND BLAMELESS BEFORE HIM IN LOVE

Scripture Reading — Ephesians 1:1-23

"Blessed be the God and Father of our Lord Jesus Christ, who hath blessed us with all spiritual blessings in heavenly places in Christ:" (Ephesians 1:3,4)

"The heavenly place:" My child that is where all spiritual warfare begins and ends. You have been blessed in this that you are ordained to conquer on that high sphere, for you have been chosen.

Long, long ago, **before** the foundations of the world were laid, you were chosen to be given this opportunity to be born and live on this planet. I gave you, My beloved child, an appointment to earth. Now you are on it for one purpose: to be holy and without blame before Me in love.

"Holy!" A more misunderstood word in the Christian vocabulary has not been found. But you are called to a holiness that is the "mark of heaven" upon your life and soul. It is a way of life like unto Mine. I said to Abraham, "Be ye holy as I am holy." It is being like Me. The closer you are to Me, and the better you know Me, the more you will know what holiness is.

I call you to be without blame before Me. Even as I said to Abraham, "Walk before Me and be thou perfect" so I say to you, "Be holy without blame before Me in love. It is all before Me. What others think of you is unimportant. It is before Me you walk and live and have your being."

June 12

YOU ARE CREATED TO DO GOD'S WORKS

Scripture Reading — Ephesians 2:1-22

"For we are his workmanship, created in Christ Jesus unto good works, which God hath before ordained that we should walk in them." (Ephesians 2:10)

Just as surely as a man is permanently changed after he is circumcised and can never return again to being uncircumcised, so it is when you are reborn, re-created by the mighty hand of Jesus.

My Son, Jesus, was there when we created the heavens and earth. Is He not sufficient to re-create a new creature out of you? Did He not create you to begin with; can He not re-create you and all those whom I have ordained unto good works?

What "good works" do I demand of you? Even the works that My Son did.

I love to give, to sacrifice, to undo the works of Satan and make him powerless to afflict in such a way that he can destroy you and others, and hinder all from living a holy life. These are the works to which you are ordained.

I have ordained My Son to work these works in you, to re-create a new mind in you, to loosen you from the powers of darkness which in the past held you in bondage, that you might be free to have this great work of grace wrought upon you, that He can make you worthy to be fit into the temple of God, even the living temple. If you are ordained to it, shall you not succeed in the end?

June 13

ROOTED IN LOVE

Scripture Reading — Ephesians 3:1-21

"For this cause I bow my knees unto the Father of our Lord Jesus Christ, Of whom the whole family in heaven and earth is named, That he would grant you, according to the riches of his glory, to be strengthened with might by his Spirit in the inner man;" (Ephesians 3:14-16)

My servant Paul prayed daily for the saints to be made strong in the spirit. This is where true strength is needed. What is the use of much physical strength if the spirit is weak?

Samson had physical strength but his spirit was weak, and that soon caused him to lose his physical strength.

You must ask Me daily to give you much spiritual strength. You have still many mountains to climb, many victories to win, many sermons to preach, many miles to travel, many nations to reach, all for Me, not for yourself. If you always remember "it is for Me," this will help you. I love you, My child and I want to use you, but your spirit is not strong enough to carry the burden.

Remember that your spirit can be strengthened by My Spirit. It takes Spirit to strengthen spirit. The Holy Spirit puts strength into you as you abide close to Me.

I must dwell in your heart at all times, so that your tree of life will extend its roots down, deep in love.

It is in the love of Christ alone that you can be filled with all the fullness of God. Be strong, therefore, My little one, through My love. For love roots you and fills you to make you a strong and fruitful tree. I can do exceedingly abundantly more than you can ask or think.

June 14

HOW TO WALK WORTHY OF YOUR HIGH CALLING

Scripture Reading — Ephesians 4:1-12

"I therefore, the prisoner of the Lord, beseech you that ye walk worthy of the vocation wherewith ye are called, With all lowliness and meekness, with longsuffering, forbearing one another in love; Endeavouring to keep the unity of the Spirit in the bond of peace." (Ephesians 4:1-3)

Walk worthy of the vocation wherewith ye are called! This isn't just a suggestion. This is a command. There is nothing more distressing than to see those whom I have called to walk in the "high-calling walk," grovel around down deep in the things that are not becoming to a saint.

Sometimes it will cost you great humility, for you must begin, continue and finish this walk, even as I did while on earth.

There are certain qualifications needed to enable you to walk worthy of the vocation wherewith ye are called. And without these you will never make it.

They are lowliness, meekness, longsuffering, forbearance, love, unity, peace!

Lowliness is the ability to live a normal life, not esteeming yourself to be anything which you are not, giving God the glory for all you are.

Meekness is the yielding of your own spirit and will to Mine alone, letting Me lead you, guide you, and use your life for Myself.

Longsuffering is the strength of God to wait for others, who are doing wrong, to awaken, have their eyes opened, turn from their wrong ways and change.

Forebearance is letting others be themselves, whether right or wrong, trusting in My power to change what is wrong, not criticizing, but carrying their iniquity for them.

Love is the gift of God, compassion, not limited by circumstances or conditions.

Unity is the ability to work for a compromise, even though you may not agree to conditions.

Peace: Peace of heart comes when you have done your best to bring peace between two apostles, letting Me work it out. Peace is when you say and do nothing, simply handing your case over to Me!

June 15

GROWING INTO THE MATURITY OF CHRIST

Scripture Reading — Ephesians 4:13-32

"Till we all come in the unity of the faith, and of the knowledge of the Son of God, unto a perfect man, unto the measure of the stature of the fulness of Christ:" (Ephesisans 4:13)

"From whom the whole body fitly joined together and compacted by that which every joint supplieth, according to the effectual working in the measure of every part, maketh increase of the body unto the edifying of itself in love." (vs. 16)

My child, wait for others to grow up. The body of the bride is like a "freak." It is not a perfected body. Far from it, it is not "fitly joined together and compacted by that which every joint supplieth." One leg is shorter than the other, one finger on each hand is undeveloped. One hip is the size of that of a 10-year old child and the other of a full grown man. The body is not growing together. It is a pathetic sight. All because the whole body has not been renewed in the spirit of the mind (vs. 23). It is the brain which sends signals of growth. And this it cannot do if part of the brain is not the rejuvenated "Christ brain." Parts of the body grow and parts are retarded. That is the picture of My bride.

I am waiting for her to grow up, so that she will be fully developed. This will bring the unity of faith that My bride does not have now. Part believes this, part that, and part another thing. She is like a school house with many degrees of living and levels of knowledge, from beginner to graduate. That is how her understanding concerning My Word is varied. How can she be one?

But I would have her hasten to become equalized, fully developed into a perfect body, even one that fits the measure of the stature of Christ in all His glory and fullness. If she does not mature to full growth, even into the stature of His fullness and glory, My Son would be unequally yoked through eternity.

I, Jehovah, was unequally yoked to Israel, and I gave her a bill of divorcement after much pain and suffering. Now My Son is seeking out a new bride, even spiritual Israel.

June 16

FOLLOW GOD AS A LOVING CHILD WOULD

Scripture Reading – Ephesians 5:1-33

"Be ye therefore followers of God, as dear children; And walk in love, as Christ also hath loved us, and hath given himself for us an offering and a sacrifice to God for a sweetsmelling savour." (Ephesians 5:1,2)

"Wherefore be ye not unwise, but understanding what the will of the Lord is." (vs. 17)

Even as a little child follows you around, hanging on to your skirt because she loves you and doesn't want to lose you, but keeps holding your skirt, lest in any sudden movement you should turn and get away from her; so you, with the same worshipful love, should hang onto My skirt, and follow Me wherever I go. I will lead you wisely and lovingly. When the little child follows you, you often have to do things for yourself or others, but when you follow Me, all I do will only be for your good.

I am your example of the walk of love. I have only one purpose: to love, and give My life for others as a sacrifice unto My Father for a sweet-smelling savour. There are sacrifices which are not a "sweet-smelling savour." They are lives which appear to be lives of sacrifice but are only done for self. From these lives comes only a stench into My nostrils. Your motives **must** be pure. Everything you do must have a good, clean, holy purpose. And that is the only way you can be like Me. I am the pattern Son.

If you keep this in mind, you will not be unwise. For you will know the will of God more perfectly when you follow Me closely. Love is the key to following closely. For love never wants to be far away from the loved one. And in the closeness is the knowing what My perfect will is, even the life of sacrifice, the life that is lived for **others**.

June 17

HONOUR AND OBEY YOUR PARENTS

Scripture Reading — Ephesians 6:1-29

"Children, obey your parents in the Lord: for this is right. Honour thy father and mother; which is the first commandment with promise; That it may be well with thee, and thou mayest live long on the earth." (Ephesians 6:1-3)

For every good deed that is done, there is a reward. But the reward of long life and prosperous living is one that comes by way of honouring that source from which you have sprung.

When you honour your parents, it is like watering the roots from which you have sprung. This is the law of everything that grows.

The roots of the trees are fertilized by the fruit and the leaves that fall from the tree which enrich the soil and bless the tree so that it can produce even better leaves and fruit.

You may grow out into great branches and reach far out in every direction, but only if you bless and strengthen your roots will you live a long and healthy life, one that will not easily be shaken by the storms of life that **shall** surely come to shake you and try you.

"That it might be well with thee." Prosperity is promised to those who obey their parents in the Lord. This can be interpreted in two ways:

1. Children, obey your "parents in the Lord" (spiritual parents);
2. Children, obey your parents "in the Lord" (when what they ask of you is My will).

Both interpretations are correct according to the laws of heaven. Both are truth. When you honour the ones above you, both spiritually and naturally, you receive great benefits of prosperity and long life.

June 18

PUT ON THE WHOLE ARMOUR OF GOD

Scripture Reading – Ephesians 6:10-22

"Wherefore take unto you the whole armour of God, that ye may be able to withstand in the evil day, and having done all, to stand." (Ephesians 6:13)

This is the evil day. But I want you to take dominion over the evil day. I gave Adam (Genesis 1:28), Noah (Genesis 9:2), and My disciples (Luke 10:19, 9:1, Matthew 10:1) dominion. And you have it through My blood (Revelation 12:11) and through the armour which I have given unto you to wear in these evil days. Without this armour, you will fail. **Stand therefore.**

1. Loins girded with truth: Truth is a most essential characteristic. First be honest to yourself, then to Me, then, with discretion of what you reveal, with others. It protects your loins (your strength).

2. **Breastplate of righeousness:** Your heart is protected by its purity and innocence. Many die of heart attacks because the heart cannot stand the burden of guilt. Not all of My saints die of heart attacks who are thought to. I simply still the hearts of some of them and take their spirits to Me.

3. **Feet shod with Gospel of peace:** It is the feet that carry the soldier into battle. If your feet are feet of peace, they will bring peace with them wherever they carry you.

4. **Shield of faith:** Have faith in me and in My ability to work in the hearts and lives of others. Faith's shield is not only a protection for the heart, but it is wrapped all the way around you.

5. **Helmet of salvation:** Your mind needs to be covered at all times with the thought of My great salvation provided for you, body, soul, spirit and mind. I redeemed your mind. Stay in My redemption. The word salvation also means healing.

6. **Sword of Spirit:** My Word is not only for your protection, your defence, but it is for the purpose of attacking the enemy. The first five parts of armour protect the soldier, but the sword makes him dangerous to the enemy. He hates the Word of God. Satan is convicted by My Word and so also are his hosts of demons, when it is used **against** him in the anointing of the Holy Spirit.

7. **Watchfulness of prayer:** A fully armed and armoured soldier is helpess when he is sleeping. Therefore prayer is vital, for it is the alerting of the spirit, the open line of communication with headquarters which gives the soldier his commands.

June 19

HIS KISSES ARE BETTER THAN WINE

Scripture Reading — Song of Solomon 1:1-17

"Let him kiss me with the kisses of his mouth: for thy love is better than wine." (Song of Solomon 1:2)

This kind of intimate kissing takes place only in privacy, whereas the drinking of wine is something you do in the presence of others who are also feasting and revelling.

My bride is so "in love" with Me, that she is more content in the privacy of My arms than in the house of feasting and banqueting.

She becomes more "intoxicated," lost, in the bliss and ecstasy of My love than she does in all the fine cooked up, planned programmes and schemes of man.

This bride doesn't even need, nor desire, conventions, services, meetings, Bible studies, because she has more in one hour in My presence, alone with Me, than in three days in the halls of learning, the chapels of chaplains.

So she runs from them, for they only break her heart and cause confusion, because she cannot feel My closeness to her in man-made and man-conducted religious charades.

She wonders at her own peculiarity and almost feels guilty because she cannot be "lifted" by the wine from the bottle.

But I understand, for she has drunk from the wine of My kisses, that have made her delirious with joy and transported her out of the natural into the supernatural, the bliss of heaven. How then can the man-made "wine" suffice, when she is drunk from the grapes of Eshcol?

June 20

COME RUN WITH ME

Scripture Reading – Song of Solomon 2:1-17

"My beloved is like a roe or a young hart: behold, he standeth behind our wall, he looketh forth at the windows, shewing himself through the lattice." (Song of Solomon 2:9)

Yea, My precious one, I am as the young hart longing for your nearness, looking for your companionship, waiting, waiting for your attention.

I silently come from the wilds close to your garden. I'm looking through the lattice of your window for glimpses of you, My beautiful bride.

Oh, how I long for you to come and run with Me, over My hills, over My fields, over My mountains. Running and skipping and leaping, as together we rejoice at the coming in and the going out of the day.

How long, My bride, will you remain busy in the confines of your daily activities? When will you turn from all these things that demand your attention and come away with Me?

You grieve in vain, you mourn in ignorance. Your loneliness is not necessary. I am right here beside you, looking at you, My bride, through your lattice. Turn and see Me. I stand here watching you like a love-sick lover. Can't you see Me? Come, open the door and come away. Come now, My love, My fair one.

June 21

HOLD ON TO THE LORD

Scripture Reading — Song of Solomon 3:1-11

"It was but a little that I passed from them, but I found him whom my soul loveth: I held him, and would not let him go, until I had brought him into my mother's house, and into the chamber of her that conceived me." (Song of Solomon 3:4)

My beloved, hold on to Me, even as I reminded you of how a child holds on to your skirt and will not let you go.

There are hard trials coming; pains and fears and dangers lie ahead. You will need to feel My presence close to you more than ever. Reach out to Me for comfort and strength. Feel My presence close to you in these hard places.

Live so close to Me that I can feel your heart beat and can feel the very vibrations of your being. Your whole being will cry out to Me like the blood of Abel cried out. You won't need to speak a lot of words, even as I didn't need to speak many words to My Father. He heard My heart beat. He read My pulse, My blood pressure. My very blood stream spoke to Him all that I was feeling.

Bring Me into the intimacy of your life. Don't exclude Me from ANYTHING! Share all with Me. Be open-hearted with Me. I will never grieve nor disappoint you.

June 22

ALL THAT YOU ARE

Scripture Reading — Song of Solomon 4:1-16

"A garden inclosed is my sister, my spouse; a spring shut up, a fountain sealed....A fountain of gardens, a well of living waters, and streams from Lebanon." (Song of Solomon 4:12,15)

My beloved, I love you with such a great love that it is impossible for you to comprehend. You have known great love, and you have loved deeply, but all the loves you have ever known together can only **begin** to reveal the great magnitude of My love for you, My sister, My spouse.

If you read this 4th chapter of the song of love every day, many times a day, for many days, and meditated deeply on it, you could begin to comprehend the greatness of My love for you.

I love you because of all that you are. You are much that you don't even know you are. Within you are potentials, beauties, precious gems yet undiscovered. I see these in you and love you.

To the world, to your companions, even to your dearest family members, you are a garden enclosed, a spring shut up, a fountain sealed, because you have never been fully released into your greatness. But I look within, I see behind the closed door of the interior façade of your life. I know that one day you will break through to be all that you were meant to be. And then you will water the earth. For you are a garden of fountains, a well of living water, flowing waters, a stream pure and clean, flowing from the snows of Lebanon's peaks, the source of which is in the clouds.

That is you **behind Me.** Go forth today and let this water of life flow out of your being onto this nation where I have sent you.

June 23

I AM COME INTO YOUR GARDEN

Scripture Reading – Song of Solomon 5:1-16

"I am come into my garden, my sister, my spouse: I have gathered my myrrh with my spice; I have eaten my honeycomb with my honey; I have drunk my wine with my milk: eat, O friends; drink, yea, drink abundantly, O beloved." (Song of Solomon 5:1)

My beloved one, I have taken great delight and pleasure in you. I enjoy sitting and listening as you speak about the things of God. Your heart's expressions are the delight of My soul. Sometimes you make Me laugh by the way you express the feelings of your soul with the humour which the Holy Spirit has given you. Then it is that I taste of your spices.

Other times, the agony of your soul, the tears of your eyes, the pain, fears and longings you endure, becomes My cup of myrrh and pain.

What is yours is mine. I share it all with you. Whatever grows in your garden is Mine also.

But there is more good than bad, more happy than sad, more to make Me rejoice, than to cause Me to grieve, for you are My joy, My bride. I love to be near you. Please contemplate on Me and feel My nearness. Do not relegate Me to the stars. I am here beside you, seeing you every minute, listening to your every word, dancing with you. I'm going with you. I'm in your garden, feasting together with you of the blessings of the Lord.

June 24

MY DOVE IS BUT ONE

Scripture Reading – Song of Solomon 6:1-13

"My dove, my undefiled is but one; she is the only one of her mother, she is the choice one of her that bare her. The daughters saw her, and blessed her; yea, the queens and the concubines, and they praised her." (Song of Solomon 6:9)

My dove, My undefiled, you are very special to Me. There is only ONE like you. Many times you long for someone else to be like you in every way, with the same heart beat, the same vision, the same burden, the same gifts and callings so that you can "retire" or take it more easy while that other one will carry on with your vision.

But there is no one ever like you. You are one of a kind. Some have your vision in part, but none can take your place.

Just when you think you have found and developed and trained that second "you," she or he disappoints you, leaves you to follow her or his own mission and calling and you are again "but one," the "only one," the "choice one."

All I can do is to take of the Spirit which is upon you and put it on them. But I cannot make them another "you."

I do not manufacture identical humanoids. That is the work of the anti-Christ. I make each one different, and this difference is for eternity. So do not be disappointed with others. They are what they are. You are you, the blessed one, the praised and honoured daughter.

June 25

A PALM TREE GIVING LIFE TO OTHERS

Scripture Reading — Song of Solomon 7:1-13

"This thy stature is like to a palm tree,...I said, I will go up to the palm tree, I will take hold of the boughs thereof:" (Song of Solomon 7:7a,8a)

You are beautiful to Me, like the elegance of the palm. The palm stands tall, and when you walk in the Spirit you stand tall too.

It is only in the spirit realm that you can be like the palm, for in the natural realm you are like any other tree of the woods.

I call you to the elegance and the distinction of the high calling of "Spirit-living."

In Hong Kong there were many missionaries, but very few

touched the lives of the people of the Walled City. So I sent Jackie Pullinger, and she became a "palm tree," standing tall and courageous among the dens of iniquity.*

Many came to her and "took hold of the boughs thereof," and she gave them life and strength through her own spiritual greatness which she had received through Me.

So you too, as you grow in the Spirit, will become like the palm tree. You will love not only the nations, but the people, the poor, weak, sickly, sinful, disturbed, pesky, obnoxious, offensive, and they will come and take hold of the boughs of your life and receive strength and life.

June 26

LOVE, THE SEAL OF IDENTITY

Scripture Reading — Song of Solomon 8:1-14

"Set me as a seal upon thine heart, as a seal upon thine arm: for love is strong as death; jealousy is cruel as the grave: the coals thereof are coals of fire, which hath a most vehement flame." (Song of Solomon 8:6,7)

There is no power as great as love. But there is a power which is related to a great love which is very powerful, and that is jealousy. For the greater the love, the greater the jealousy can be, if there is reason to doubt the faithfulness and fidelity of the loved one.

This is why the lover calls, "set me as a seal upon thine heart, as a seal upon thine arm." For there is the feeling that there should be some mark to identify and remind that loved one that no matter where they must go, or what they do, they will see that seal, that mark, and remember there is one who loves faithfully and who can never change and that they must remain faithful to that one.

The tortures of jealousy are very terrible and very cruel. But love is stronger. The mark of love is faithfulness, purity, loyalty, fidelity.

---

*"Chasing the Dragon" by Jackie Pullinger is available from End-Time Handmaidens, P.O. Box 447, Jasper, Arkansas 72641.

No token of ring or chain is reliable. The jealous heart looks beyond these trappings and searches for the vibrations of pure love, faithfulness and devotion.

This is the identity marking which you need towards Me, My beloved. No chain, or cross, or nice words of love, but only pure devotion to Me will suffice. When your heart strays from loving Me and is devoted more to working for Me and serving Me than loving Me and wanting to be near to share with Me, I surely will feel it and know it. Let your love and vibrations for Me, and not My gifts, be your seal of dedication.

June 27

YOUR VESSEL PERFECTED THROUGH LOVE

Scripture Reading — Philippians 1:1-11

"And this I pray, that your love may abound yet more and more in knowledge and in all judgment; That ye may approve things that are excellent; that ye may be sincere and without offence till the day of Christ; Being filled with the fruits of righteousness, which are by Jesus Christ, unto the glory and praise of God." (Philippians 1:9-11)

My beloved, this is the prayer of the Holy Spirit which the Spirit prayed through Paul for the believers of Philippi (Acts 16:12-40). The first convert of their area was a woman, Lydia. She was as zealous in her new-found faith as she had been in her business. She immediately believed the Gospel message and was baptized. Then she opened her home to Paul and his party. After Paul was released from prison, he returned to her home and left from there to continue his ministry. It was the first church of Macedonia (today's Europe).

To you, My child, I say, let your love grow and grow, just like Lydia's love grew. The true sincere love, which she had for Me when she worshipped on the river on the Sabbath, opened her heart to greater truth and knowledge and gave her the spirit of true judgment, so that she was able to accept the truth when she heard it.

Pure love does not blind the eyes, it opens them to truth. I desire that you be sincere, without offence, till the day of My appearing. For you may hide the flaws from others, but never from

Me. I will not put My fruits of righeousness in a vessel that is unclean and filled with offensive rubble. Let love purge your vessel now.

June 28

ALL, FOR THE FURTHERANCE OF THE GOSPEL

Scripture Reading — Philippians 1:12-18

"But I would ye should understand, brethren, that the things which happened unto me have fallen out rather unto the furtherance of the gospel;" (Philippians 1:12)

My beloved, you may not understand everything now, but there is a time coming when you will see that all of your disappointments have been My appointments. Not only does everything work together for good for you, but also for Me. That is the wonderful thing about it. My Gospel is perpetuated and propagated more widely because of the things which you have had to suffer.

Paul, My servant was wise. He knew that not all preach out of love for Me or for the love of souls, or even with the pure motive of a Divine calling. Some preached out of envy, because they were jealous of Paul and wanted to copy him and be like him; others preached out of strife, to prove their point, and some preached because they wanted fame. But he knew that even though their motives were not pure, I would use the message they preached to the furtherance of the Gospel.

Paul rejoiced. I call you to rejoice! Rejoice! Rejoice! Rejoice, because Christ is preached. For in one way or another your life is influencing others. It may not be as you desired, or as I desired, but it shall be for My glory in the end. Rejoice!

June 29

TO LIVE FOR CHRIST

Scripture Reading — Philippians 1:19-21

"For to me to live is Christ, and to die is gain." (Philippians 1:21)

My beloved, if you could but see for one moment the glory of heaven, the peace, the rest, the comfort, the joy, the presence of loved ones, the rewards, the revealed presence of the God-head, how you too would long to come home!

Paul had seen this during one of his great trials and times of suffering, and it never left him. He always remembered it and faithfully strove towards the goal of the heavenly abode of the righteous.

But Paul knew the value of every minute here on earth. He saw how he was needed to minister, bring comfort, exhort and teach My children, and he knew that his only purpose for living was **not** for self, but "for Christ."

Teach My people this vital truth, even to live for Christ. There are many who do not understand this truth. They become weary in the sufferings of life; the trials and testings overwhelm them. So they need to know that everything they suffer, all the trials, the tests, the weary miles of travel, the leaving home and loved ones, is only "for Christ." The years in prison, slave-camp, separation, beatings, mental conflict is only for Me. If they can understand this, it will give them strength to finish their task, and then they will all begin so great an entrance into glory.

June 30

LIVING FOR OTHERS

Scripture Reading — Philippians 1:22-27

"But if I live in the flesh, this is the fruit of my labour: yet what I shall choose I wot not." (Philippians 1:22)

Paul knew that under any circumstances it would turn out for good, whether by life or by death. He knew that for himself personally, death was far better than life.

But love compelled him to think about and care for those whom he loved, even the church of Philippi, where his first convert had been the woman Lydia.

So, because of love, he reached out and accepted a longer life which he knew was needful for them. **They** needed him.

There is no way that you can live to please yourself. Your life belongs to others, and you are dedicated totally to helping others. The long life I give you is for others; the strength, the courage, the endurance, the inspiration to work is for others. Even the time when your work is finished is not your decision. It is Mine. As long as your life brings joy to others and is meaningful, I have the prerogative to give to you, and you have the responsibility to ask of Me long life.

Paul longed to live to return to give them joy and faith. Your reason to live is to give others joy and faith. He knew how they had prayed for him and that their faith would be built up as they saw God spare his life and return him to them in answer to their prayers.

July 1

THE GIFT OF SUFFERING FOR HIM

Scripture Reading — Philippians 1:28-30

"For unto you it is given in the behalf of Christ, not only to believe on him, but also to suffer for his sake;" (Philippians 1:29)

My beloved children cannot always accept the calling of suffering for My sake. Most are willing to walk only as far as "the garden of prayer" with Me. Even there, they fall asleep in exhaustion. They do not do this intentionally, but because they just do **not** have the strength to endure!

Peter, James and John (Mark 14:33) truly loved Me, but they did not have the strength to travail or intercede during the night of My betrayal. It was not until after they were endued with power from on high that they were able to travail and intercede late into the night hours. Only the power of the Holy Spirit can keep you through the night vigil of intercession.

I have given you, My beloved, the calling of suffering for My sake. You have known great heartache. Though you have not yet suffered (resisted) unto blood (Hebrews 12:4), you have known deep agony of rejection, misunderstanding, false accusation and condemnation by My other children. Sometimes this kind of suffering leaves deeper wounds than the physical suffering.

July 2

WITHOUT BLAME IN A CORRUPT WORLD

Scripture Reading – Philippians 2:1-16

"Do all things without murmurings and disputings: That ye may be blameless and harmless, the sons of God, without rebuke, in the midst of a crooked and perverse nation, among whom ye shine as lights in the world." (Philippians 2:14,15)

My beloved, you are My Kingdom of God on earth. You represent heaven to a corrupt, crooked and perverse world.

By your shining example, you make others know that there is a higher law, a life on a higher plane. You point the way to God, but only as you live by the laws I have given you through My Word.

Even as I came to earth and took upon Myself the form and life of man, and became the example of a higher life through humility, obedience and death, even the death of the cross, so you too are called to be an example of perfection.

You must work at these laws of perfection. It does not come easily to the fallen nature. But I have given you My Holy Spirit to help you and make you strong. He works in you the desire, first of all, to do My will, and then, after that, the strength to do it. My will, in your life, gives Me great pleasure. I rejoice to see you living My life again.

One of the great keys is to do it all without murmuring and complaining. For I never murmured or complained. And you are My representative, living in My likeness by another law of life than the one of this corrupt world.

> Let the love of My God shine through me.
> Let the beauty of Jesus men see.
> Let the pattern of the Son be the One, the only one
> That men will see in me.

July 3

A COMPANION WHO SHARES THE BURDEN IS PRECIOUS

Scripture Reading — Philippians 2:17-24

"For I have no man likeminded, who will naturally care for your state. For all seek their own, not the things which are Jesus Christ's." (Philippians 2:20,21)

Can you picture, My child, Paul dictating this letter to Timothy? Can you see the look that passed between these two men? Can you feel what Timothy felt at this time?

How sad, that after serving Me for all those many years, after Paul's many journeys, after his great revival at Ephesus, there was only one son in the Gospel standing with him, with the same heart and soul!

Human nature has not changed one iota. Even in 2,000 years the hearts of men are still the same. All seek their own welfare. Self-preservation has corrupted the ministry. All want their own name to have fame. They seek after recognition, honour, the praises of men, independent power to do miracles for the sake of acclaim and financial independence.

Few are willing to lose their identity in the "Pauls" who have raised them up and made them great in God. Each seek their own. The sons of the Gospel are few, very few. The daughters of the mothers in Israel, the Ruths, are few, very few.

Timothy cared for the Philippians because Paul cared. Paul's burden was Timothy's burden. It came naturally. There was no pretence, not putting on a burden, rather a sharing, because they had one heart. **Pray for Me to give you Timothys and Ruths in the Gospel.**

July 4

SERVING IN YOUR PLACE

Scripture Reading — Philippians 2:25-30

"Because for the work of Christ he was nigh unto death, not regarding his life, to supply your lack of service toward me (to serve me in your place)." (Philippians 2:30)

Epaphroditus, whose name means "the beloved," was sent by the church of Philippi to minister unto Paul and to help him in the work of the Gospel. He took their place and did for Paul what the church of Philippi could not do.

Not all are called to go, but all are called to send a substitute or to stand behind those who are called, by their prayers and by their moral and financial support.

This "beloved" of the Lord, Epaphroditus, became very sick, even unto death. Paul knew how his loved ones would grieve if he died. Not only that, but Paul felt the responsibility for his life and that he should not die under Paul's care. Just like you feel responsible for all the souls who journey with you to the nations of the world and to Israel. Did I not promise Paul in the stormy seas, through My angel, "and, lo, God hath given thee all them that sail with thee"? (Acts 27:24)

I have given you this promise for those who labour with you, that, like with Paul, "I may have mercy on you also, lest you should have sorrow upon sorrow." For many whom I send you will "not regard their life," will work recklessly and foolishly and dangerously to serve Me in your place, for you cannot always go to these places and more. And I will spare them as I spared Epaphroditus, that they may return to you in joy again.

July 5

COUNT ALL THINGS LOSS FOR CHRIST

Scripture Reading — Philippians 3:1-8

"But what things were gain to me, those I counted loss for Christ. Yea doubtless, and I count all things but loss for the excellency of the knowledge of Christ Jesus my Lord: for whom I have suffered the loss of all things, and do count them but dung, that I may win Christ," (Philippians 3:7,8)

My beloved, I call you to this same kind of dedication. Don't ever love anything or anyone overly much. Love with My God-love.

Then the pain of losing and the pain of parting will not overwhelm you.

Everything that is precious to you is only on loan to you for a little while. What I gave you yesterday, I can take away today. You would be a fool to hang on to anything or let your heart strings wrap around it.

When you were still very young, I taught you not to love anything overly much. You have learned your lesson well. But as soon as you forgot, I taught you again by example and experience the pain of parting from something you loved too much. Now I teach you again.

If you can accept this loss as coming from My hand, because I love you and want only what is best for you, then you shall find healing and comfort.

It still pains you to lose all things because you are still hanging on to them. Even your reputation has become important to you now. You prize your ministry, and it is special, but My high calling is always one step above **your** ministry. My high calling for you is the perfect will of God which perfects you, the **real** you.

Your only obligation is to win Me. Do not strive for anything else, only to win Me. For in Me is the excellecy of the knowledge of Christ, which is the dearest treasure you can have.

July 6

YOU ARE RIGHTEOUS THROUGH HIM

Scripture Reading — Philippians 3:9; Psalm 139:13-17

"And be found in him, not having mine own righteousness, which is of the law, but that which is through the faith of Christ, the righteousness which is of God by faith:" (Philippians 3:9)

My beloved child, I love you because you are you. I made you. I put into you what I designed for you to be and to have. I take pride in My accomplished work. You are to Me what a beautiful building or bridge is to its architect and engineer who designed it. Even as he takes pride in the finished product, I take pride in what I have created in you. "For we are his workmanship, created in Christ Jesus unto good works, which God hath before ordained that we should walk in them." (Ephesians 2:10)

And this work of creation did not finish at your birth, but it is continuing. I am making you presentable to the whole of My creation. It does not matter if you are not acceptable to yourself or to others, just as long as you are acceptable to Me, and that you ARE. You are My beloved bride. I love you. I have given you My righteousness. Your own righteousness is acceptable to the law of society, but no one can be perfect by his own efforts, not matter how much he tries. Don't you see that?

Just have faith in My love for you and that I see you through love. I have called you and put My Word in you. The message you bear is not your own; you are simply the instrument, the vessel that contains My message.

I have purchased for you forgiveness, healing and the righteousness of God through My death on the cross. Accept it and rejoice!

July 7

FELLOWSHIP IN SUFFERING

Scripture Reading — Philippians 3:10-13; John 17:20-26

"That I may know him, and the power of his resurrection, and the fellowship of his sufferings, being made conformable unto his death;" (Philippians 3:10)

My beloved, it is impossible to know Me without entering into My life's experiences.

When you love someone dearly, you desire for them to share in your joys and your precious treasures. You take them to places where you have been. You promote their ministry, their gift, so that they can also have honour. You introduce them to your friends. No great man takes honour unto himself. The Maestro shares the glory of the thunderous applause with the first violinist and he, in turn, shares it with the whole orchestra.

But to really love and to truly share, one must enter the valley of pain together with those whom you love. You must weep together, be rejected together.

This is why My children in the prisons and torture chambers of the world know Me like none of My other children. They have accepted the suffering that they may truly know Me.

To reject suffering only proves your lack of knowing and understanding Me.

Because I love you and want to draw you even closer to Me, I have permitted you to fellowship with Me in suffering. For I have much glory and much blessing still in store for you.

Great glory accompanies great suffering. They cannot be separated. And it is true that you must, through much tribulation, enter into the Kingdom of God. (Acts 14:22) With every hurt, you are one step further into the glory of My Kingdom.

July 8

RUN TO OBTAIN THE PRIZE

Scripture Reading — Philippians 3:14-29; II Timothy 4:7,8

"I press toward the mark for the prize of the high calling of God in Christ Jesus. Let us therefore, as many as be perfect be thus minded:" (Philippians 3:14,15a)

My beloved, press forward. Keep your eyes upon the prize, not the end of the race. At the end of the race is only a ribbon. Think beyond that ribbon. Think about the prize which is the result of breaking the ribbon.

I have bequeathed to you the great honour of the high calling of God in Christ Jesus. This is the greatest honour that I can give an earthling. There is no higher honour. You have been chosen to represent your race, your sex, your heritage. Run for them. Many eyes are upon you. You are compassed about by a great cloud of witnesses who are watching you. Remember that. (Hebrews 12:1)

Run with patience this life's race that is set before you, always looking to Me. I am your start and your finish. I am your inspiration, your trainer, your encourager, and I am the final goal. You will run into My arms.

Press forward, your eyes on Me. If you look at others who are competing with you, you will surely be hindered. Keep your eyes on Me and surely you shall receive the everlasting crown that fadeth not away. (I Corinthians 9:24,25)

July 9

A NEW BODY FASHIONED FOR US

Scripture Reading — Philippians 3:20-21

"Who shall change our vile body, that it may be fashioned like unto his glorious body, according to the working whereby he is able even to subdue all things unto himself." (Philippians 3:21)

Praise Me, My child! You shall not always be as you are now. I made this body which you now possess, and I am the only one who can change it for another one which is like unto My resurrected and glorified body. I had different bodies Myself. I surely can give you another body.

1. I had My pre-incarnated body, which Moses, Abraham and David saw.

2. I had My body, created in the womb of Mary, which was fashioned by the workings of the Holy Spirit. This work lasted nine months.

3. I had My body which was the same as the last, but it was a resurrected body with flesh and bones, and had the ability to pass through doors that were closed. I could do the same with My human body, which I received in My mother's womb. I could translate Myself, walk on water and make Myself invisible. Not all that I could do is fully recorded. You can do the same if you have faith. Peter did!

4. I have My glorified body which John saw in Revelation (Revelation 1:13-16; I Corinthians 15:42-44).

One day soon you also shall be transformed from a corruptible and weak body into one like Mine. Even now, day by day anticipate it and expect it. You can have a foretaste of it in this life, like Enoch, Elijah and Philip did.

July 10

HELP THE WOMEN WHO LABOUR IN THE GOSPEL

Scripture Reading — Philippians 4:1-5

"And I intreat thee also, true yokefellow, help those women which laboured with me in the gospel, with Clement also, and with other my fellowlabourers, whose names are in the book of life." (Philippians 4:3)

My beloved, I call you to be a "true yokefellow." You are not called to bear the yoke alone. You are yoked to others. In fact, you are even yoked to Paul himself who laboured with many of My daughters in the work of the ministry. You are called to stand at his side and bear his yoke which I gave him.

Can you think how great the agony of My servant, Paul, would be, if he were to return to the scene of his labours and see the desolations of Corinth, Ephesus, Philippi and Malta? His heart would break. Oh, where is the church? What has happened to the church? Surely this is another world from the world of Paul's time.

Pick up this yoke. Wear it all your life. Help the women who laboured with Paul. Remember your sisters of yesterday. Ask for their burden. Help them finish the work they started. Help My daughters of today who labour in My fields. Encourage them. Help them bear the burden. Their names are in the book of life with all their deeds. What you do for them will be recorded eternally.

July 11

PRAISE INSTEAD OF WORRY

Scripture Reading — Philippians 4:6-9

"Be careful for nothing; but in every thing by prayer and supplication with thanksgiving let your requests be made known unto God. And the peace of God, which passeth all understanding, shall keep your hearts and minds through Christ Jesus." (Philippians 4:6,7)

My beloved, it is in your hearts and minds where the source of all disturbance lies. You cannot keep peace in your being unless you have My help. But My help is available.

I do not want you to be worried about anything. Have I not said, "Let not your heart be troubled"? I want you to have perfect peace in all your activity. Never be overly troubled and disturbed about what is happening all around you to the world, to others, and even to yourself. Remember I am in control.

Worry will age you. It will sicken you. It will frustrate you and make you powerless. It will confuse you so that you will not make the right decision under pressure. Worry is Satan's key which he uses to make many of My children powerless and weak in exploits. Worry will shackle your arms to your side, your feet to the stocks, so that you will not be able to do exploits for Me. Let your requests always be announced to Me, not only by prayer and supplication, but with thanksgiving, for in thanksgiving lies great power to release you from chains of doubt and worry. As you praise, you have My peace.

July 12

THE ABILITY TO ADJUST TO ALL SITUATIONS

Scripture Reading - Philippians 4:10-12

"I know both how to be abased, and I know how to abound: every where and in all things I am instructed both to be full and to be hungry, both to abound and to suffer need." (Philippians 4:12)

This is a high place of perfection because it is the ability to adjust to all situations.

Some of My children are not like that. They have known hunger and great deprivation in the past, but since I have blessed them they have learned to live in a state of abundance, and they are spoiled. They would not be willing to lay off that wealth or high scale of living. They have become proud and spoiled.

Paul was flexible. In the past life before his conversion he had known wealth and position and honour of men. But also, for My sake and the Gospel's, he met men of great wealth, was given honour and positions of great responsibility. But there were many times when he experienced just the opposite.

He knew the pain of suffering for Me and the shame of rejection. One day he was praised and feasted and wept over, and the next day he was slandered, hungry, hated and cursed. He could enjoy a great feast in a great house, knowing he might eat nothing for three days, except bread and a little fruit. For many years he never tasted a home-cooked meal. But he was content, for his source of joy was not in carnal things nor circumstances, but in Me.

July 13

DO ALL THINGS THROUGH CHRIST'S STRENGTH

Scripture Reading – Philippians 4:13-18

"I can do all things through Christ which strengtheneth me." (Philippians 4:13)

My child, if you will accept it, you are capable of handling every situation that you come up against. Things may not always work out according to your plans, but I have My own plans for you and if you will accept them, you will be glad later for My intervention. You may not always understand at the time just why I changed your plans, but you will later, and that is when you will rejoice.

Sometimes you may feel incapable, weak, or fearful of doing certain things that I demand of you, but if you will believe this one scripture then you will never fail to accomplish all that I call you to do, or to fulfil every plan that I have for your life!

I will not demand more of you than what My grace will enable you to do. You are not going to succeed because of your inherited strength or qualification of character, but through Me. I am the one who will strengthen you so that you shall accomplish all My will. Do not rely on yourself, rely on Me. I am your source of enablement. I will strengthen you physically and spiritually. You will succeed in **all** things, not some things, but all things. Believe Me for this, and it shall indeed be established in your life.

July 14

ALL YOU NEED IS SUPPLIED THROUGH CHRIST

Scripture Reading — Philippians 4:19-23

"But my God shall supply all your need according to his riches in glory by Christ Jesus." (Philippians 4:19)

My beloved, sometimes your greatest need is not for finances but for grace, for love, for patience, for understanding.

It is true that when Paul wrote these words to the Philippians, he was talking about financial needs because they had given of their finances and Paul wanted them to understand that I would repay them for all they had given to Paul, My servant.

But today your greatest need is for the strength and grace to rise above the flesh realm into the higher realm. You are always on exhibition and you usually do not fail Me. Do not fail Me now.

There is a turmoil within your breast. You have been hurt. You have been treated unfairly and rudely in a way that is unjustified, but leave it with Me. Sometimes you want to take the case in your hands and handle it, but I will do a better job than you can. The one you want to train and teach to be Christ-like, I, too, want to train and teach. Let Me do it. Don't be warped by the same spirits that warp those whom you love. Rise above. Be seated in heavenly places with Me.

I now heal your memories. I heal the hurt. I heal your spirit. Accept My healing. I told you to do certain things and you forgot. Remember, if you are not perfect, how can you expect perfection from others?

July 15

TRAINED AND PREPARED FOR PERFECTION

Scripture Reading — Colossians 1:1-11

"For this cause we also, since the day we heard it, do not cease to pray for you, and to desire that ye might be filled with the knowledge of his will in all wisdom and spiritual understanding; That ye might walk worthy of the Lord unto all pleasing, being fruitful in every good work, and increasing in the knowledge of God; Strengthened with all might, according to his glorious power, unto all patience and longsuffering with joyfulness;" (Colossians 1:9-11)

My beloved child, you need wisdom and spiritual understanding to fit every situation. New problems need new wisdom and understanding in how to deal with each situation. You are being trained and prepared for perfection. Your aim, your goal, must always be My aim and goal for you. Satan will try to destroy you and keep you from attaining the goal of perfection. Remember he is very subtle and will use every available person to try to rob you of the true graces. Be wise to his cunning deeds, so that you can walk worthy of Me, and be pleasing to all, for all are watching you. You have no idea how great is your influence on others. Your fruitfulness in the the fruits of the Spirit will enable many to also become fruitful.

As you abide by the rules of love, which are patience, longsuffering and joyfulness, you will make other lives become fruitful also. It is how you react to what they do to you that counts, not what they do.

For you are called to increase in the knowledge of God. When you know Me, you also know the workings and dealings of the evil one. As you know Me, you are given strength with all might, according to My glorious power and not your own feeble supply. In Me is all the patience, longsuffering and joyfulness you need for every situation, no matter how difficult.

July 16

DELIVERED FROM THE POWER OF EVIL

Scripture Reading — Colossians 1:12-19

"Who hath delivered us from the power of darkness and hath translated us into the kingdom of his dear Son: In whom we have redemption through his blood, even the forgiveness of sins:" (Colossians 1:13,14)

My beloved, you are delivered out of all powers of darkness. I have Myself delivered you. Satan has no right or authority over you.

Yes, the earth is cursed; I cursed it. It has the imprint of Satan on it. And I created you out of the dust of the earth. In your very existence is the imprint of Lucifer. But I have delivered you, with his imprint still upon you, out of the satanic powers of darkness.

I have not only delivered you from his kingdom, but I have translated you into My Kingdom, so that you now walk and live in the Kingdom of light. The ones who control it are My Father and I. No evil can enter this Kingdom. It is **My** Kingdom. My Father has given it to Me, and you are now a citizen of this Kingdom.

You have been redeemed out of the kingdom of darkness by My blood and you have no sin. I have forgiven them all. Satan only has authority over you when you have unforgiven or unrepented sins. But all sins that you have repented of are forgiven and do no longer exist. So you can now dwell in My Kingdom. No powers of darkness can reach you in My Kingdom.

July 17

RECONCILED IN CHRIST

Scripture Reading — Colossians 1:20-22

"And, having made peace through the blood of his cross, by him to reconcile all things unto himself; by him, I say, whether they be things in earth, or things in heaven. And you, that were sometime alienated and enemies in your mind by wicked works, yet now hath he reconciled In the body of his flesh through death, to present you holy and unblameable and unreproveable in his sight:" (Colossians 1:20-22)

Beloved, without Me there is no reconciliation. It is only in My body that you can be reunited. When two friends fall apart, it is because one or both are not close enough to Me. For as you enter into the cleft of the Rock, even into My torn and bleeding side, you cannot help but be reconciled.

It is in My blood that you find peace. It is not in much discussion, proving to others your innocence in the case or arguing, or even praying or fasting, but in My blood that you are reconciled. Claim My blood to cover every case where there is disunity, strife or alienation of any kind, and then, enter into an even closer relationship with Me.

It is wicked works that separate people, such wicked works as suspicions, murmuring, criticism of other people's weaknesses, pride and the desire for power, and just plain lack of love.

I died and gave My body to the bruisers, that all hate, all anger, all striking at each other between two parties could be vented on Me. I hung there on the cross like a boxer's "punching bag" that people can vent their anger, frustrations, hurts, rebellion on My body, and having done so, can go in peace, for in every blow I receive I return peace to the one who strikes Me. If you want to strike someone who has hurt you, strike Me; I will heal you and you shall go in peace.

July 18

CONTINUE IN FAITH

Scripture Reading — Colossians 1:23

"If ye continue in the faith grounded and settled, and be not moved away from the hope of the gospel, which ye have heard," (Colossians 1:23a)

Continue in the faith, grounded and settled and not moved away. So many times I give My children promises concerning their lives, but they lose them, simply because they let go too easily.

I have spoken to you concerning this great trial and testing. I have touched you and I have released you. I have told you by dreams, by the voice of My Holy Spirit, to "get out of there." Leave the situation in My almighty hands. Stop trying to do it yourself. Start to praise Me now! Right now! Don't think about the trial, the test, the conflict, the pain, the hurt. Forget it all. Think about My promises to you. Hang on in faith. Look into My face. See My love, My faithfulness, My loyalty; what more do you need than Me?

I command you to be grounded and settled and not moved away from My word to you and from the healing and release I have given you. Your test came from Satan. He has tried to destroy you, your calling, your ministry, but his power is broken by Me. You have been released. He has no more power over you. Today I proclaim liberty to the captives. Lean on Me alone! I will do unto you all that you require, and much, much more!

July 19

WORTHY TO SUFFER FOR THE BODY OF CHRIST

Scripture Reading — Colossians 1:24-29

"Who now rejoice in my sufferings for you, and fill up that which is behind of the afflictions of Christ in my flesh for his body's sake, which is the church:" (Colossians 1:24)

Yes, My beloved, you too can rejoice when you are counted worthy to suffer on behalf of the church. For few of My children realize the great honour, the rewards and the workings of grace that are wrought in the lives of My children when they suffer for My name's sake. My children flee from suffering. They fear to suffer for Me. They have forgotten My teachings that "except a corn of wheat fall into the ground and die, it abideth alone: but if it die, it bringeth forth much fruit." (John 12:24)

Yes, it is the blood of the martyrs that is still the seed of the church. It was the blood of the Jews in the holocaust that birthed the land of Israel. And it shall be the sufferings of My children in these days that shall birth the coming revival.

Many have paid the great price, but not all, and there is yet a great working of grace to be wrought in many of My children's lives before I can recognize that they have died with Me.

Even as I died in My flesh to bring you to peace and to present you holy and unblamable and unprovable, so you must die to the flesh to bring peace and purity into your own life and the lives of others.

July 20

KNIT TOGETHER IN LOVE

Scripture Reading — Colossians 2:1-10

"That their hearts might be comforted, being knit together in love, and unto all riches of the full assurance of understanding, to the acknowledgement of the mystery of God, and of the Father, and of Christ;" (Colossians 2:2)

My beloved, it is a wonderful thing when hearts are knit together in love. That which is knit together has great strength and beauty.

A thread of wool alone is weak, but when it is knit, it is very strong. As you are knit together in love, you will have great strength and protection, and nothing can ever separate or destroy you.

Satan will attack the love which My children have for each other from Me and try to destroy it by unravelling it. But as you stay close to Me, I will give you strength to overcome all evil attacks upon you.

When two or more colours are used for knitting a pattern, it adds great beauty to the work, but it is important that the strings of wool be twisted over on the other side so that it does not make a hole where the one colour of thread stops and the other starts.

So you must bend to the other side, in order to blend into My pattern. You must give of yourself, your ideals, your will; your very heart's love must be surrendered, in order to keep the pattern united, so that you cannot trace where one thread stops and another starts, except by the pattern.

Give a little more of yourself. I have a plan, a beautiful pattern for your life and it shall be fulfilled.

July 21

THE TREASURES OF WISDOM AND KNOWLEDGE

Scripture Reading – Colossians 2:11-13

"In whom are hid all the treasures of wisdom and knowledge." (Colossians 2:3)

Yes, I do know all things. There is absolutely nothing that I do not know. All the treasures and wisdom of all creation, seen and unseen are known to Me. I am the origin of all wisdom and knowledge.

My child, stay close to Me. Let Me be your tutor, your revelator, to reveal to you the hidden secrets and mysteries.

Learn from Me. Do not learn from worldly teachers or instructors unless they have received their knowledge from Me. "Because the foolishness of God is wiser than men; and the weakness of God is stronger than men." (I Corinthians 1:25)

In their blindness and rebellion against Me, they search for TRUTH, when I am the way, the truth and the life. I am the One who will instruct them in all things. Yet they have rejected Me.

My beloved, you need instruction in godly wisdom and knowledge. As you come close to Me, you shall be endued with My power from on high and My hidden wisdom and knowledge, and thereby you shall be able to teach many the glorious truths which are hidden from the foundations of the world.

July 22

THROUGH HIM WE CAN TRIUMPH OVER SATAN

Scripture Reading — Colossians 2:14-29

"Blotting out the handwriting of ordinances that was against us, which was contrary to us, and took it out of the way, nailing it to his cross; And having spoiled principalities and powers, he made a shew of them openly, triumphing over them in it." (Colossians 2:14, 15)

Yea, My beloved, when I hung on the cross, naked and in shame, I was making an open show of the glorious victory over all principalities and powers with their sins.

Men thought they were making an open show of Me, hanging Me there, for the world to see. But they did not realize that it was the reverse of what they thought.

I am victor! I am the triumphant Lord! And you are too; the thing the evil one does to destroy you is the very thing I will use to lift you up and make you great in the Kingdom. Remember, "If God be for us, who can be against us?" (Romans 8:31)

And I am for you. Every minute of My life I am for you. But I also am for your enemies and those who hurt you for I love them also. I am trying to change them. You need to pray for them with

My love. Evil forces work against them and use them. But your prayers for them will be more effective to set them free than any other prayers. Not only will they be delivered, but you too will be blessed and delivered. Remember that, "the Lord turned the captivity of Job, when he prayed for his friends: also the Lord gave Job twice as much as he had before." (Job 42:10) I called them friends; even those who accused, maligned and ridiculed Job I called friends.

Did I not also call Judas "friend" on the night he sold Me and betrayed Me with a kiss? (Matthew 26:50) Go thou and do likewise.

July 23

THE NEW YOU

Scripture Reading – Colossians 3:1-12

"If ye then be risen with Christ, seek those things which are above, where Christ sitteth on the right hand of God. Set your affection on things above, not on things on the earth." (Colossians 3:1,2)

"Mortify therefore your members which are upon the earth; fornication, uncleanness, inordinate affection, evil concupiscence, and covetousness, which is idolatry:" (vs. 5)

"But now ye also put off all these; anger, wrath, malice, blasphemy, filthy communication out of your mouth." (vs. 8)

"And have put on the new man, which is renewed in knowledge after the image of him that created him:" (vs. 10)

My beloved, this is the key. This is really the only way you can win the victory over every evil that would come against you. Look again at the truths and I shall teach you.

First, you must desire to be raised above it all. Then seek for the higher things. Your mind will be taken up with it. What your mind dwells on, that is what affects your heart. The heart cannot be touched, except through the mind (through knowing, by sight, sound, touch, etc.). Don't tell someone something, and he will not grieve. So do not dwell on evil, hurt, wrong. Dwell on My love.

Second: Remember you have died to everything in the past. Put to death by godly principles everything that would rob you of your peace, including inordinate affection. It is by loving something or someone too much that much of your peace will be taken from you, for that one, sinner or saint, has power over you, to hurt you, or be used to give you pain. So let all your love be for **Me** and I will give My love (with your spirit and flavour) to them.

Third: Don't talk about it. Talking aggravates the situation and will not allow it to die. It also seeks for companionship with the grievances. If you are dead, how can you keep a grievance alive? Filthy communication is not only dirty, it is **everything** that defiles.

Fourth: Put on My image. **You** put it on yourself. It is not something I put on you. You can live in it, walk in it and be it. Christ in you is the hope of glory. I went up to Jerusalem to be crucified for your sake. If you suffer, it is not the new you. It is the old, dead body, that is already crucified. Your spirit has risen above it and dwells here with Me.

July 24

TRUE GREATNESS

Scripture Reading — Colossians 3:13-22

"Put on therefore, as the elect of God, holy and beloved, bowels of mercies, kindness, humbleness of mind, meekness, longsuffering; Forbearing one another, and forgiving one another, if any man have a quarrel against any: even as Christ forgave you, so also do ye." (Colossians 3:12,13)

This is true greatness. The wonderful thing is that it is truly possible for every one of My children to possess these precious fruits of the Lord's Spirit.

These characteristics are the true destiny and fulfilment of the elect of God who are the holy and beloved people. You are in My elect company when you put off the former evil things Paul mentioned which are unbecoming to the glorious saints. I am making out of you a holy people who shall possess bowels of mercies, hearts of kindness, humility of the mind, longsuffering in spirit, with grace to forbear and forgive.

Strive after these glorious, heavenly characteristics, for then you shall be like the great saints of all time. This is the nature of the angelic hosts. You must always strive to attain unto this perfection. Do not settle for anything less when you can have all this, if you will only try. It is available through the indwelling power of My Holy Spirit. For this is His nature, and when He is in control He will live His life through you, and you will be as the Lord in character of beauty.

July 25

DO ALL FOR JESUS

Scripture Reading — Colossians 3:23-25

"And whatsoever ye do, do it heartily, as to the Lord, and not unto men;" (Colossians 3:23,24)

My child, you are serving Me. If you were serving others, you would get discouraged, because many times it would seem as though your work was done in vain. There is more criticism than appreciation from man. Man is ungrateful, proud, boastful, forgetful of good done for him, and critical after finding fault with that which I am leading you to do.

But your service is not for man, but for the sake of Christ. Therefore there shall be a just and eternal reward given to you for every kind deed, for every loving thought expressed.

There is no crime in serving your enemy. I have told you to do good unto him, for in so doing you will heap coals of fire on his head.

Many of My children need deep inner healing. They have wounds and scars which are putrified. But you must not let the stench of their wounds drive you away from trying to help them and heal them. Be a good nursing mother to all that I give into your care.

See past their weakness to the cause of it, that you may have compassion upon them, for if their wounds are not healed, the infection will take a limb and eventually a life. Many are sickly in soul and I must amputate their members. Others die ahead of time because poison has entered their blood stream and killed them. Go quickly, bringing healing to all to whom I send you.

July 26

GIVE AND DO WHAT IS RIGHT

Scripture Reading — Colossians 4:1-5

"Masters, give unto your servants that which is just and equal; knowing that ye also have a Master in heaven." (Colossians 4:1)

No matter how high you rise in your station of life, there is always someone who is higher than you. I, the Lord your God, am above you and greater than you. I watch everything you do. You are My servant, My handmaiden, and as you treat your servants and handmaidens, that is exactly how I will treat you.

When you give those who work with you or who are under your care, true love and kindness, understanding and longsuffering, bearing their weaknesses and mistakes with true compassion, I will do the same for you. You set the chain of command. You lay down the laws and orders with which you will be treated and judged by the way in which you treat and handle others.

Always remember, I am seeing it all. When your motive and your love is misunderstood, I see that also, and I will step in and pass judgment.

Strive at all times to be just with all who are under you. Do not let one feel less loved than another. Love all equally. You may not be able to trust all the same way or give the same responsibility to each one, but you must love each one for the good which there is in each one, for each one has a special disposition and gift I have given them to help them to help you, so you can do much for Me.

July 27

LET YOUR SPEECH BE WITH GRACE

Scripture Reading — Colossians 4:6-10

"Let your speech be alway with grace, seasoned with salt, that ye may know how ye ought to answer every man." (Colossians 4:6)

More problems are created because of lack of grace in speaking than in any other way. No man whose tongue runs away with him can be a diplomat. Mark the one who speaks seldom, and you will see a man of wisdom.

But it is not enough to be silent, or a person of few words. It is vital that one also speaks with grace when one does speak.

Never justify your ill-spoken words. There are times when you need to repent of words that you have spoken, even though they were words of truth, because they were not seasoned with the salt of grace, but rather they came out of a bitter and angry heart.

I have died that you can be delivered of all bitterness and anger. Your speech will not portray these influences. You have died to bitterness and anger. Your speech is alive with grace and love, for these are the truths and realities of your life.

Every problem which arises, every discussion which takes place, must be under My supervision. Speak, knowing I am listening. I will always give you the right answers. If I give you no answer, be silent. For silence is better than words ill-spoken. Remember, more lives have been destroyed by words than by the sword.

"To have one's speech flavoured with grace" does not mean to always say "yes" to everything. It may mean the ability to say "no" with a smile.

July 28

TAKE HEED TO FULFIL YOUR MINISTRY

Scripture Reading — Colossians 4:11-18

"...Take heed to the ministry which thou hast received in the Lord, that thou fulfil it." (Colossians 4:17)

There are many tricks that Satan will devise to hinder you from fulfilling the high calling of God which is upon your life. He will even let you do God's service, so that you will think you are in My high and holy will, just because you seem to be serving Me.

But it is only through great humility, the willingness to be led by Me, and utter obedience to the still, small voice, that you will indeed be able to fulfil the calling and destiny which is upon your life.

To every one of My predestined, elect ones, I have given a special calling and gift to enable them to fulfil their eternal destiny. But many never use these gifts for Me. Some never even discover these gifts. They lie dormant in their lives until death.

Do not let Satan lie to you that you are proud because you use My gift. It is a special "something" that you have received just from Me. I desire to see you use this gift. It pleases Me to see that no one's talents are wasted, for many are not used because of a false humility or fear.

Seek My face each morning, that you may fulfil My calling for that day.

July 29

PATIENCE WORKS PERFECTION

Scripture Reading – James 1:1-11

"But let patience have her perfect work, that ye may be perfect and entire, wanting nothing." (James 1:4)

More great and wonderful blessings have been missed because of lack of patience in the hearts of My children than for any other reason.

So often I want to lead you by a way that you had not expected, you had not planned; but you were totally unprepared for it, and you had your mind made up as to what you wanted to do, and so you did not have the patience to wait one more day, go one more mile, rest one more hour, so that I would be able to work out this special surprise and blessing which I had prepared for you.

Oh, My child, slow down! Don't be so tense! Don't try to hurry Me up. Relax! You need to know how to relax. You cannot have patience unless you can relax on My arm and let Me lead you and guide you even in a path that you had not expected to walk.

Patience is never in a hurry. It believes that all things work together for good. It knows that there is a Divine plan that is being worked out. It has rest in times of unexpected delays and enjoys the scenery along the detour. It does not hasten to return to the originally planned highway, because it expects to find a diamond where it walks. Patience not only makes the way you travel and your journey perfect, but it also perfects you so that you too will be perfected as you are led in My pathway. (Hebrews 10:36)

July 30

BLESSED ARE THOSE WHO ENDURE

Scripture Reading — James 1:12-17

"Blessed is the man that endureth temptation: for when he is tried, he shall receive the crown of life, which the Lord hath promised to them that love him." (James 1:12)

Temptation is the crucible of the soul, the instrument I use to purify and remove the dross in your life. I have only one desire for you, that you might be perfect.

Through the ages I have selected certain of My children in whom I want to show My glory. I have allowed them, like Job, to experience greater trials, greater fires of temptation than others.

The more special ones have been permitted, like the mystics of old, to experience the "dark night of the soul," that terrible time of utter despair where you feel all is lost, even your soul, and you cry out like My Son, "My God, my God, why hast thou forsaken me?" For several hours he endured this dark night of the soul but He came through to resurrection life that you may know there is victory for everyone who lives through this terror. You also will come forth in the glory of the resurrection, for though it seems that I have forsaken you in that hour, still I have not. I am standing behind the veil, watching, listening, caring.

And even while I seem to be so far away, I am holding in My hands your crown of life.

> Hang on My child, when all seems hopeless,
> Soon the victory you will see;
> There is not a trial or testing
> That you suffer without Me.

July 31

HIS CHOSEN FIRST-FRUITS COMPANY

Scripture Reading — James 1:18-27

"Of his own will begat he us with the word of truth, that we should be a kind of firstfruits of his creatures." (James 1:18)

Salvation surely is extended to the "whosoever." But there is a chosen company, a kind of "first-fruits" of all My creation whom I am choosing out of all the earth who will portray My highest perfection to the world.

A husbandman has a garden full of fruit, but only a very special specimen is selected to be taken to the country fair, and put on display for all to see and admire and finally be selected by the judges for the grand prize.

So it is with My first-fruits company. Not all of My garden is worthy of praise or deserving of a prize. Some of My fruit is marred. It still belongs to Me. I will not cast it from My garden, but I can take no pride and receive no honour from it.

Therefore, I say unto you, strive to let Me plant you in the sunshine, to prune you, to water you, to do with you what I know is missing, that you might become the object of beauty and value that I would have you to be.

Pruning is very hard to endure. It is the cutting off of the most intimate and cherished relationships on your same vine that I might single you out for My special attention, that the entire sap of the vine may feed and nourish you alone to make you a choice first-fruit.

Trust Me to work out in your life all that is necessary to accomplish My plan for your eternal spirit. The first-fruits company is a lonely company, a separated company.

> I am come into My garden
> For the first-fruits company;
> All the first-ripe of the harvest,
> I will soon take home with Me.

August 1

THE ROYAL LAW OF LOVE

Scripture Reading – James 2:1-11

"If ye fulfil the royal law according to the scripture, Thou shalt love thy neighbour as thyself, ye do well:" (James 2:8)

There really is only one law for heaven and earth and that is the law of love. All other laws and commandments are built around this mighty and perfect law. If everyone lived by this law, there would not be any need for any other commandment to be written or given to man, for love for others would dictate to each heart the action of man that would be well-pleasing.

No one loves himself less than he loves others. For one cares tenderly for oneself, feeds oneself, clothes oneself, warms and cools oneself, prides and honours oneself, rests oneself, defends and protects oneself and even weeps in pity for oneself. Most of what you spend, you spend for yourself. The thing that concerns you the most is your own well-being.

But I call you to a higher law. **Others** first, yourself last. You know how obnoxious are those who live by the law of self-preservation: "after me, you come first." This is the law of the world, even for best of friends. But the law of heaven is "God first, others second, myself last." Whatever you would that men should do to you, so ye even do to them. This is the law I gave Israel and this is the law I give you. (Deuteronomy 10:12)

August 2

JUDGE WITH MERCY

Scripture Reading – James 2:12-26

"For he shall have judgment without mercy, that hath shewed no mercy; and mercy rejoiceth against judgment." (James 2:13)

Everyone is judged according to the way he has judged others. If you demand perfection of others, it (perfection) shall be demanded of you.

This is why it is so important that you are not critical of others nor seek to know the details of their mistakes and sins, because you can be ensnared to be quick to pass judgment on a case, not knowing the full extent of their situation.

If you are to hear or read about someone's faults, first of all, receive this information with reservation. Do not let it anger you nor arouse your emotions. Shelve it temporarily! Then, when it persists, pray for mercy to be given you before you go into handling any situation. Try to "find in the Spirit" the faulty one. This will enable you to become merciful in your heart towards the one who has failed.

You must always strive to have mercy for **everyone** at **every time**, knowing that some day you will need mercy, and the only way in which you will receive it will be according to the amount which you stored up for others.

I did not pass judgment even in the most sinful cases. I came with mercy for sinners. You are My followers. Come with mercy. It is greater than judgment, much greater.

August 3

THE DIFFICULTY OF BEING A LEADER

Scripture Reading — James 3:1

"My brethren, be not many masters, knowing that we shall receive the greater condemnation." (James 3:1)

Yes, it is much more difficult to be in a place of leadership, whether it is in the religious world or in the secular. The leader is the one who is attacked, blamed, criticized and defamed. He must have more wisdom than the ones whom he leads. He will be the first to be attacked and shot at by the enemy. Satan will first of all attack him. And if he falls, his judgment will be greater because his fall will destroy more lives.

Before anyone accepts the role of leadership, he must realize these terrible responsibilities and the consequences if he fails.

Through My servant James I mentioned the three ways in which a leader can fall: envy, strife, and by the tongue.

The leader will be attacked by demons of envy. There will be many who will be jealous of his position. He himself will be tempted to be jealous of other leaders.

Strife is the result of rebellion and disobedience in the ranks. There will always be those who cannot come into submission to spiritual leadership which I have put in the body. As a leader, you will be personally offended when those in your care rebel. This strife could eat at your soul. Do not allow this to happen. When you cannot deal with a situation because of rebellion, just hand the case over to Me, and be at peace among you. I will break the neck of the rebellious one, for I am the Master of the masters.

August 4

THE POWERFUL TONGUE

Scripture Reading — James 3:2-13

"Behold also the ships, which though they be so great, and are driven of fierce winds, yet are they turned about with a very small helm, whithersoever the governor listeth. Even so the tongue is a little member, and boasteth great things. Behold, how great a matter a little fire kindleth!" (James 3:4,5)

The tongue is the most powerful member of your body. It can calm the sea, kindle a forest fire, sway a multitude, destroy a nation, heal a nation, change a life, move a mountain, build a city, save a world, or destroy it.

When you speak, something happens. You influence another person, or persons, in one way or another, good or evil. You can create hate in the heart of your hearer, or you can give birth to love and healing.

The bit in the horse's mouth will not only give direction to the horse it controls, but all those who are in the vehicle which the horse is pulling. The rudder of the ship will take the ship across the seas to new and glorious horizons, or crack it into a floating iceberg and sink every soul on board, even to the destruction of the vessel.

You have a tongue! I have given it to you! Every day it controls your life and the lives of others. If you speak negatively it will destroy you and others. If you speak with faith, love and courage, it will bring healing, comfort, blessing and salvation to the world.

It will kindle a fire: either a fire of comfort and glory, or a fire of destruction and hell.

Dedicate your tongue to Me, to be used by Me alone, and it will bless an end-time world.

August 5

ENVY PRODUCES STRIFE

Scripture Reading — James 3:14-18

"This wisdom descendeth not from above, but is earthly, sensual, devilish. For where envying and strife is, there is confusion and every evil work. But the wisdom that is from above is first pure, then peaceable, gentle, and easy to be intreated, full of mercy and good fruits, without partiality, and without hypocrisy." (James 3: 15-17)

Yes, it is true, My child, one of the greatest reasons for confusion (not flowing in the Spirit) is envy. When someone seeks for their own rights, their own way, their own profit and gain, their own position, power and acclaim, it hinders them from "flowing in the Spirit." It is only as you let the Holy Spirit lead you, as you bow in complete submission to Him, that you can indeed rise above confusion and every evil work.

If you look daily at the problems in families, churches and organizations you will find that all of the serious problems arise because of envy and a spirit of striving amongst the members. One wants to be more important than another; one wants to control, one is greedy for gain.

I want to lead you into that high realm which is the law of the Kingdom of God, where you live by the laws of peace and gentleness, and where you are easily led (not pulled or driven), but led by My Spirit. I desire for you to have a life that produces much good fruit because every act is one of mercy.

Be not partial to certain ones, ignoring or hurting others who seem to you to be of lower degree. Put all partiality aside. It is not becoming to a true saint.

August 6

YOUR LIFE IS IN MY HANDS

Scripture Reading — James 4:1-17

"Go to now, ye that say, To day or to morrow we will go into such a city, and continue there a year, and buy and sell, and get gain: Whereas ye know not what shall be on the morrow. For what is your life? It is even a vapour, that appeareth for a little time, and then vanisheth away. For that ye ought to say, If the Lord will, we shall live, and do this, or that." (James 4:13-15)

My child, your life is in My hands. It is true that it is sometimes necessary to make plans even for a long time ahead. But your heart must always be open for a change of plans.

It is important that you realize that this scripture is speaking about the need of My children to walk softly before Me. Never decide what you are going to do without consulting My Spirit which dwells within you. Many lives suffer terrible shipwreck because people plan heedlessly what they will do without consulting My high will.

The scripture refers much to those in business, whose one sole aim is to amass wealth, and who seem to have forgotten the brevity of life, or how soon it can be broken off, even in the midst of their years. Always remember, your life is as a vapour. Never live to get earthly gain. For one minute after the death angel touches you, it will be lost to you forever. The only thing that you will possess through eternity is what you gave to Me.

And you give to **Me** by giving to others. Don't ever give to others hoping for it to be returned to you, for that is not giving; that is business. Give, expecting nothing in return, and you will have it stored up for you as a true, eternal security. Many amass fortunes that last only till they stop breathing. That is foolishness. Put your treasures in the bank of heaven where it is eternally secure for you.

August 7

GOD HAS HEARD THE CRY OF THE SUFFERING MULTITUDES

Scripture Reading — James 5:1-6

"Behold, the hire of the labourers who have reaped down your fields, which is of you kept back by fraud, crieth: and the cries of them which have reaped are entered into the ears of the Lord of Sabaoth." (James 5:4)

These are indeed the last days. The climax of the days of My grace upon a sinful nation has come. I will now allow you to destroy yourself, oh people of earth!

It is the same cry that I heard in Egypt which I am hearing now, even the cry of My people who love Me and who are suffering under the hands of their cruel taskmasters. As I came down then, I am coming again, and I will judge the situation. I will raise up mighty deliverers who shall come against the cursed system and the economy of the nations shall collapse, for it has become the god of the people. And all of My people who have made wealth their god shall collapse together with the unrighteous mammon.

My child, love not the world, nor the things that are in the world, for the world passeth away, and the lust thereof, but he that doeth the will of God abideth forever. (I John 2:15,17) The only way that you can survive is by hating the things of this world and loving that which belongs to the eternal world, even the souls, the true riches of heaven and Me, your Lord.

As poverty increases, judgment and lawlessness and angers and wars and revolutions shall increase. It is the poor who shall revolutionize the nations. Their wail and their cry shall be heard. The day of the Sabbath is at hand.

August 8

HE IS WAITING FOR THE FIRST-FRUITS

Scripture Reading — James 5:7-20

"Be patient therefore, brethren, unto the coming of the Lord.

Behold, the husbandman waiteth for the precious fruit of the earth, and hath long patience for it, until he receive the early and latter rain." (James 5:7)

All creation waits for the coming of the Lord. And if you thought about it, and meditated on how glorious will be the change, you too would be filled with greater longing and desire for My return. For I shall come in great power and great glory to this fallen generation.

I am even now preparing groups of saints who shall be mightily used by My Spirit to prepare the world and to work for its transformation immediately after My arrival.

The glory and the might of My Kingdom shall indeed be wondrous. I, Myself, long greatly to return and rule over this sin-cursed planet. For the sin grows steadily worse, and with it the suffering is multiplied. An evil committed in Chicago has an impact on the Philippine Islands. But, before I come (and My coming will bring great judgment), I must patiently wait for the fruit to all be brought in, even the first-fruits company, these glorious overcomers who are now being perfected through the latter rain. For the latter rain is falling and My precious children are coming into maturity, and soon I will have My quota. Then I'll be here with you.

August 9

MANY INFALLIBLE PROOFS

Scripture Reading — Acts 1:1-26

"To whom also he shewed himself alive after his passion by many infallible proofs, being seen of them forty days, and speaking of the things pertaining to the kingdom of God:" (Acts 1:3)

My child, there is not a shadow of doubt that can shroud the works and the miracles that I do. My life, My Word, and My works are infallible. All that I have spoken to you, or given you to speak, is also infallible.

An evil generation would cast doubts upon the holy record of My life. It would do the same concerning your life and your dedication. It would like to steal the Word you speak and make it appear as "one that dreameth." But I will not allow it. I will bear witness to your life and your ministry. I will let none of your words fall to the ground. As I stood with the child Samuel, the despised prophet Jeremiah, the woman Mary of Magdalene, so I will stand with you and bear witness with many infallible proofs.

I do not leave Myself without a witness. I proved My resurrection with many infallible proofs, both by sight and sound. They saw Me and they heard Me speak to them.

The things concerning the Kingdom have come down to the level of mankind. You can see the reality, feel the reality of My presence with you. It is not something you need to imagine. I am real. This is no fantasy, no illusion. I am not a spirit. I am body. As I was, so I am, and ever will be THIS SAME JESUS. I will return again with the same body, and you will see Me and you will know Me.

August 10

I SAW THE LORD AT MY RIGHT HAND

Scripture Reading — Acts 2:1-28

"Thou hast made known to me the ways of life; thou shalt make me full of joy with thy countenance." (Acts 2:28)

David "saw" Me by the way I led him, protected him, blessed him, used him, anointed him and made him great. All of David's greatness was made possible only because I always stood at his right hand, and all this was 1,000 years before I came to earth by way of Bethlehem.

Now it is nearly 2,000 years after Bethlehem, and you know Me so much better than David knew Me. You have the record of My life, My love, My sacrifice and My power. You also have My promise, "Lo, I am with you alway, even unto the end of the world." (Matthew 28:20)

How much more should you have reason to believe and have hope and faith and joy! I am not only at your right hand, but I also go before you into every place that you go. I will open doors — I will close them also! The latter is for your sake as much as the former. It is all ordained "by the determinate counsel and foreknowledge of God." (Acts 2:23)

Even as David was "not moved," so you also must not be moved by fears, threats or intimidations. I stand at your right hand as you go forth today and set your feet on the soil of every nation. I will continue to make known to you the ways of life, even abundant resurrection life. I will fill you with joy as you see Me in every tomorrow of your life.

August 11

THIS REBELLIOUS GENERATION

Scripture Reading — Acts 2:29-42

"And with many other words did he testify and exhort, saying, Save yourselves from this untoward generation." (Acts 2:40)

This is indeed a perverse and rebellious generation. I call on you to come out of their way of thinking as well as their way of acting, doing, and being.

You must never be like they are. Their stench must never be on your garments. Never model yourself after them.

You are a precious and dedicated servant of Mine. You are different. You are not "one of the crowd." I brought you out from among the worldly friends. Then I brought you out from most of your old Christian friends. I know it is a lonely walk and sometimes even a rejected life. But you must go the "Calvary Road." It never was popular, nor will it ever be.

You save yourself from this perverse, rebellious generation by following in My footsteps and taking the pathway of loneliness and rejection. At first it will be painful, but in the end you will be glad and rejoice for all the way that I have led you, even though it was painful.

There is a terrible judgment coming on this generation. By coming out from the crowd, you save yourself from what is coming upon them. There is a way of deliverance possible. I was numbered with the transgressors, that you need not be numbered with them.

August 12

THEY DENY THE HOLY AND JUST ONE

Scripture Reading — Acts 3:1-17

"But ye denied the Holy One and the Just, and desired a murderer to be granted unto you; And killed the prince of life,..." (Acts 3:14,15a)

My child, if they did it to Me, is it any wonder that they do it to you? Even My children do not want holy and just leadership. They are fearful of the judgment that is theirs when they come face to face with true holiness and the justice of God.

And so it is, they run to others who are not pure, but who will let them continue in their ways of sin and rebellion without condemning them. And how can the leaders they choose condemn and correct them, when they themselves live in sin and rebellion against My holiness and integrity?

Does My Word not say of these children of Mine that in the last days they will "not endure sound doctrine; but after their own lusts shall they heap to themselves teachers, having itching ears; and they shall turn away their ears from the truth, and shall be turned unto fables"? (II Timothy 4:3,4)

If they killed Me (the Prince of Life) because of their ignorance (Acts 3:17), even though they were My people, then they will be cruel to you also. Because through the hardness of their hearts, and their unwillingness to clean up their lives in the way My Spirit is striving with them to do, they shall surely become even more ignorant concerning My leadings through My anointed leadership that I have raised up and in whom the Prince of Life dwells.

August 13

IN THEE SHALL ALL THE NATIONS BE BLESSED

Scripture Reading — Acts 3:18-26

"Ye are the children of the prophets, and of the covenant which God made with our fathers, saying unto Abraham, And in thy seed shall all the kindreds of the earth be blessed. Unto you first God, having raised up his Son Jesus, sent him to bless you, in turning away every one of you from his iniquities." (Acts 3:25,26)

My beloved children of Israel shall accomplish in a few years a task of evangelization which the Gentiles have not been able to succeed in accomplishing in two millenia. They started the work of bringing salvation to the world and they shall complete it. In a few decades men like Paul succeeded in "turning the world upside down." (Acts 17:6)

The world of this generation has yet to see such dedication and zeal and anointing as the early church, the almost 100% Jewish church, had.

Look at the army of Israel. See how she fights and how I fight with her. See how her business men succeed in everything they set their hand to do. See how in a few (three) decades, she has covered the earth with fruit and vegetables grown in the desert.

When I give her her hidden oil and restore rain to her in full, and when I wipe out her enemies before her eyes, she shall rise again in My name to bless the entire world. Be one with her. Love her. I have made My covenant which shall never be broken.

August 14

THEY HAD BEEN WITH JESUS

Scripture Reading — Acts 4:1-14

"Neither is there salvation in any other: for there is none other name under heaven given among men, whereby we must be saved. Now when they saw the boldness of Peter and John, and perceived that they were unlearned and ignorant men, they marvelled; and they took knowledge of them, that they had been with Jesus." (Acts 4:12,13)

It will show! If you have been in My presence, the Lord of glory, the architect of salvation, more than in the presence of men, My people will know it. It shall be seen. I love you, and as you love Me and draw nigh to Me, I will leave My glory and My fragrance upon your life.

Even as John and Peter went through great trials, so you too have known hurt and suffering and rejection. But it is these very things which have made you a vessel for My glory.

Peter and John spoke with boldness. Be not fearful of anyone. Speak My Word with great boldness. I have brought you here. You have a message for them that is more than a certain subject or topic. It is your very life, your presence, the fact that you have walked with Jesus that will speak to these people. Be not fearful to stand before them.

This day prepare your heart to seek My face, to receive My anointing in a new way to give My people, who will open their hearts and listen, a new word from Me.

The common people heard and fasted. The leaders rejected My message and turned their hearts. They are colder and harder. I have not sent you to them. But those who have heard, in whose heart a flame was lit, shall come out of their camps to you, for they too have been with Jesus.

August 15

SPEAK THE THINGS WHICH WE HAVE SEEN AND HEARD

Scripture Reading— Acts 4:15-37

"For we cannot but speak the things which we have seen and heard." (Acts 4:20)

This is the thing that makes your testimony richer and with greater impact than scores of others. You have "been there," you have seen and you have heard.

But I want to warn you that, while it has a great impact on the common, ordinary folk, it is the leaders who "have not been there, have not seen or heard," who resent what you say. They cannot bear your words. It makes them uncomfortable. It shows them up.

They have not been through or seen many things, such as:

1. the lands of persecution,
2. the dangers of prison and death,

3. the valley of separation and loneliness,
4. the nights of weeping and travail,
5. the struggle with self and dying to it,
6. the days and weeks of fasting,
7. the life of a mystic and saint,
8. the purity of absolute holiness in thought, word and deed,
9. the absolute commitment to My call,
10. the heart ablaze with My love and compassion,
11. your discerning of their sins.

Nevertheless, I call you to speak of these things, even the miracles of God you have seen and the secrets of eternity which I have whispered in your ear.

August 16

WE OUGHT TO OBEY GOD RATHER THAN MAN

Scripture Reading — Acts 5:1-32

"But Peter and John answered and said unto them, Whether it be right in the sight of God to hearken unto you more than unto God, judge ye." (Acts 4:19)

"Then Peter and the other apostles answered and said, We ought to obey God rather than men." (Acts 5:29)

There is a high law that governs the one who is wholly committed unto Me. He lives to please Me only and always.

The law of obedience to Me is very high, but one must live it always, not only now and then. Because, if you will only live by it when it suits you, then you will be unprotected when Satan comes against you.

Either you live under the laws of man or you live under the Divine order of the Kingdom of God and the laws of heaven. The two do not mix.

Peter and the apostles were not ordinary men when they spoke these words. Though they were human, still they had moved into the new realm of Kingdom-living. There could be no compromise. They knew they had to obey Me and Me only at all times. If ever they stepped out from this covering they would be in danger.

This was a radical change from the former concept of living under the law of the governing religious body of Jewry. But when revival comes to you it will call you to a new way of life, a new commitment unto Me. If your spiritual leadership cannot flow with My Divine order, then you must decide whose servant you will be, Mine or man's. The price will be very great. But the cost of failure is also very great.

August 17

REJOICE THAT YOU ARE WORTHY TO SUFFER

Scripture Reading — Acts 5:33-42

"And they departed from the presence of the council, rejoicing that they were counted worthy to suffer shame for his name." (Acts 5:41)

The courage, the testimony and witness of My servants of the early church was without precedent. They had such tremendous courage because they believed that it was all for My glory, and so they were able to "count it all joy when they endured these trials and testings."

Today's Christians have difficulty in this modern world in accepting suffering and shame. They have never been schooled to realize what the terrible cost of discipleship can be. Many live in an atmosphere that considers itself Christian. Therefore there is little or no opposition to those who truly are Mine.

Because the society is "Christian" it gives the impression to My children that whatsoever is accepted by a Christian society is permissible with Me, just as long as it does not break the laws of the land.

As a result the world has entered the church. There is very little difference between sinner and saint. So few saints ever suffer shame for My name's sake. And in nations where they do (for many still do), it is misunderstood by My other children, who think that the suffering saints should rise up, "take the kingdom and overthrow the tyrants." They do not know the joy there is in suffering for Me.

They do not realize the work of grace, the glory of My presence, that is worked out in those who suffer for My name's sake.

Never look at suffering as something to escape from or to avoid at all costs. But rather accept it as a special privilege given by Me to selected members of the bridal company.

August 18

THE SPIRIT BY WHICH HE SPAKE

Scripture Reading — Acts 6:1-15

"...and they chose Stephen, a man full of faith and of the Holy Ghost,...And Stephen, full of faith and power, did great wonders and miracles among the people....And they were not able to resist the wisdom and the spirit by which he spake....And all that sat in the council, looking stedfastly on him, saw his face as it had been the face of an angel." (Acts 6:5a,8,10,15)

Not only did they choose Stephen, I chose him too. He was born and ordained to be the first recorded martyr of the early church. He was great through the indwelling power of the Holy Spirit in his life.

It was the Holy Spirit within him who did the wonders and miracles among the people. My Holy Spirit, not you, does everything which it appears that you do.

It was My Holy Spirit who gave him the great wisdom whereby he spoke in such a manner that they could not resist, (discredit) the things he said.

But the thing which was more wonderful than the things which he said was the spirit in which he said them. I want to work on the spirit of man, while man is more interested in the words of man.

My child, of all the greatness of Stephen, all signs and wonders and words, nothing was of such high importance as that innermost purity of his soul.

It was that inner purity which shone forth in the hour when he sat before the council, and heard the lying accusations and felt the hatred directed at him, and in spite of it all his face was as the face of an angel. Perfect love had lifted him above the darkness of man's heart and placed him in the heavenlies, where he, through the Holy Spirit, was comforted and shielded from accusations, and even from the pangs of death.

August 19

NOT SO MUCH AS TO SET HIS FOOT ON: YET HE PROMISED

Scripture Reading — Acts 7:1-19

"And he gave him none inheritance in it, no, not so much as to set his foot on: yet he promised that he would give it to him for a possession, and to his seed after him, when as yet he had no child." (Acts 7:5)

Just because My promises to you are not immediately fulfilled does not mean that I have not spoken. There is always a time element which is involved in every situation. I promised Eve that her seed would bruise the serpent's head 4,000 years before it happened. I promised Abraham his seed would inherit the promised land 400 years before it happened. I promised Israel the land of Canaan 40 years before they entered in.

Sometimes promises are not fulfilled because My people are slow to meet the conditions. Other times there is a delay because "the cup of iniquity" has not yet been filled and My laws of love and grace must continue to be extended until I know it is time to judge and remove the one who is an obstacle in the way, so that I can fulfil My Divine plan for that life that I have chosen to use.

In the case of Abraham's descendants I not only had to wait for the iniquity of the Amorites to be filled (Genesis 15:16), I also had to wait until the evil deeds of Egypt against My children had reached their zenith, for I knew how great and terrible would be the judgments upon Egypt and it had to equal their evil deeds which they had done to My people.

I call you, My child, to hang on in faith, trusting Me and believing Me. I will fulfil every promise I have given to you. But you must wait until I will judge the one to whom you are in bondage, and after that you shall come forth and you shall serve Me. (Acts 7:7) Hang on, even when there isn't a single sign of a miracle.

August 20

HE SUPPOSED HIS BRETHREN WOULD UNDERSTAND

Scripture Reading — Acts 7:20-33

"For he supposed his brethren would have understood how that God by his hand would deliver them: but they understood not." (Acts 7:25)

Not many receive the deliverers that I send to them. Many times My "Moseses" suffer terrible rejection and sorrow from the very ones whom they love and want to help.

Moses was not able to realize the spiritual depravity and darkness to which his brethren had sunk. So many years of hardship and slavery had turned many of them into beast-like, craven creatures whose only thought was survival. They could not believe that someone loved them enough to care about their suffering, least of all that "prince" from the palace of Pharaoh who drove about in fine chariots and who wore costly raiment.

It was only as Moses returned to them, 40 years later in the humble robe of a shepherd, walking as they did, and doing My mighty miracles, that they were able to accept him.

I commissioned him to perform miracles, not only to bear witness to the authenticity of his calling before Pharaoh, but also to prove to "the brethren" that he was the one who would set them free and deliver them. (Exodus 4:1-5) And although they were glad to hear his message (Exodus 4:31), later when the testings came, they turned against Moses. (Exodus 5:21)

People are feeble, even My people. Today they will praise you and seemingly love you, but tomorrow they will crucify you. So you must live for Me, serve Me, obey Me. Never do anything to please man. Be courteous, be loving, be humble, but live for Me and care only to fulfil My will in your life.

> I came unto My own dear planet,
> And My own received Me not,
> If you too would walk My pathway
> This must also be your lot.

August 21

AND HE, BEING FULL OF THE HOLY GHOST, SAW THE GLORY OF GOD

Scripture Reading – Acts 7:34-60

"But he, being full of the Holy Ghost, looked up stedfastly into heaven, and saw the glory of God, and Jesus standing on the right hand of God," (Acts 7:55)

My child, it is the Holy Spirit who reveals heaven to you. Did I not say "...he will guide you into all truth: for he shall not speak of himself; but whatsoever he shall hear, that shall he speak: and he will shew you things to come. He shall glorify me: for he shall receive of mine, and shall shew it unto you." (John 16:13,14)

The Holy Spirit is the revelator. He reveals to you the truths which you teach. You could not know the secrets of heavenly things without the wisdom given to you by the Holy Spirit.

More and more as you yield yourself to Him, He will take over your life, fill you with Himself, and give you wisdom and knowledge concerning Me and My Father.

I said, "He shall teach you all things" and as you minister unto My people, "he shall bring all things to your remembrance." (John 14:26)

He is in you, as He was in the saints of old. He enables you to live a full life before the world. And He makes the way of heaven open to you, even as He makes the Word of God open to you.

It is the Holy Spirit who enables you to see the glory of God. Lean much on the Holy Spirit. He is your comforter, your strength and your helper. Do not grieve Him. Obey His Word to you. He is your key to greatness.

> The Holy Spirit is your covering;
> He, My glory shall reveal;
> He will teach you heaven's knowledge,
> And My glory, He'll make real.

August 22

THE LORD CAUGHT AWAY PHILIP

Scripture Reading — Acts 8:1-40

"And when they were come up out of the water, the Spirit of the Lord caught away Philip, that the eunuch saw him no more: and he went on his way rejoicing." (Acts 8:39)

Philip was led by My angel into Gaza's wilderness to reach one seeking soul who would hear and believe and receive the message of salvation. The Gospel filled Ethiopia 2,000 years through the influence of this one man. Never despise the day of small things.

It is not always the great crowds or the seemingly great impact that has the greatest results. The great revival of Samaria did not last long; where is it today? But the revival that came to Ethiopia through one man is still in evidence this day. And the powerful, iron fist of Marxism cannot block it out. It can only purge it in the fires of persecution. My church in Ethiopia shall not die.

When Philip had finished his work, the Holy Spirit was so mightily upon him that he was lifted up bodily and translated to Azotus. And in that same powerful anointing he preached the gospel in city after city until he came to Cæsarea.

Philip was living in Cæsarea when Paul passed through there years later on his way to Jerusalem. (Acts 21:8) It was here that Paul was kept prisoner under Felix (Acts 23:33, 24:3) and Festus (Acts 25:1), and here he stood before King Agrippa (Acts 25:13-27). It was here that the Holy Spirit was poured out upon the Gentiles. (Acts 10:1-48) All this time Philip lived in this city and left a great impact upon it. His four daughters were free to prophesy because of the Roman influence. My Spirit knows where to send you for the sake of your children, so they, too, can serve Me freely.

> The Spirit caught up Brother Philip,
> Carried him from A to Z,
> Now He's preparing for the transport
> Of the church triumphantly.

August 23

YOU ARE A CHOSEN VESSEL TO BEAR HIS NAME

Scripture Reading — Acts 9:1-43

"...for he is a chosen vessel unto me, to bear My name before the Gentiles, and kings, and the children of Israel: For I will shew him how great things he must suffer for my name's sake." (Acts 9:15,16)

My child, you are a chosen vessel unto Me. You were chosen from your mother's womb. (Jeremiah 1:5) Your life is not your own. It is Mine completely. I have a plan for it from the beginning of time. This is not some last minute arrangement. All creation is built around My last-day plan.

You are chosen, not only to be My beloved bride, but to fear My name. You carry My name on your heart, like the high priest carried the names of Israel before Me. Every day, every place you go, My name is there on your heart. (Exodus 28:29)

Man has not chosen you. Had man chosen you, you would be answerable to man. But no man wanted or desired you, so you are Mine.

I chose Paul from his mother's womb. (Galatians 1:15) He knew this and what it meant. So he "conferred not with flesh and blood." (Galatians 1:16) I have many whom I have chosen and who work directly under My leadership. Neither can they work under any other. You are such a one, to hear My voice and obey it.

But you must remember that to be chosen to such a high calling means suffering. There is a great honour and glory attached to the high calling of God and so a large measure of suffering is permitted in your life. It gives balance and maturity and even more glory. (II Corinthians 12:7)

August 24

WHILE PETER YET SPAKE THESE WORDS

Scripture Reading — Acts 10:1-48

"While Peter yet spake these words, the Holy Ghost fell on all them which heard the word." (Acts 10:44)

Peter did not give them the Holy Ghost; I did while they were sitting there, listening to Peter. My Spirit was poured out upon them from on high.

It was a wonderful event, one of the greatest in recorded history. Suddenly, without any ritual of man, or decision of man, or concession of man, I sovereignly gave them the same glorious experience which I had given My faithful Jewish disciples in Jerusalem. If man would have had any say in the matter, he would have deliberated for hours over this situation. There would have been endless discussions as to whether or not the Gentiles were worthy.

Laws would have been laid down from Jerusalem. The Jewish doctors, performing the act of circumcision, would have been called down from headquarters. (Acts 11:2) The house of Cornelius would have been searched for idols from top to bottom. Pots and kettles would have been scoured and cleansed. All pork would have been thrown out. The men and women would have had hours of lecture.

Man always delays and interrupts what I am seeking to do. So I have to work around man rather than via man. That is what I did at the house of Cornelius. I had Peter there that day because if I had not used him, the apostle of Pentecost, he would have fought and argued the hardest of all against this whole episode. Now he was put in a position where he had to defend it.

Sit back and watch the Holy Spirit work. (Acts 15:7-11) He will do My sovereign will. Let Him have His way.

August 25

AND THE HAND OF THE LORD WAS UPON THEM

Scripture Reading — Acts 11:1-30

"And the hand of the Lord was with them: and a great number believed, and turned unto the Lord." (Acts 11:21)

It was ordinary followers of Mine who are not even named here who had My hand upon them in such a way. They were among the persecuted from Jerusalem, Judea, and other Jewish cities where strong opposition and persecution had broken out. Much of this persecution had been fomented by Saul in his days before I stopped him on the road to Damascus and he was converted. That is why he had to suffer. For whatsoever a man sows, he **must** also reap.

These dear ones who went out from their homes had lost or given away all their possessions. They had nothing to lose now. They went out preaching boldly to the Jews in other cities. Although their name is not mentioned by Luke, I have kept the record.

There will always be the unnamed who will do My works unknown to man. My hand shall be upon them and I will walk with them in a mighty way. But the earthly recorders will forget to mention their names.

Do not feel badly if you do not have earthly acclaim. The recognition and honour of man is a very temporary and treacherous thing. The most important thing is that you seek for **Me** to know you and to work with you and to use you and seek for My hand to be upon you and for Me to use you to turn many to Me — many, many, many, by My Holy Spirit working with you and My hand resting upon you.

August 26

BUT PRAYER WAS MADE WITHOUT CEASING FOR HIM

Scripture Reading — Acts 12:1-25

"Peter therefore was kept in prison: but prayer was made without ceasing of the church unto God for him." (Acts 12:5)

When My people pray, I begin to work. Satan had pulled a fast one on the church when Herod had James beheaded. The church could have stopped that too, but they did not really expect it to happen. They did not realize that Herod would stoop so low to buy the favour of men. So, like many of My children today, they were caught off guard sleeping. And that is how James was killed.

But when Peter was also arrested, the body of the church rose up together and began to pray and call upon Me mightily. This set in motion the armies of heaven. This began to undo the powers of Satan who had risen up to destroy the leaders of the early church. This turned the judgment and evil that Herod tried to do to My children back on himself and destroyed him. For the thing he had done was so very low and depraved that the lowliest of creatures (worms) ate him up.

When someone seeks to do you evil, and you begin to pray, then that evil turns back on that one, and if it was very powerful, then the vengeance will be very powerful, (unless that one repents).

Remember King Saul (I Samuel 31:1-8), Jezebel (II Kings 9:30-37), Judas (Matthew 27:3-5, Acts 1:17-19) and the enemies of Daniel (Daniel 6:24), Haman (Esther 7:9,10) and many others.

It was not the hand of those they tried to destroy that caused their fall and destruction. Neither David nor Elijah, nor Daniel, nor Mordecai, nor Myself took joy at the destruction of our enemies nor sought their death. But their evil ways turned upon themselves when My people prayed. Look and see how David, Elijah, Daniel, Mordecai, Esther and the early church prayed, and remember again the power of prayer.

August 27

AS THEY FASTED THE HOLY GHOST SAID...

Scripture Reading — Acts 13:1-5

"As they ministered to the Lord, and fasted, the Holy Ghost said, Separate me Barnabas and Saul for the work whereunto I have called them....So they, being sent forth by the Holy Ghost, departed...." (Acts 13:2,4a)

The Holy Spirit always knows My will perfectly. If you will listen to Him carefully, He will clearly show you and give Divine instruction according to My will.

So many of My children make terrible mistakes because they do not listen to the Holy Spirit nor do they even seek Him for a moment to receive guidance.

These are the closing days of the dispensation of the Holy Ghost. He, like Me, is the same yesterday, today and forever. It would do you well to honour Him and teach more people concerning His great office. He will honour those who honour Him. The church almost died in the middle ages because they forgot or neglected the presence of the Holy Ghost in it.

He is your friend, your comforter, your co-worker. Because He lives inside of you, He is very close to you, always standing there, wherever you are, ready to help you. Do not look to the skies for the Holy Spirit. He is inside of you. He is living in the church. The church is His body which He is bringing together. Like Eliezer of old, He is searching for a bride for the Father's Son and He has come bearing rich gifts for her. Please Him who has separated you and your partner for the work of God.

August 28

THE RIGHT TO TRANSMIT TO OTHERS WHAT WE HAVE LEARNED

Scripture Reading — Acts 13:6-13

"Then Saul, (who also is called Paul,) filled with the Holy Ghost, set his eyes on him, And said, O full of all subtility and all mischief, thou child of the devil, thou enemy of all righteousness, wilt thou not cease to pervert the right ways of the Lord? And now, behold, the hand of the Lord is upon thee, and thou shalt be blind, not seeing the sun for a season. And immediately there fell on him a mist and a darkness; and he went about seeking some to lead him by the hand." (Acts 13:9-11)

Does it not seem strange that the same thing should happen through the ministry of Paul as what had happened to him? (Acts 9:8) Even as Saul (Paul) was smitten blind on the road to Damascus as he too tried to pervert the right way of the Lord, so also was Elymas, the sorcerer and magician, smitten blind for the same reason.

This shows you that there is a great law of transmitting that is parallel with the law of sowing and reaping. That law is this, that whatever God has done or worked in your life, you have the power and the right to pass it on to others.

Paul had been smitten blind because of his evil ways. So now he had power to smite others with this same affliction. Notice, he was blind only for a while, and he also sentenced Elymas to be blind only "for a season."

Everything that has become a part of your life, you are able to pass on to others, otherwise it would not be yours. Where I have judged you and dealt with you and corrected you, you must share of these experiences with others. In this way the sufferings and judgments of the past are not in vain.

Look into the past! In every way I dealt with you and made demands of you, you can call others (through My Holy Spirit) to the same degree of dedication and righteousness and correction. You can never deliver to others that which you have not yourself experienced.

Let the hurts and scars of yesterday's mistakes serve to bring others to righteousnesss and the fear of God.

August 29

YOU ARE A LIGHT TO THE ENDS OF THE EARTH

Scripture Reading — Acts 13:14-52

"For so hath the Lord commanded us, saying, I have set thee to be a light of the Gentiles, that thou shouldest be for salvation unto the ends of the earth." (Acts 13:47)

Paul knew his calling. It is so very important that you know your calling and My will for your life.

So many of My children wander aimlessly through life like a ship abandoned at sea, without a captain to direct its journey. That is why so many lives are ship-wrecked.

There are many whom I cannot use because they do not want Me to control their lives. Their own strong and stubborn will forces Me to stand to the side and watch them aimlessly drift with the tide, until they finally end up on the rocks, a useless and permanently damaged vessel. It is not that I am unable to still rescue that vessel, but the situation is such that the entire cargo and the crew and the "attachments" of that vessel are so intertwined with that one's life that it is almost impossible to get that one to leave his doomed wreckage and to be transferred into another ship, even the ship of salvation.

I have called all My children to be lights unto the world. I want this whole world to be lit up, with the light of My glory shining through My vessels. I want you to know My ultimate will for your life. I don't want you to flounder about, not knowing My high calling for your life.

Greater doors of ministry are opening to you. You will not have to knock on those doors. They will knock on your door, asking for you. Go forth wherever I send you. I will not waste your time in places where My Holy Spirit is not free to work through you. I have your whole life planned out. The future is as a blue print as clear and concise as the past is a record. Only obey Me in every detail. I will give you strength for each task and for each day.

August 30

THROUGH MUCH TRIBULATION WE ENTER THE KINGDOM OF GOD

Scripture Reading — Acts 14:1-28

"Confirming the souls of the disciples, and exhorting them to continue in the faith, and that we must through much tribulation enter into the kingdom of God." (Acts 14:22)

Paul and Barnabas had served Me on this first missionary journey with much suffering and great opposition. The very gates of hell opened up as strong spirits came out to fight against and try to destroy these courageous men. But they learned the price of discipleship.

Yea, it is not an easy road. There will be many times you will be rejected, and there will be the temptation to be treated like some great one "fallen down from heaven." This is more dangerous for the soul than rejection.

Always remember you are a person "of like passions" as those who would put you on a pedestal. Remind them of it when they seek to lift you up as some great one.

The pathway before My children is one of much tribulation. As you teach them this, you can prepare their hearts to go through many hardships for My name's sake.

Exhort My people to continue in the faith, and not to despair when the way gets hard through tribulation. There are dark days ahead—days of tribulation, and even much tribulation. You are a faithful child of Mine. You have suffered many things. Let the things you have suffered make you strong to help and exhort others.

If you had not tasted tribulation, you would not be able to teach it. It was after Paul and Barnabas experienced tribulation that he returned to the churches to tell them to prepare their hearts to suffer as they enter the Kingdom of God.

August 31

I RETURN TO BUILD THE TABERNACLE OF DAVID

Scripture Reading — Acts 15:1-21

"After this I will return, and will build again the tabernacle of David, which is fallen down; and I will build again the ruins thereof, and I will set it up:...Known unto God are all his works from the beginning of the world." (Acts 15:16,18)

Never let go of this prophetic promise. First, all the Gentiles needed to be visited. And indeed because I am no respecter of persons I have given the Gentiles 2 millenia of time, even as I gave Abraham and his descendants, the house of Israel.

After I have finished working among the Gentiles and showing them My glory, I shall return and build again the tabernacle of David which is fallen down. I will raise up the ruins thereof and set it up. My works are planned from the beginning. Nothing is done by accident. All is in decent order, planned from the foundation of the world. Because it is in the original design, the gates of hell cannot prevail against it. My will shall surely be accomplished to the full.

"After this..." That time is now! I am returning to the house of David. I Myself am going to set it up. The gates of hell shall not prevail against it. For I have decreed it, and even as I decreed the reconstruction of this planet after it fell into ruin and was without form and void, I spoke, "Let there be light" and the work of creation was begun. So today I declare "Let there be light on the household of David and Abraham" and creation has begun its work of restoration.

September 1

BARNABAS' DETERMINATION

Scripture Reading — Acts 15:22-41

"And Barnabas determined to take with them John, whose surname was Mark. But Paul thought not good to take him with them, who departed from them from Pamphlyia, and went not with them to the work. And the contention was so sharp between them, that they departed asunder one from the other: and so Barnabas took Mark, and sailed unto Cyprus;" (Acts 15:37-39)

This is one of the sad, but true stories of the New Testament. Both Barnabas and Paul were faulty, in that both spoke sharp words, and both found it hard to relent a little.

You must realize, Barnabas was a Levite (Acts 4:36) and Paul was a Benjamite. In many ways these two tribes were much the same. In fact, Saul was more of a Levite than the Levites. He was overly zealous in the religion of the Jews and he carried much of that over into the Christian faith. Paul demanded complete dedication and loyalty and sacrifice, and he had no time for foolishness. (Acts 22:2-5)

Barnabas had the strong will of a Levite. And John Mark was of the tribe of Levi because his mother was Barnabas' sister. (Colossians 4:10)

Up until then, Paul's strength made most of the decisions, but when Mark came back on the scene, the united strength of the two Levites (Barnabas and Mark) was too strong for Paul to influence Barnabas, as he previously had. So nothing could move Barnabas' determination.

Often two dear friends, who get along beautifully for years are parted when a third person influences the one who has the subordinate position. At that time the one who did the leading finds himself losing that "flowing together," that beautiful "oneness." This is a very painful experience for that one. And in his hurt Paul said some strong words against Mark which angered Barnabas because Mark was his sister's son and like a son to him. Barnabas was more hurt than angry, because he hurt for his family name and reputation.

That is why Barnabas left. He took John Mark and ran off, protecting his "protégé" and leaving Paul stranded alone in Antioch. Paul waited upon God because he needed a partner. The Lord gave him Silas and he had the recommendation and the blessing of the church as the two of them began Paul's second missionary journey. Now there were two teams. I used it for good, but it had been a painful thing for Paul.

September 2

THE SPIRIT DID NOT PERMIT IT

Scripture Reading — Acts 16:1-12

"After they were come to Mysia, they assayed to go into Bithynia: but the Spirit suffered them not....And a vision appeared to Paul in the night; There stood a man of Macedonia, and prayed him, saying, Come over into Macedonia, and help us. And after he had seen the vision, immediately we endeavoured to go into Macedonia, assuredly gathering that the Lord had called us for to preach the gospel unto them." (Acts 16:7,9,10)

Immediately after Paul and Silas left Antioch they met Timothy. I gave Timothy to Paul as a son in the Gospel, to comfort him, and help him, but also, so that Paul would train him. As Barnabas now was training John Mark, Paul was training Timothy. Both of these young men became apostles in their own rights and giants in the early church.

It was also after this that Luke, the writer of Acts, began to journey with Paul and his team. ("We" endeavoured to go, assuredly gathering that the Lord had called "us."), etc..

Paul, in his hurt and grief after the split-up with Barnabas, wanted immediately to do some dangerous and desperate thing. He was going to go to Asia. Had he gone, he and those with him would immediately have been killed by the barbarians of that time. But I had a plan for Paul and also for Europe. First, I sent the Holy

Spirit to stop him from going into Asia. I will stop you from doing what is destructive to your life and ministry. Only be sure you obey My voice.

Next I gave Paul a vision, clear and concise, of a man of Macedonia calling, "Come over and help us!" Paul and his companions knew that this was direct guidance and they, with great joy and relief at knowing My will, prepared to go as soon as they could, and they "came a straight course."

My guidance is always clear. Unless you have this guidance, do not do anything. But once I have spoken, make a "straight course" directly to My highest will.

September 3

WHOSE HEART THE LORD OPENED

Scripture Reading — Acts 16:13-24

"And a certain woman named Lydia, a seller of purple, of the city of Thyatira, which worshipped God, heard us: whose heart the Lord opened, that she attended unto the things which were spoken of Paul." (Acts 16:14,15)

"And they went out of the prison, and entered into the house of Lydia: and when they had seen the brethren, they comforted them, and departed." (vs. 40)

Lydia's heart was open to Me before Paul and his companions found her. In fact, it was in answer to her heart's cry for more of Me that I gave Paul the vision of the man of Macedonia whom he saw crying, "Come over into Macedonia, and help us." (vs. 9)

This strong-hearted and prosperous woman opened her house to My children and to Me for the ministry.

"Lydia" is Greek, and it means "born of God." My hand was on the life of this woman from her mother's womb. Everything in her life, her birth, her education, her life as a businesswoman, her moving from Thyatira to Philippi, was preparation for that Sabbath day by the river side when she gathered with certain other women to pray. She did not know when she got up that morning what an important appointment she had with Me. She did not know that My messengers were on their way and that before the day was out she would hear for the first time about My saving grace, My life and My love.

She did not realize when she dressed up that morning that the gown she was wearing would be her baptismal robe. In fact she knew nothing about baptism.

Neither did she know when she left her house that morning that it would never be just her house again, that I would henceforth use it as My house where My children would have a home and where I would build My first church in Europe. Lydia, "born of God," was indeed born of Me, and predestined to be the great key person to Europe. I have many Lydias in these days. Find them. Their hearts are open, they are waiting.

September 4

PRAISES SHAKE THE WORLD

Scripture Reading — Acts 16:25-40

"And at midnight Paul and Silas prayed, and sang praises unto God: and the prisoners heard them. And suddenly there was a great earthquake, so that the foundations of the prison were shaken: and immediately all the doors were opened, and every one's bands were loosed." (Acts 16:25,26)

This would never have happened if Paul and Silas had grumbled and complained instead of praising and singing. All the grumbling and complaining in the world would never open one prison door. Instead, it would seal up the prison of self even more.

When you complain you hinder My powers from operating. Demon spirits take your negative words and build chains to tie up and bind situations, making it even more evil and difficult to deliver. That is why I said, "Let your communication be, Yea, Yea; Nay, Nay: for whatsoever is more than these cometh of evil!" (Matthew 5:37) Every time you speak evil concerning someone you bind up that person into that condition with another cord, another chain of bondage.

Your negative words in a difficult situation bind your spirit too into greater bondage, so that your spirit is not free to look out of the "window of My promise" and see the avenue of escape that is even then being prepared for you as well as for the others.

When Paul and Silas sang praises, the positive word came against all the negative deeds that had ever taken place in that dreadful prison, and the two forces of positive and negative (good and evil) were set in motion until there was a great shaking that was described as an earthquake. This earthquake was used to break walls loose and spring gates open, loosening chains and setting people free.

When Paul and Silas praised, they showed Satan that they were not afraid of him or his tactics. They set for all time the pattern of attitudes which all My children should have when they come into difficult, frightening and painful situations.

Go forth praising Me today for **everything**, and watch Me open prison doors and set men free. But remember your praises will not only set others free, they will also deliver you out of every difficult situation. Read Isaiah 60:18 and meditate on these words.

September 5

THESE THAT TURN THE WORLD UPSIDE DOWN

Scripture Reading — Acts 17:1-15

'And when they found them not, they drew Jason and certain brethren unto the rulers of the city, crying, These that have turned the world upside down are come hither also; Whom Jason hath received:" (Acts 17:6,7a)

Any man or woman whom My Spirit is using is going to turn the world "upside down."

If you do not want to cause a ripple and want to live a quiet, peaceable life without any friction from others, then don't ask the Holy Spirit to use you.

But if you truly want your life to be lived under the power and impact of the Holy Ghost, then get ready for trouble. You will be attacked from inside, and from outside. You will be an adversary of Satan and your name will be known in hell.

As long as there is no fire of the Holy Spirit burning in you, making you powerful against all demonic activity, you will not be troubled much by Satan. Remember, on the battle field the soldier who is not firing his gun is not noticed by the enemy. But when he does fire he draws attention to himself, and he immediately is under attack from the enemy, for firing draws out firing.

I want to use you to "turn this generation upside down" making it a new and glorious generation, but you must prepare for the cities where you go to be put in an uproar, and your very dwelling place to be assaulted. But fear not, I will protect you and deliver you and you shall finish your vital work for Me in spite of all the devils of hell.

September 6

THE SPIRIT STIRRED WITHIN

Scripture Reading — Acts 17:16-34

"Now while Paul waited for them at Athens, his spirit was stirred in him, when he saw the city wholly given to idolatry." (Acts 17:16)

In verse 5 you read how one man can turn the world upside down. Now you read of the impact on a man's soul when a city is full of evil. Paul's soul and spirit were filled with great sorrow and anger to see a whole city of the greatest intellectuals of his time given over to Satan. As you serve Me, you will see many things in many lives that will distress you and fill your heart with grief.

Serving Me is not an easy thing for the soul that is sensitive. You will feel great soul-pain at the spiritual condition of these. While it is true that you will shake nations and turn them upside down, it is also true that cities, nations and churches to which I send you will shake you and turn your heart to sadness and weeping when you see the spiritual death and plight which they are in.

Do not think it a strange thing when you visit a nation and you are made to weep when you see the sad state of the spiritual condition of those people.

I have brought you here and I have allowed you to see the plight of My people. Where is the love that My people need? Where are they today in spiritual growth? Many who loved one another yesterday cannot speak to each other today. Your spirit is stirred within you at the spiritual condition of My people, but I, too, am grieved for the spiritual condition of this city, this nation and I now command men everywhere to repent, for the day of judgment has been set, and it is fast approaching.

September 7

THEY OPPOSE THEMSELVES

Scripture Reading — Acts 18:1-8

"And when they opposed themselves, and blasphemed, he shook his raiment, and said unto them, Your blood be upon your own heads, I am clean: from henceforth I will go unto the Gentiles." (Acts 18:6)

When you have done all you can and there is nothing left, then shake off the burden; don't carry it with you; leave the place and go to another place free of the responsibility and the pain of others' mistakes. Leave the mess behind. You cannot carry the faults, failures, the wrongs of the last group of people with you. You must be ready to pick up the burden of the next place to which I send you. You cannot carry both burdens. It will kill you. It would be like trying to carry all the suitcases and baggage of the past years together with that of today's with the new fashions in clothing. You cannot wear yesterday's garments. They do not fit any longer. Shake them off.

The tragedy is that "they opposed themselves" when they closed up their hearts and were critical and did the things they have done. They were harming themselves. I wanted to bless them, but I could not. Their spirits were not open to receive. They did not oppose you; it was themselves they opposed. When people do not receive My messengers, it is to their own harm and grief.

When you do not receive the anointed word that I send to you, you are opposing yourself. It is you who will be harmed. Think how terrible it would be if I told one of My servants to shake off his raiment and leave you, and that now your blood would be on your own head. You are going to be fully responsible for every servant of Mine you reject. That would be a terrible thing. Live so close to Me that it can never happen to you, My child.

September 8

MUCH PEOPLE IN THIS CITY

Scripture Reading — Acts 18:9-17

"Then spake the Lord to Paul in the night by a vision, Be not afraid, but speak, and hold not thy peace: For I am with thee, and no man shall set on thee to hurt thee: for I have much people in this city." (Acts 18:9,10)

My beloved child, I have a work for you to do right here where you are. There are many hungry hearts here. They are Mine. They have been chosen from the foundations of the world. Although they do not know Me yet, I know them. They are Mine and I will bring them to a saving knowledge of Me.

Lift up your eyes. Behold, the sheep of My pasture. They are precious to Me. I am going to visit them and pour My Spirit out on their hungry hearts. Be not fearful to speak out clearly the message I have given you. The storms may blow. There may be terrible opposition from the evil one. But I have placed you here to leave a message with these people. Hold not your peace. Do not be afraid of what they may think or say. They cannot hurt you. I am with you. I am here to protect you and watch over you. I will stay with you until you have touched all those lives which you are ordained to bless.

Beyond that you need not worry. Do not feel badly because you cannot go to other places. I brought you here to this place. It is here that you have an appointment for Me. If I wanted you other places, I would have sent you there also. Be faithful. Speak loud and clear, and the message shall live on.

September 9

IF GOD WILL

Scripture Reading — Acts 18:18-28

"But bade him farewell, saying, I must by all means keep this feast that cometh in Jerusalem: but I will return again unto you, if God will. And he sailed from Ephesus." (Acts 18:21)

There will be many times in your life when you will be strongly tempted to stay in a certain place. It was this way with Paul when he came to Ephesus with Priscilla and Aquila. (vs. 18) He had been with them a long time and he loved them dearly. Priscilla was as close as a sister to Paul. To leave them both and depart for Jerusalem was not easy. Paul had to renew his vows. He had shaved his head, for the calling of the Nazarite vow was upon him. It was a time when he had to say good-bye to loved ones and go forth with a deeper dedication and even more of a spirit of separation from others upon his life.

Paul was never permitted by Me to hold onto anything. So deep was his consecration that I took from him all that was precious; John Mark, Barnabas, Timothy, Priscilla and Aquila and many other things. He could never clutter his life with things nor people, no matter how precious, nor share the hours with others which belonged to Me.

So it is, I call you to the same "giving up" of all that is precious. I am the only precious thing that you can cleave to. All you have is through My grace alone. You could lose it all tomorrow, but you will never lose Me.

You must be ready to say good-bye to your "Ephesuses," knowing that, if it is My will, you shall return. Never look back when you leave a nation. If it is My will for you to have a future part in that harvest, know of a certainty I will bring you back. If not, you are better off never to return. Finish your work and sail on. Always know, if it is God's will, you shall return. If it is My will, I will give you back your family, your friends, your possessions.

September 10

SPECIAL MIRACLES

Scripture Reading — Acts 19:1-20

"And this continued by the space of two years; so that all they which dwelt in Asia heard the word of the Lord Jesus, both Jews and Greeks. And God wrought special miracles by the hands of Paul:" (Acts 19:10,11)

Never before had anything quite like this happened. I opened up the flood gates of glory over the life of My servant Paul when he came to the great city of Ephesus.

"Moreover the law entered, that the offence might abound. But where sin abounded, grace did much more abound:" (Romans 5:20) Yes, even in that great and idolatrous city, I poured out My Spirit in a mighty way. There will always be certain places where I can do more than in other places.

It all began when Priscilla and Aquila arrived there months earlier. They laid a foundation in Ephesus by their teaching and their prayers. (Acts 18:24) They had asked Me to send Paul back to them. They had been witnesses to the works I had done in Corinth during the 1½ years Paul was with them there. (Acts 18:11) But there never had been a revival with signs and wonders among the Gentiles like there was in Ephesus. It was to be Paul's greatest revival. It was to shake all of Asia Minor.

It was as a result of this revival that the seven churches of Revelation sprang up in that area.

Do not be distressed if you see greater miracles of faith take place in some places more than in others. I will work My works in times and ways to fit certain times and needs.

I did **special** miracles by the hand of Paul because of many reasons. As I send you forth from nation to nation, you will see My power working on your behalf to do special miracles in some places more than in others. Expect it. It is the time of My visitation on your life and ministry, and on those to whom I send you.

September 11

PURPOSE IN YOUR SPIRIT

Scripture Reading — Acts 19:21-41

"After these things were ended, Paul purposed in the spirit, when he had passed through Macedonia and Achaia, to go to Jerusalem, saying, After I have been there, I must also see Rome." (Acts 19:21)

My child, you must purpose in your spirit to do that which is My will for your life.

Paul purposed in his spirit to go to Jerusalem and then to Rome while he was in Ephesus. After that, he had many miles to backtrack and many months to wait and to serve Me in Macedonia and Greece, but he never forgot what he had purposed in his spirit and what he had set his heart to do.

So you too must be firm in the thing which I have put in your heart to do. Do not look to the left or the right. Always remember that today's obstacles must not be permitted to block out the vision of yesterday.

Little did he know the price it would cost him and the terrible suffering which lay ahead. He would endure beatings, long years of imprisonment and suffering from loneliness and separation from his beloved "son" Timothy, who was dearer to him than all else. This "free spirit" Paul, who would come under no apostolic leadership (Galatians 1:16, 17; 2:6, 11) nor authority of man, was now facing years of being My prisoner. Paul, who would get on a ship tomorrow and sail to the farthest point, would not be able to leave his prison cell for years. He who loved the wind, the sunshine, the stars, the rain, would sit in the darkness of dungeons. He who loved to read and study and debate, would weep for a script to feast his soul on and a man to converse with.

Paul could only go through those years of suffering because he had purposed in his spirit to see Rome. Don't let anything keep you from fulfilling that which I have put in your spirit to do!

September 12

TRAIN OTHERS BY EXPERIENCE

Scripture Reading — Acts 20:1-6

"And there accompanied him into Asia Sopater of Berea; and of the Thessalonians, Aristarchus and Secundus; and Gaius of Derbe, and Timotheus; and of Asia, Tychicus and Trophimus." (Acts 20:4)

These are seven men listed who travelled with Paul on the last of his three recorded missionary journeys. Look at them again a little more clearly:

1. **Sopater** came from Berea, the city in Macedonia near Thessa-

lonica, where the people were "more noble" than those in Thessalonica in that they received the Word with an open mind and searched the scriptures daily. It was here also that not a few honourable great women and men believed. (Acts 17:11,12) Sopater means "life from father."

2. **Aristarchus** came from Thessalonica. In Acts 27:2 he was with Paul when he was loaded on the ship in Cæsarea to be sent as a prisoner to Rome. In Colossians 4:10 Paul calls him his fellow prisoner. He is also mentioned in Philemon 24. Aristarchus means, "the best leader, the best regent." He had also been arrested in Ephesus and brought into the theatre. (Acts 19:29)

3. **Secundus:** He came from Thessalonica and is only mentioned here. His name means "the second."

4. **Timotheus (Timothy)** of Derbe and Lystra was like a son to Paul. His name means, "Honour be to God, honoured by God."

5. **Gaius** of Derbe was mentioned as being Paul's host in Romans 16:23. He was also arrested in Ephesus with Aristarchus (Acts 19:29). He was baptized by Paul (I Corinthians 1:14) and John III was written to a well-beloved elder by the same name (Gaius). Gaius means "man of this earth."

6. **Tychicus** delivered Paul's letter to the Ephesians (Ephesians 6:21) Paul called him a beloved brother and faithful minister in the Lord. (Ephesians 6:21,22) He also delivered Paul's letter to the Colossians (Colossians 4:7) and was called "a beloved brother, and a faithful minister and fellow servant in the Lord:" Paul said he had sent him to know how they were and also to comfort their hearts. In II Timothy 4:12 he mentions sending him from Rome to Ephesus. When writing to Titus, Paul speaks of sending Tychicus to Titus, so Titus can come to him at Necapolis. (Titus 3:12) His name means "lucky."

7. **Trophimus:** He was an Ephesian. He accompanied Paul on his last journey to Jerusalem when he was arrested. (Acts 21:29) Paul tells Timothy that he had to leave him at Miletum, sick. (II Timothy 4:20) His name means "nourished."

Paul took these men with him to train them for the high calling of God. They were from many different cities, different languages and backgrounds, different ages, and different countries. Paul knew that the best way to give them a missionary vision was to take them with him on his journeys. They suffered with him, were arrested in his place, falsely accused, imprisoned with him, knew sickness, experienced sea voyages and ship-wrecks, cold and heat and the joy of serving Me.

Paul trusted them to take his letters (epistles) to the churches and to faithfully give an honest report to the Christians.

I want you to train those whom I have given you by letting them experience your travels, your suffering, your rejection. Experience is the best teacher. Don't think that anyone is indispensible to his or her job. I can use any of My vessels in any way I desire.

Some will succeed, others will fail and disappoint you. Do not be hesitant to take with you on your missionary journeys all of those I have called for this purpose.

> Please come back and labour with me;
> The fields are white, I need you so;
> Let us glean the golden harvest;
> I need you, this you surely know.
>
> Once we laboured close together,
> Hand in hand we sowed the grain,
> Smiled and laughed and wept as sisters,
> Now, I work alone again.
>
> You said you'd be my faithful daughter,
> Promised you would share my load,
> But you've skipped off o'er the hill-top;
> Left me to walk this lonely road.
>
> Can you hear me calling to you?
> Does your heart remember me?
> Must I labour till the sunset
> Alone, without your company?

September 13

TALKING TILL MORNING

Scriptrue Reading — Acts 20:7-12

"When he therefore was come up again, and had broken bread, and eaten, and talked a long while, even till break of day, so he departed." (Acts 20:11)

The fellowship among My children is the closest thing to heaven that there is. The angels love to stand around and listen when My children talk together about the things which give glory to My name. If you could see the angels, you would see them smiling and nodding their heads as they remember with you some of the wonderful things which I have done in your life and the lives of your friends whom they know as well as you know them. Yes, they know them even better than you do. And they were there helping when all these wonderful things happened.

But when you say things against My children and repeat malicious gossip, even though it is true, the angels shake their heads, put their fingers in front of their lips and say, "Shh!" If only you could see them, you would spare some of these words which you now so freely speak.

That is why you feel so badly after you have spoken negatively against one of My children. You have made the angels feel very sad because they know that you don't know the full story. You are judging without all the evidence. Their sadness gives off vibrations which you feel. This makes your spirit sad also. They want you to talk about the things that will bring joy and victory.

In Malachi 3:16 it says that when you speak the glorious things of God, I hearken and take notice, and special mention of every godly conversation is recorded for all time. The true jewels of My Kingdom are those of My children who order their conversation aright, even for the glory of God.

Paul had so much to share with My children at Troas. He had been there seven days, but on this last day they still wanted to fellowship. The excitement of Eutychus being raised from the dead made them all wide awake. They ate their "midnight snack" and talked and talked until day break. There was always one more miracle to talk about, one more blessing to share, one more answer to prayer. Don't be afraid to talk all night about Me, even though you have to pack to leave the next day. Just remember Philippians 4:8: "Finally, brethren, whatsoever things are true, whatsoever things are honest, whatsoever things are just, whatsoever things are pure, whatsoever things are lovely, whatsoever things are of good report; if there be any virtue, and if there be any praise, think on these things."

September 14

HOUSE TO HOUSE

Scripture Reading — Acts 20:13-21

"Serving the Lord with all humility of mind, and with many tears, and temptations, which befell me by the lying in wait of the Jews: And how I kept back nothing that was profitable unto you, but have shewed you, and have taught you publickly, and from house to house," (Acts 20:19,20)

My beloved servant Paul could only be as great as he was because of his humility. Without humility of mind he would have been too proud to accept the suffering and bear the reproach. He went forth weeping.

You, too, have been called to walk this same pathway of humility, tears and temptations, and the "lying in wait" of your enemies.

Satan tried many times to destroy Paul through those people who hated Paul. You too have experienced this same kind of dreadful hate. Only as you stay close to Me in My love can you be strong enough to overcome the fears that you might be tempted to have because of those terrible vibrations your spirit will receive from the hatred of your enemies.

Paul kept nothing back. He preached the whole counsel of God. He not only preached publicly to great crowds, but he was also humble enough to preach from house to house, even to smaller groups. Never be too proud, or think yourself so big that you cannot teach and preach in house meetings. For there will be times when I can work in a mightier way in a cottage than I can in a synagogue (or church building). Always be ready to serve Me with all humility in any place that I send you.

September 15

BOUND IN THE SPIRIT

Scripture Reading — Acts 20:22-23

"And now, behold, I go bound in the spirit unto Jerusalem, not knowing the things that shall befall me there: Save that the Holy Ghost witnesseth in every city, saying that bonds and afflictions abide me." (Acts 20:22,23)

Bound in the Spirit! You cannot do your own will or choose to go your own way. Your life is bound in the Spirit. Ever since the Holy Spirit said, "Separate me Barnabas and Saul for the work whereunto I have called them," Paul was bound by the Holy Spirit when he fasted in Antioch. I did a work in his spirit that was so great that it bound his spirit with My Holy Spirit.

When you make a total commitment of your entire life to My will a wedding takes place wherein your spirit is wedded and sealed in with the Holy Spirit. This brings your whole being under submission to the will of the Holy Spirit for the rest of your life. He becomes your guide, your comforter, your way-maker, your power, your covering. He will, from that time on, work His works through your life and plant His seeds of grace into your life, even the seed of My Word which shall bring forth fruit unto life.

Many people criticize Paul for going to Jerusalem when he had been warned repeatedly of the dangers he faced. Let it suffice to say he was "bound in the Spirit." I warned him because I am faithful to My own beloved. I will not lead them into something for which they are not prepared in their spirits. I warned Paul so he could be ready in his spirit to suffer for My name's sake.

I too knew My own future and what awaited Me the last time I went up to Jerusalem, but knowing the suffering that awaits you is not an excuse to escape or flee from it. (John 12:27)

Paul wanted two things. He wanted to die for Me in Jerusalem and he wanted to go to Rome. My Spirit gave him both desires. He died to self and glory and fame and honour in Jerusalem, the city where he had known great honour and power, and then he went to Rome. When you are bound in the Spirit, nothing of what you face will move you.

September 16

MOVED BY NOTHING

Sripture Reading — Acts 20:24-25

"But none of these things move me, neither count I my life dear unto myself, so that I might finish my course with joy, and the ministry, which I have received of the Lord Jesus, to testify the gospel of the grace of God." (Acts 20:24)

My beloved, faithful child, it is I who have made you strong in Spirit so that no matter what opposition comes against you it can not daunt you.

When you said "yes" to Me and gave Me your life, I put My Holy Spirit's seal upon you so that you would be able to fulfil the covenant of dedication which you made with Me.

There is nothing that is powerful enough to move you if you are willing to suffer and bear rejection and the prejudices of others against your calling.

You need never defend your calling, nor seek to prove who you are, nor show your credentials. All such actions are beneath a person of your calibre and calling.

When Paul's apostle's credentials were called into question he did not answer by showing the lists of converts, the cities he had preached in, the nations he turned upside down, the many miraculous healings. The proof of his calling was in his suffering and the persecution he bore for Me.

Yes, there are many who can tell about the long years of "successful" ministry, the churches built, the members added to the church, but few can show the wounds and the scars of a soldier's life in combat.

Neither is it in vain that you should not be numbered with the applauded and acclaimed. You have not been celebrated as a star by men. But still you stand fast in your calling, that none of man's opposition need ever move you from that which you have purposed in your heart.

September 17

FREE FROM THE BLOOD OF MEN

Scripture Reading — Acts 20:26-35

"Wherefore I take you to record this day, that I am pure from the blood of all men." (Acts 20:26)

Not many of My children can say that they are free from the blood of all men.

I said to Ezekiel that if he would not warn the wicked to flee from his wicked way, to save his life, the same wicked man would die in his iniquity, and I would require his blood at Ezekiel's hand. (Ezekiel 3:18)

The blood of generations of lost souls is upon My children. This generation of lost souls is the greatest of all time. Nations like China (over 1,000 millions), India (700 millions), Bangladesh (90 millions), the Philippines (50 millions), Indonesia (150 millions), Japan (118 millions), Malaysia (14 millions), Hong Kong (52 millions) are teeming with souls. Asia alone is the home of nearly two thirds of the 4,000 million souls on this planet. I need missionaries. I need men like Paul and women like Priscilla who will do My work with a heart abandoned to Me and a great love for the lost. But alas, I have too few who care, who go, who pray, who give and sacrifice to send others. I want to send you as lights to the nations in the uttermost parts of the earth. But each man cares only for himself.

I spoke to A. C. Jeffries, My missionary pioneer to Indonesia, in a dream. I showed him the millions of souls marching to hell. When he awakened he saw blood on his hands. He rededicated his life, even in old age, unto Me, and went to India where I used him in a mighty way. Age is no barrier for being used by Me for soul-winning. Tell the older people who have reached retirement to dedicate their lives unto Me and to go out and preach and teach and live for Me among the lost of this last generation.

My child, I can send you anywhere and I can open any door. There is nothing too hard for Me. Make no excuses. Fast and pray for a burden for souls. I need an army. I will use whoever is willing to offer up this life. My Holy Spirit will work through anyone, man or woman, adult or child, without exception.

Pray for Me to give you a love and a burden for the lost. Ask Me for a vision, for without a vision the people perish. (Proverbs 29:18) The angels are grieving for the multitudes who are going to hell. They weep for the lost. More are going to hell in this one year than in centuries of the past. Hell is enlarging its borders to make room for the millions of Asia alone. Put this burden on My people. Awaken them. I will work with you to sound the alarm.

September 18

SAYING GOOD-BYE

Scripture Reading — Acts 20:36-28

"Sorrowing most of all for the words which he spake, that they should see his face no more." (Acts 20:38)

Yes, My child, good-byes are always sad. It is hard for you to break off that beautiful relationship and companionship which comes through love and confidence.

But "good-byes" will always be necessary. This is because you live in a temporary abode. Only in heaven are there no "good-byes." But be of good cheer. Because you live in a temporal world, even your "good-byes" are only for a little while. For you will meet every living soul on the other side. Some you will only see at the judgment seat, others you will share eternity with. And your relationship with them will be so much better and sweeter than it is down here. For here you all have imperfections which mar your friendships, but in heaven, all spirits are perfect.

True friendship is a blending of two spirits (not 2 bodies). That is why two of the most perfect bodies put together still can disagree and even detest each other.

Love is inspired through the spirit and not the magnetism of the body. That is why you can lay your life down and still love strongly after "death."

Let your spirit be set free to love. And think not that because a loved one has left to go away, or passed on into the higher plane of that eternal abode, that you have in any way "lost" them, for this is not true. True friendship is eternal. It is cemented together by Myself, standing with My arms around you and your loved ones. You must prepare your heart in the coming days to say many sad goodbyes, but do not grieve overly much, for you will meet again and that will be a day of great joy.

September 19

READY!

Scripture Reading — Acts 21:1-16

"Then Paul answered, What mean ye to weep and to break mine heart? for I am ready not to be bound only, but also to die at Jerusalem for the name of the Lord Jesus." (Acts 21:13)

After Agabus, the famous prophet, had earlier prophesied the dearth that would come to all the earth (which came to pass in the days of Claudius Cæsar [Acts 11:28]), he was respected as one of the great prophets of all time by the early church. When therefore, he was moved by My Spirit to come from Judea to Cæsaria to give Paul this prophetic warning, it was an overwhelming thing. All of the people who loved Paul and who were with him all this time were convinced that all these fears and anxieties for him were genuine. Paul was in great danger.

When Agabus took Paul's girdle and bound his own hands and feet, he demonstrated clearly and unmistakably Paul's future bondage. He also said Paul would be delivered up to the Gentiles.

When Paul was apprehended by the Jews in the temple of Jerusalem after this prophecy had been given, the chief captain of the Roman battalion stationed there seized him and bound him in two chains (one for Paul's hands, and one for his feet), thus fulfilling Agabus' prophecy to the letter.

Paul's greatest test in fulfilling what he felt was his highest and most supreme sacrifice was seeing his beloved companions suffer on his behalf. When they had heard Agabus' prophecy they immediately wept so terribly, and begged Paul with such entreaties not to go to Jerusalem, that he could hardly stand it.

It is not for your sake alone that you suffer when you answer My call. You are ready in your spirit to make all final commitments of life and death; you know that your loved ones also must suffer when you make that total commitment to Me, and this is hard. It breaks your heart to see them weeping and hurting because of your dedication to Me. Some do not understand it when you have to leave family and loved ones to answer My call. But you are bound in the Spirit. It was only because Paul was bound in the Spirit that he could face the bondage of the Roman chains.

Do not let the tears of your dearest companion untie those bonds of commitment wherewith you are bound to My will. Do not let their tears and pleas loosen you from your vows to Me. You must face your Jerusalem. It is My will. You are not alone. I am with you.

September 20

KNOWING WHEN TO SPEAK

Scripture Reading — Acts 21:17-40

"But Paul said, I am a man which am a Jew of Tarsus, a city in Cilicia, a citizen of no mean city: and, I beseech thee, suffer me to speak unto the people." (Acts 21:39)

There are times when it is proper to quote your credentials and to share with others the greatness of your pedigree.

While it is true that Paul did not often speak about his noble birth, his education, his rank in the religious world, and his suffering as My missionary, still there were times when he was released by My Spirit to reveal and speak about who he was.

So you too must be wise in what you say to others concerning who and what you are. There are times when it is wiser to be silent, and there are times when you can tell portions of your past; then there are times when you can reveal even more. But in every life, there are certain things which must never be spoken nor revealed. For instance, Paul said there was given him a "thorn in the flesh," but he never revealed what it was. Also Paul never mentions his private life, whether he was married or had children. He remains completely silent concerning his private life, and so do I.

You do not need to satisfy a curious world by telling them all they hunger to know. Speak only what I bid. I too did not tell the curious the secret of My birth, My life, My destiny. Learn from Me to speak only that which the Father bade you speak.

September 21

DEPART: I WILL SEND YOU FAR AWAY

Scripture Reading — Acts 22:1-21

"And he said unto me, Depart: for I will send thee far hence unto the Gentiles." (Acts 22:21)

There is no doubt about it. You will always live a more effective life and give a greater testimony among the heathen than you can at home amongst your own people.

Paul was known by all in Jerusalem. He said that the high priest and all the elders of Jerusalem could bear witness to who he was. (Acts 22:5)

But as he sought to share his experience of conversion with them, they would not receive his testimony of conversion. (vs. 18) So while he was praying and seeking My face, I told him "Make haste, and get thee quickly out of Jerusalem:"

Never be guilty of not honouring the anointed of the Lord whom I send to you. There are so many who despise and reject and look down on those who are familiar to them. Familiarity breeds contempt because we see each other's mistakes and weaknesses so clearly when we know them. That is why I often have to separate families before I can use them. It is so sad, but it is true. The parents always see their children as their children, and not as My anointed vessels, and the children see their anointed parents only as mom and dad, and not as My anointed vessels.

As long as you stay where you are, I cannot use you to your fullness. I need to send you far away to the heathen. There you will be accepted as My anointed handmaiden and servant. Honour and respect will be given to you and you will turn many to righteousness.

Do not force yourself to stay where you are not accepted and respected. Arise and go far away. There I will use you and give you great honour.

September 22

WITH A GREAT SUM I OBTAINED THIS FREEDOM

Scripture Reading — Acts 22:22-30

"And the chief captain answered, With a great sum obtained I this freedom." (Acts 22:28)

Freedom is the greatest treasure that you can have in life. There are many kinds of freedom:

1. Freedom from **sinful habits.** Many who think they are free are bound by habits which control their thoughts and their actions. No matter how strong in character or physique you are, the chains of bondage from your habits bind you up. You are not free as long as you need to satisfy that strong urge within.

2. Freedom from **depression, criticism, complaining, etc.** Many who live right lives outwardly are full of strong negative thoughts and words. This is a terrible bondage which darkens the whole life and, when spoken, darkens the lives of others.

3. Freedom from **miserable relationships.** So many are suffering because of wrong marriages and wrong relationships. Many go through agonizing ordeals only because they feel "indebted" to someone. But if they were willing to let go, I could set them free from these chains of bondage.

4. Freedom from **want of any kind.** In Me is the supply of all that you need. I am the provider. As you look to Me alone, I will do such great and exceedingly mighty things for you, even beyond all that you can think and comprehend. You do not need to live a beggarly life. Rejoice in Me; I will do great things for you as you rejoice and are grateful to Me for what I have done. You are free because I obtained this freedom for you. It cost Me everything. And it cost you a great price to enter into it. Be careful you do not let your soul become ensnared into bondage again.

> I paid the price to set you free
> From all that would destroy your soul;
> If you will only look to Me
> I'll meet your need, and make you whole.

September 23

"THOU MUST BEAR WITNESS IN ROME ALSO"

Scripture Reading — Acts 23:1-35

"And the night following the Lord stood by him, and said, Be of good cheer, Paul: for as thou hast testified of me in Jerusalem, so must thou bear witness also at Rome." (Acts 23:11)

I spoke it, and I did it. When you make a full commitment of your life to Me, there are not enough people or demons to hinder Me from fulfilling My plan in your life.

And strong winds can blow your plans away, but My plans are different. That is why your life must be totally and completely yielded to Me. I will fulfil all My will in your life as you are yielded to Me.

The hatred against Paul was so great that 40 men decided to fast without food or water till he was killed. They had powerful, influential friends in high government places who could co-operate to kill Paul. They hid their plans carefully, but I knew all about it.

When people and demons plan against you, I know all about it and I know how to destroy their plans. In the same night that they made their plans, I, Myself, visited Paul and told him that he would stand for Me in Rome, even as he had stood and borne witness for Me in Jerusalem. He had faithfully and courageously testifed before the angry mob and also before the angry council. He had turned the anger they had towards him and directed it in such a way that they turned against each other — Saducees against Pharisees and Pharisees against Saducees. Thus was he saved temporarily. I gave him this wisdom. I will give you wisdom against your adversaries and I will fulfil all My will through your life.

September 24

A RINGLEADER OF THE SECT OF THE NAZARENES

Scripture Reading — Acts 24:1-27

"For we have found this man a pestilent fellow, and a mover of sedition among all the Jews throughout the world, and a ringleader of the sect of the Nazarenes:" (Acts 24:5)

I, too, was called a Nazarene. In fact, it was fulfilled concerning Me, "He shall be called a Nazarene." (Matthew 2:23) I was called a Nazarene for 3 reasons:

1. I was raised in Nazareth and so it was that I was identified with the city where I grew up.

2. The word "Nazarene" means "a green branch, set apart, dedicated to Jehovah, and prince." The same word in Hebrew is used in Genesis 49:26 ("set apart from his brethren") and in Numbers 6:2 (a vow of a Nazarite). So Paul was given this name because he was My dedicated disciple and follower.

3. In Zechariah 6:12 the prophet called Me "a branch." You too are a branch, a green, living branch because you have been grafted into My root. You have been dedicated, separated from the crowd whom you call your brethren.

Paul was accused of being a troublemaker and a ringleader. All those in opposition must prepare their hearts to be shot at and suffer more intense opposition than others.

They called them a sect. Oh, how you hate it when people say you belong to a sect! Everything that is not the conventional is termed a "sect." It has become a word that has strong negative vibrations. But do not fear, you belong to a great crowd of noble princes and warriors who all were accused of belonging or promoting what the religious world calls "a sect." I was the founder of the "sect" called the Nazarenes. Paul was a ringleader and if you follow on in true dedication as a green branch, separated from your brethren, you will become a leader (ringleader) too, just like Paul. And that will make you a prince.

September 25

"NO MAN MAY DELIVER ME UNTO THEM"

Scripture Reading — Acts 25:1-27

"For if I be an offender, or have committed any thing worthy of death, I refuse not to die: but if there be none of these things whereof these accuse me, no man may deliver me unto them. I appeal unto Cæsar." (Acts 25:11)

There are times when you need to fight for the right to live. You do not need to wilfully submit to death. Life is the most precious gift you have. Cherish every moment of it.

You daily have an enemy, called the angel of death, the destroyer, whose one aim is to cut short a person's life span. You can readily submit to him, or you can escape him. Some have escaped his cold clutches many times, simply because they have obeyed warnings I have given them in dreams or premonition, or because they have wrestled in prayer, pleaded the covering of My precious blood, or just refused in their spirit to submit to death before their work was finished.

Paul had not "finished his course" yet, and he knew it, so he wrestled for his life. He knew that if he went to Jerusalem, he would be killed by his treacherous, religious enemies who were filled with hatred against Paul because he preached the pure Gospel and had turned many people to believe in Me.

Paul also knew what route to take because I had told him in Jerusalem, "so must thou bear witness also at Rome." (Acts 23:11)

When you know your work is unfinished and I have commissioned you to do a certain thing, you must stand on that Word until it is fulfilled. Do not let the light go out in your lamp of flesh until the last letter is written, the last sermon is preached, the last nation has been visited.

September 26

NOT DISOBEDIENT TO THE HEAVENLY VISION

Scripture Reading — Acts 26:1-32

"Whereupon, O king Agrippa, I was not disobedient unto the heavenly vision:" (Acts 26:19)

It is a glorious victory for anyone to be able to report after years of service to Me that they were not disobedient to the heavenly vision.

Every true calling to the ministry is based on a heavenly vision. Some are closer visions than others. It is not often that I meet someone on the road of life like I met Paul on the way to Damascus and shine down on him with a brightness that is greater than that of the noonday sun. Often it is only in the spirit of man that the heavenly calling and vision is given; even so, it is as real and as important.

You have been given a heavenly vision for these last days. The Father wants to reach into your heart with His heavenly light and expand that vision in even a greater way. Accept what He wants to do.

Behold, My child, I am the Light of the world, and I want to let My light and My glory shine out through your life to the world.

Every true vision from heaven is accompanied by My light which enlightens the spirit of man. I lighten your spirit and body with the glory of this light of heavenly revelation, not only temporarily, but permanently. This light will remain in your being all the days of your life, as long as you stay obedient to the heavenly vision. But if once you begin to become disobedient to the heavenly vision, this light will begin to become dim in your spirit and it will turn to darkness within you.

Stay obedient to the heavenly vision which I have given you. Do not be afraid to do all I require of you. It is by the power of your vision that all will become a reality. The vision has power to create into the tangible all you see in the Spirit.

September 27

ALL THAT SAIL WITH THEE

Scripture Reading — Acts 27:1-24

"Saying, Fear not, Paul; thou must be brought before Cæsar: and, lo, God hath given thee all them that sail with thee." (Acts 27:24)

Life is like an ocean voyage. Some vessels are small and have a limited household, others are larger and have a larger number in the household.

You started life all by yourself. I expanded your capacity to love and to share of My goodness to you with others. You have increased the size of your boat to meet the size of your heart, your love and your vision.

Some have gotten off your vessel at one of the ports where you stopped in the past and they are no longer with you today, but you can claim them, you can travail for God to give you all the souls who have sailed with you.

I could have saved Paul all by himself. Some did not deserve saving. The owner of the ship had not believed Paul. The centurion had chosen to disregard Paul's warning (vs. 11), but Paul asked Me in true intercession to save the lives of all those with whom he was sailing, and I sent My angel to tell him that I had heard his intercession and would save everyone.

You too can claim everyone who sails with you. When you go out on a journey, claim protection for everyone on the ship, on the plane, in the car, or whatever vessel you use. You can do it, just like Paul did.

Also you can claim the salvation of every member of your household. Ask Me fervently to save the souls of every one of those members of your family who "sail with you" on the sea of life. With Me nothing is impossible. I will work in such a way as to bring each and every one of those whom you love safely to the haven of rest, even the ones who did not believe and who chose to disobey the warnings you have given them.

"...lo, God hath given thee all them that sail with thee."

September 28

STAND STILL AND WAIT FOR THE LIGHT

Scripture Reading — Acts 27:25-32

"Then fearing lest we should have fallen upon rocks, they cast four anchors out of the stern, and wished for the day (daylight). (Acts 27:29)

Sometimes all you can do is wait and pray. After weeks of being helplessly tossed about in the stormy seas in the darkness of the stormy night, the sailors could "feel" that there was land nearby. They sounded the depths and found that they were fast approaching some kind of country. But they knew that they would never survive shipwreck on the rocks if it took place in the darkness of the night.

In spite of the fact that Paul had told them that all lives would be saved, they still did the wise and careful thing.

Don't take anything for granted. Don't risk your life just because you feel you can't get killed or injured or become sick. Take the necessary precautions of survival like these trained and wise sailors did.

Remember, there are days coming when you will not know which way to turn or what to do. When you are in the dark about your future, then cast out your anchor and wait. They cast out four anchors, one for each direction. There are times in your life when you dare not move forward, backward, left or right. In that hour don't be tempted to do something which you should not do. Stand still and see the salvation of your God.

I am with you in the darkness. Just hang on, praying, waiting, listening, sounding the depth. Cast your anchor and pray for the light to come, so that you can see which way to go. Don't let friends or foe coerce you into making even half a step, for if you do not have guidance you will be cast on the rocks and all will be lost. Wait, My child, wait.

September 29

TAKE SOME FOOD: FOR THIS IS FOR YOUR HEALTH

Scripture Reading — Acts 27:33-38

"Wherefore I pray you to take some meat: for this is for your health: for there shall not an hair fall from the head of any of you." (Acts 27:34)

There comes a time in every life when the Holy Spirit will lead you from your fast. It comes to you with a sense of release, of accomplishment, of having done all you can do.

The ship-wrecked crew were still being tossed by the stormy

waves. The darkness of night was upon them, but Paul knew that he had prayed through and that he had the victory even when there were no signs of it, so he announced, "it is time to eat."

You do not need to fast until you see the victory, but until you know in your heart that I have heard your prayers.

Every cry that ascends to Me from earth has to pour through different degrees and types of testings.

1. Is the one who prays sincere and worthy?
2. Is it the best for that life, or would something else be better?
3. Does that one truly desire this request with all his or her heart?
4. What will the result be if I answer that prayer?
5. Is that one praying out of any ulterior motive which would result in a negative way?

Remember I do not see like you see. I know what is best. And when I release the answer, there may be a time element of delay in seeing the answer, but you have the answer in your heart. That is when faith believes it is done and you should then eat, for your life on earth is constructed in such a way that nourishment is necessary for your health and survival. Be happy and eat, knowing I have heard your prayers, and all is well.

September 30

WHERE TWO SEAS MEET

Scripture Reading — Acts 27:39-44

"And falling into a place where two seas met, they ran the ship aground; and the forepart stuck fast, and remained unmoveable, but the hinder part was broken with the violence of the waves." (Acts 27:41)

There comes a time of extreme testing to every life, every ministry. The storms of life run many vessels into perilous waters. I have seen many ministries which started out under My anointing break apart and be destroyed in the violence of the storms.

When the ship was driven against the rocks, the forepart (the bow) stuck fast and held, but the back part began to be broken into pieces.

It is not enough for the leaders of a ministry to know My will and hold fast in the storm if those who are in the back part (the followers, or the disciples) are tossed about with unbelief and rebellion.

There are many times when your vessel will sail into areas where two seas meet. These are treacherous waters. It is in such places that many ship-wrecks take place. Remember, My child, when you come to where two seas meet, that there are two mighty currents flowing in two opposite directions. These two currents work in opposition against each other. Any vessels caught in the midst are in danger of being destroyed, especially if there is violence caused by storm and wind.

You cannot, as a sailor on life's sea, always avoid these treacherous areas; your brave little ship must trust the Helmsman to navigate you safely through treacherous shoals and hidden reefs. For if you get stuck in these rocks by your strong will, the ships will be broken at the place where two seas' currents meet.

Not many understand and know My will. Let them do what they will. **You** trust Me to help you lead your crew of dedicated prisoners safely through the storms into the Fair Haven.

October 1

THE KINDNESS OF BARBARIANS

Scripture Reading — Acts 28:1-6

"And the barbarous people shewed us no little kindness: for they kindled a fire, and received us every one, because of the present rain, and because of the cold." (Acts 28:2)

"In the same quarters were possessions of the chief man of the island, whose name was Publius; who received us, and lodged us three days courteously." (vs. 7)

There is kindness in every heart. Even the Barbarians can show love and concern. They had not yet seen the miracle works which Paul did in My name on the island. But they had compassion and concern as they saw these 276 men who were washed in by the stormy waves. It was cold and raining and the men all had only the clothes which they were wearing. The people were poor. There were no homes for all these strangers. But they did what they could. They made a huge bon-fire to warm the shivering men and dry their clothing.

Paul would have had to live out in the open if I had not performed the miracle with the viper. For when the viper clung to his hand, the superstitious people thought he was an evil man who was doomed to pay for his sins. But when he suffered no harm they thought him a "god," so they lodged him with the chief man. Sometimes it takes "vipers" to prove who you are. I have many ways of showing your greatness to the people.

Thus, Paul was singled out and given a special abode where he performed the miracle of healing in My name. They lodged him and the ones who travelled with Paul courteously.

When you go to a strange place you may often feel unwelcome and maybe even unloved, but if you will begin to minister in My name, you will open the hearts of the people to Me and even Barbarians will receive you kindly. Never be afraid of the natives of the land. There is more kindness in some Barbarians than in some Christians.

October 2

HONOURED WITH MANY HONOURS

Scripture Reading — Acts 28:7-31

"Who also honoured us with many honours; and when we departed, they laded us with such things as were necessary." (Acts 28:10)

People's hearts will always be touched through the anointed ministry and their lives will be changed. It is so wonderful to see My people's hearts opened up to a spirit of generosity and love and giving to those who have blessed them through the touch of the Holy Spirit.

The people of Melita were Barbarians, but when they saw the

miracle-working power of God in operation in their lives through the ministry of My servant Paul, and when they were healed of their sicknesses, they were full of gratitude.

The thing that causes people to give to a ministry in a joyful way is not a lot of letters appealing for funds, or sad stories, or the like, but a true spirit of gratitude.

And nothing will make Barbarians or Christans more grateful than to see and feel the mighty workings of God in their lives.

You need to reach out to those who are falling off, not in a scolding, threatening way, but in a way of ministering to them in love. There is so much to disappont them and to try to rob them of their loyalty to My work. But when My people see true love and caring, their hearts are opened.

Paul needed clothes; everything had been lost at sea. So they gave to him many wonderful gifts. He had more when he boarded the ship "Castor and Pollux" three months later than he had had when he started out from Cæsaria.

Paul's heart was warmed and comforted to see this love and to know I was still using him in working miracles after all those years as a prisoner. He knew that all things worked together for good.

October 3

YOUR WORDS ARE THE KEY TO UNITY

Scripture Reading — I Corinthians 1:1-19

"Now I beseech you, brethren, by the name of our Lord Jesus Christ, that ye all speak the same thing, and that there be no divisions among you; but that ye be perfectly joined together in the same mind and in the same judgment." (I Corinthians 1:10)

My child, as you look closely at these words of wisdom, you will see that divisions come among you because of the things that you say. I said you must be careful to "speak the same thing." That means, you must be on guard to avoid getting into arguments. There is no end to troubles that have come into the world simply through words.

Words are so powerful, that if you knew how powerful they are, you would set a more diligent guard over your mouth than you would over gold and diamonds. Words are harder to guard than costly jewellery. Words are always seeking to escape from the prison of wisdom.

Many times you know that you should not say certain things, but you disregard My Holy Spirit within who gently nudges you to keep silence. And My Spirit is faithful to warn you, if you will listen to Him, because He does not want you to lose your peace and happiness. Remember "God is not the author of confusion." (I Corinthians 14:33)

As you guard your words it will promote unity among the members of your household and those with whom you live and work. This unity will lift you into positions of truth and leadership so that you can give righteous end-time judgment.

October 4

GOD CHOOSES THE FOOLISH

Scripture Reading — I Corinthians 1:20-31

"For ye see your calling, brethren, how that not many wise men after the flesh, not many mighty, not many noble, are called: But God hath chosen the foolish things of the world to confound the wise,..." (I Corinthians 1:26,27a)

Only I, your God, could speak these words to you and not anger you. If anyone else said it you would be hurt and angry. But I say it, and you accept it, because you know that I speak with love and from the viewpoint of the eternal wisdom and knowledge of all time.

Look around at what the world calls "knowledgeable, intelligent, wise and clever" and you will see that it is heavily influenced by the fruit of the tree of the knowledge of good and evil, even the satanic source of evil.

Satan was in the garden of Eden. His resting place was this tree. He tempted Eve to eat of the fruit of this tree, and when she did, she fell from the high place of purity of conscience and innocence.

The wisdom of this world is derived from this source. It looks appealing, but its source is evil and its outcome is destruction.

So seek not after the so-called "wisdom" of this world, nor the promotions and acclaims which the world can give you, but rather after the wisdom and knowledge that is born of My Spirit and is eternal because it is truth and not theory.

Man has rejected truth and substituted learning, and because of that he will never come to the knowledge of truth. I created the innocent and put them on My world at the beginning. Now, in this end-time, I take the guilty and re-create in them the innocence which they lost, through the power of My blood, the workings of My Holy Spirit in their lives, and the words which I have spoken, for they are life. Let My Spirit guide you, read the words that I have spoken, and keep your thoughts washed in My blood. If you do these things, you shall enter again the "age of innocence."

October 5

KEEP YOUR EYES ON THE LORD

Scripture Reading — I Corinthians 2:1-7

"For I determined not to know any thing among you, save Jesus Christ, and him crucified. And I was with you in weakness, and in fear, and in much trembling." (I Corinthians 2:2,3)

Abide in Me, My precious one. You will be safe here in the cleft of My rock. I will be your covering. I will watch over you, protect you and guide you all the days of your life. You are Mine.

As Paul arrived in Corinth he was attacked by Satan. He had just experienced two terrible rejections: the beatings and imprisonment in Philippi and the uproar at Thessalonica. Evil men had been hounding him as far as Berea. He had had to escape from there and after he had borne witness among the pagans on Mars Hill, who were not as vicious as the Jews (they simply mocked and ridiculed My servant), he came to Corinth in weakness, in fear and in much trembling. But I was with him.

It was in this city of Corinth that I appeared to him in a vision by night and said to him, "Be not afraid, but speak, and hold not thy peace: For I am with thee, and no man shall set on thee to hurt thee: for I have much people in this city." (Acts 18:9,10) He stayed there a year and six months teaching My Word among them. I blessed his work mightily. Many pagans believed, forsook their idols and a church was born at Corinth. From there he went to Ephesus where one of the greatest revivals of all time took place.

Why did Paul say "I determined not to know anything among you save Jesus Christ and him crucified"? Because the Corinthians were some of the most argumentive people on the face of this earth. They argued and reasoned about everything. They tried to copy the philosophers of Mars Hill. So Paul refused to enter their long, complicated discussions. He kept his eyes on Me.

You will live among all kinds of people: murmurers, fault finders, boasters, etc.. You must determine to know nothing but Me, your crucified Saviour. Keep your eyes on Me. Even when you are afraid and weak, rely on My power and presence to take over your life and your ministry.

Never rely on your ability to preach great sermons or to prove all doctrine; only rely on My presence to be with you and to work signs and wonders and miracles to bear witness to all that I am with you.

October 6

THE SPIRIT WORLD REVEALED TO US BY THE SPIRIT OF GOD

Scripture Reading — I Corinthians 2:8-16

"But as it is written, Eye hath not seen, nor ear heard, neither have entered into the heart of man, the things which God hath prepared for them that love him. But God hath revealed them unto us by his Spirit: for the Spirit searcheth all things, yea, the deep things of God." (I Corinthians 2:9,10)

My beloved one, it is only by My Holy Spirit that you can begin to know all the wonders and glories that I have prepared for you. You can never realize how important it is to be filled with My Spirit. Your being has its own spirit, which is the real "you" that I Myself created. I love it, and I never want to destroy it. I only want to perfect it. But the only way your spirit can be made perfect is by My Spirit coming inside you and influencing your spirit.

Even as your personality is influenced by those around you, so your spirit will be influenced by My Spirit within you.

And as My Spirit comes to live in you, He will open your spirit eyes to see, your spirit ears to hear and your spirit heart to perceive and accept the spiritual world that is prepared for you.

The natural man can never understand these things because the natural man is limited to the senses of the physical. But when the spiritual man within you is enlightened by My Spirit that dwells within you, you will see into the realm of eternal day. The secrets of eternity will be revealed to you. The mysteries of the glory and greatness of your God will become as real to you as your natural surroundings, for your spiritual eyes will be enlightened to see My glory, your spiritual ears will be opened to hear My voice, and your heart will be touched to receive and accept the blessings that are prepared for you.

For much is prepared for you, even since the foundation of the world; therefore hasten to enter into your inheritance by allowing My Spirit to be in full control of every faculty of your being.

October 7

THE FIRE SHALL TRY EVERY MAN'S WORK

Scripture Reading – I Corinthians 3:1-15

"Every man's work shall be made manifest: for the day shall declare it, because it shall be revealed by fire; and the fire shall try every man's work of what sort it is." (I Corinthians 3:13)

If only all My children could see and understand these important words, how differently they would build!

It is not you who will be judged on that great and terrible judgment day when all the saints come up before Me, it is your works. The sinner won't even get there.

On that day all the multitudes who have been washed in the Blood shall bring their works before Me. It is their works that will stand trial, not them.

There will be those who bring large temples, hospitals, orphanages, rest-homes, schools, whole organizations. Others will bring their office of labour, priesthood, missionary, pastorate, doctorate, evangelistic ministry, professorship, bishopric and whatever they have done, including their musical gifts, the books they have written, and on **that** day, it all shall be judged.

In the whole light of purity there will be many tragic scenes as some who have laboured a life-time will stand empty-handed when their life's work has passed through the fires of testing.

There are many who work for Me, giving their very life, but their motive is not pure. They work for fame, honour, possessions and for an earthly kingdom which they build around themselves and their families.

Only that which is done with a pure motive will pass through the fires unharmed, to the glory of God and the honour of that child of Mine who has offered it to Me.

Why do you do what you do? Is it because you love Me and have compassion on others? Is it because you feel the pain and brokenness of a cursed world and you want to help? If you were stoned and spit upon for doing what you are doing, would you still serve Me in this way? If no one saw your good works and no one praised you or was grateful, would you still do what you are doing? Do you love Me enough for that? Then your works shall stand the fire and bring honour to your life on earth.

October 8

YOU ARE GOD'S TEMPLE

Scripture Reading — I Corinthians 3:16-23

"Know ye not that ye are the temple of God, and that the Spirit of God dwelleth in you? If any man defile the temple of God, him shall God destroy; for the temple of God is holy, which temple ye are." (I Corinthians 3:16,17)

The fact that My Spirit dwells within your being is one of the greatest truths of the Christian faith. The Hindus believe there is a part of Me in every human. How much more should you, who know Me through the Holy Bible, understand the depths of this great truth and appreciate it!

The temple was the most holy thing on earth. It was received and venerated by My people. It was so holy that no pagan could enter, and even women could enter only a certain area of it.

But I have brought you, My daughter, into a full redemption, free from all curse and all bondage. Now you cannot only enter the temple, but you **are** the temple of God. I proved this on the day of Pentecost when **all** were filled with the Holy Spirit and spoke in tongues, even "the women and Mary, the mother of Jesus." (Acts 1:14)

I want you to recognize that not only you are the temple of God, but every one of My children in whom the Spirit of God dwells is the temple of God.

I call you to honour and respect these temples which I have created. Everyone is precious. To injure wilfully, to grieve or give pain to any one of these temples is a great sin which must be judged.

Every baby, from the womb (where life begins), is a temple of God. To destroy it by aborting this temple is a grievous sin which shall be judged with the crime of murder.

Honour your temple. Be appreciative of it. Keep it clean within and without. Give it the oil and bread and fragrance that it needs. But do not clutter it with any other "furnishings" than what My Word permits. The temple must have order. Cherish it and keep it clean for Me. I do not want to dwell in an unclean temple. Do not sin. My Spirit departed from the temple in Jerusalem, and He can depart from yours also. Let My Shekinah glory rest within your Holy of Holies.

October 9

STEWARDS MUST BE FAITHFUL

Scripture Reading — I Corinthians 4:1,2

"Moreover it is required in stewards, that a man be found faithful." (I Corinthians 4:2)

Faithfulness is the one pure gift that everyone can give Me. It is not only something you can do, but what I demand of all those to whom I entrust responsibility.

Sometimes the tasks and gifts which I have entrusted to you do not appear to be so important nor great. But I would have you know that no assignment is unimportant. The seemingly little tasks are as important to Me as the greater.

The rewards for faithfulness and obedience are so great that you will be astounded at the great rewards that will be given to those who do the simplest things for Me.

Reach out to accept from Me your assignment. Be glad and rejoice in all that I ask you to do. There are no rewards for those who murmur and complain. If you are faithful, you will receive a crown of life for the little tasks.

Be faithful to all responsibilities, from rising in the morning until you retire, and even in the night you will be commissioned to serve Me upon your bed by offering up prayers and praises and communing with Me. If you are faithful in the small things, I will make you ruler over many things.

October 10

RESERVE JUDGMENT TILL SHILOH COMES

Scripture Reading — I Corinthians 4:3-6; Genesis 49:10

"Therefore judge nothing before the time, until the Lord come, who both will bring to light the hidden things of darkness, and will make manifest the counsels of the hearts: and then shall every man have praise of God." (I Corinthians 4:5)

If you can just wait. That is **all** you have to do. When you have done all that you can do and tried to figure things out and understand what is happening, and still do not, then wait! Wait until I come. Everything will be clear then. You will see that I have everything under control. I have been in control all the time, even when it did not appear to be that way.

When I come, I will reveal every activity, the hidden things of darkness, secret planning, secret ambitions, secret influences and every secret work of demons. It all shall be revealed. I will manifest all the hidden "counsels of the heart," the struggles, the fears, the desires, the longings, **all**.

And then you will praise and thank Me and be glad. You will know that I did not make any mistakes. Everything went according to My plan, I turned everything around to make it work out for My glory alone. I am Shiloh, the one who comes to solve all mysteries and to bring peace and rest and order.

October 11

YOU ARE WHAT YOU ARE BY GOD'S GRACE ALONE

Scripture Reading — I Corinthians 4:7,8; II Corinthians 3:5; Matthew 25:15; John 3:27

"For who maketh thee to differ from another? and what hast thou that thou didst not receive? now if thou didst receive it, why dost thou glory, as if thou hadst not received it?" (I Corinthians 4:7)

Listen! Let Me repeat this scripture to you by paraphrasing it to make it more clear to you.

"Who made you different from anybody else? What do you possess of talents and gifts that you have not received from Me? Now, if I, your God, am the one who made you what you are, and gave you the gifts you have, why are you proud and boastful, as though you have acquired all this by your own works, and somehow earned all I have done for you?"

Yes, My child, it is true that all you are and all you have received and all you will ever be is by sheer grace.

But I not only gave you the gift of salvation and the workings of the Holy Spirit in your life, I also gave you an appointment to live for Me, to love Me and to serve Me, that My grace and My strength might be upon you for My glory alone.

You have received so much. You could not be what you are if it were not because of others. Many have paid a great price so that you can be what you are. Always be grateful to those who loved you, prayed and travailed for you, fasted for you, and spoke kindly to you, supported and sacrificed for you, stood behind and encouraged you, admonished and counselled you, and worked to make your burden lighter.

Yes, even be grateful for those who persecuted and spoke evil against you, for without them you would not be the beautiful vessel you are.

Therefore, walk humbly and gratefully. Never be proud for one moment, as though you have "made yourself," or have acquired the gifts, talents or even purification of character by your own good works. You are what you are by My grace alone. Be grateful and give it all back to Me, together with your last ounce of strength and last breath of life, so that I can use you for My glory to even a greater extent.

Never allow Satan to put one bit of pride or self-glory in your heart, not for one moment.

October 12

GOD'S END-TIME APPOINTMENTS

Scripture Reading — I Corinthians 4:9-21

"For I think that God hath set forth us the apostles last, as it were appointed to death: for we are made a spectacle unto the world, and to angels, and to men." (I Corinthians 4:9)

Paul knew he had an appointment to endure rejection, hatred, hunger and thirst, nakedness, wandering, a life without a home, work, persecution, suffering, infamy, and death! (vs. 10-13) Do you?

He knew too that he was not the only one who had this appointment. He said "God hath set forth us...we are made a spectacle unto the world, and to angels, and to men."

This appointment was not only for Paul. It is for all who are able and willing to answer the call. It is for the apostles. So many of My "apostles" think that their calling should be entirely different. They think that because of who they are and their great ministry they should never suffer for Me in any way.

But if you are an end-time apostle with an end-time calling, it must include all of these things.

Paul said, "for we are made a spectacle unto the world, and to the angels, and to men." And this was true. He was made an example for all the universe, and heaven and earth must look at Paul and see in him the example of a true apostle.

Out of My children I am calling men and women who will be end-time apostles. But remember that this is not an easy calling, nor one of pleasure. It is a calling to pain and suffering, rejection and death.

Paul wrote these strong words to the Corinthians because they had forgotten the price of the high calling of God. He had to tell it to them straight and warn them clearly because he loved them. He said "though ye have ten thousand instructers in Christ, yet have ye not many fathers: for in Christ Jesus I have begotten you through the gospel." (I Corinthians 4:15) As a spiritual mother or father you have the authority to speak strong words.

But you not only can and must speak the truth, you must remember you are called to live a life that is an example of all these things, so that people can have the grace and strength to suffer because they have seen the example of courage and strength in you. If the apostles of faith in persecuted lands today did not show the younger ones the example in suffering and courage by laying down their lives and going to prison gladly for My name's sake, there would be no Christians left in many of these countries.

October 13

"MOURN FOR ME TO TAKE HIM AWAY FROM YOU"

Scripture Reading — I Corinthians 5:1-13

"And ye are puffed up, and have not rather mourned, that he that hath done this deed might be taken away from among you." (I Corinthians 5:2)

There was one person in the church of Corinth who was being used by Satan to cause great havoc, even so great that it was bringing My righteous anger down on the ministry and splitting My holy camp; yet in spite of this terrible tragedy, they were too proud (puffed up) to recognize the sin in their midst and to humble themselves in tears and travail for Me to judge the case and do something about it.

I told them through My servant Paul that they should mourn (travail and weep) over this one who was causing the evil and the division so that he would be removed from their midst.

This is the key to cleaning out the church. If there is one in your midst who is being used of Satan to sow the seeds of rebellion and defiantly continues to sin, then it is time for the saints to mourn and travail and agonize before Me so that I will remove that one from your midst. If you try to remove him or her, it may cause a split in the camp, but if I do it, it will be done in such a way that there will be no repercussions. I will make a clean incision, take out the malignancy and sow up the wound without leaving a scar. Therefore, cry unto Me and mourn over everyone whose life is not in Divine order and who is being used of the evil one to bring sin and evil and divisions into your midst. Mourn and weep with a pure heart, and when you do, I will surely "take him away from among you." This is the way, the only way, to deal with subversion in My camp. This is what Moses did, and it never failed. (Numbers 14:5; 16:4; 20:6)

October 14

YOU CAN KEEP THE LAW BUT STILL GRIEVE THE SPIRIT

Scripture Reading – I Corinthians 6:1-12

"All things are lawful unto me, but all things are not expedient: all things are lawful for me, but I will not be brought under the power of any." (I Corinthians 6:12; compare with I Corinthians 10:23)

Others may, you cannot. There are so very many things that you are permitted to do. But they will not be for your eternal good, nor for the good of others. That is when you need to be led, not by a set and code of rules, but by My Holy Spirit.

The thing that is perfectly all right in one situation is not acceptable in another. What you can do in New York City, you cannot do in Jaipur, India, or in Johannesburg, South Africa, or in Moscow, Russia. You need to be led by My Spirit in all details of your life.

There are things which my law may authorize you to do, but under certain conditions or situations it would not be for the best. One person can do something and get away with it, still having My blessing, but another may not.

You are free to wear what you want at all times, but it is not wise to take such liberty. You are free to eat and drink what you want at all times, but it is not wise for you to disregard certain situations or conditions. The thing that is acceptable with Me may cause your brother or sister to fall. Learn to know My still, small voice so that you can always only do the thing that is expedient. You will not regret obeying My Holy Spirit or being led by Him.

Do not allow yourself to be controlled by habits or lusts of the body. It may be lawful for you to do certain things as far as My law is concerned, but if you do them, they will get control of your life and rule you. Don't ever permit habits or strong desires to have dominion and control over your life.

Anything that is not controlled by My Holy Spirit or under the guidance of My Holy Spirit is not expedient for you to do. Live in My Spirit and you will never fail to do the right things; otherwise you may not break the law, but you will grieve the Spirit.

October 15

A BEAUTIFUL SPIRIT GLORIFIES GOD

Scripture Reading — I Corinthians 6:13-20

"For ye are bought with a price: therefore glorify God in your body, and in your spirit, which are God's." (I Corinthians 6:20)

Man sees your body, but in the spirit world everyone sees your spirit. It is possible to dress perfectly for every occasion, eat the perfect dietary foods, abstain from drinking that which is harmful or sinful, wear your hair in a fashion that is acceptable and do all things correctly outwardly, even obeying the slightest order, and yet be crippled in the spirit.

What use is it if everyone on earth admires you and thinks what a great child of Mine you are, with wonderful talents and gifts, Christian graces and poise, but underneath you are not what you appear to be on the outside.

You may preach wonderful messages, sing like an angel, teach like a scribe, but if your spirit does not glorify Me, you are two people, one on the outside, and one on the inside. This will destroy you and it will grieve Me.

I call you to perfection. Let your body be in shape physically. To the best of your ability bring it into subjection, but also bring your spirit into the subjection of the Holy Spirit, that it may have a graceful and advanced acceptance into the courts of the saints; for there it will not matter how beautiful or well-formed your body is. It will only matter how beautiful in character your spirit, the real you, is.

Today, as you go about your day's activities, let your spirit glorify Me with joy, peace, love, gentleness, kindness and thoughtfulness to others. When you have left this place, it is not your body that will be remembered, but your spirit.

October 16

EVERYTHING LASTS ONLY A LITTLE WHILE

Scripture Reading — I Corinthians 7:1-40

"But this I say, brethren, the time is short: it remaineth, that both they that have wives be as though they had none; And they that weep, as though they wept not; and they that rejoice, as though they rejoiced not; and they that buy, as though they possessed not; And they that use this world, as not abusing it: for the fashion of this world passeth away." (I Corinthians 7:29-31)

You are living in a changing world with circumstances changing daily. Surely you see this as you travel around. Many of those who were married the last time you were there, are lonely widows and widowers now. Many of those who had a mother or father whom they loved have had to say good-bye to their beloved parents as death came to claim that one.

Some whose hearts were lonely and broken and without hope are full of joy and peace and comfort now, with even greater blessings to come as they come closer every day to heaven's shore.

Everything around you and in your own life is due for a change.

Thank Me for every day that you can have the joy of companionship with your dearest friends and loved ones. Tomorrow they will all leave you.

Look at the museums. All those things were owned by someone. Clothes were worn with pride by ladies of the court, swords were proudly displayed by soldiers and princes to their friends. Who owns these things now? Certainly not the man or woman who purchased them. And the beautiful homes and palaces, they too were possessed by their owners for such a short while.

That is why I tell you to use this world and the things of this world, but don't let these things possess or control your life. Even the wife who is so possessive of her husband and the man who dominates and abuses his wife, I say to them all they only have this power for a short while.

To you who are suffering I say, take courage—you will not weep forever—soon you will rejoice. Everything is always changing. Never hang on to anything, not even today's broken heart and disappointment, for tomorrow you will again sing for joy.

October 17

PUFFED UP OR BEAUTIFUL?

Scripture Reading – I Corinthians 8:1-13

"Now as touching things offered unto idols, we know that we all have knowledge. Knowledge puffeth up, but charity edifieth. And if any man think that he knoweth any thing, he knoweth nothing yet as he ought to know." (I Corinthians 8:1,2)

Everything that is puffed up will one day be deflated. The greatest knowledge and wisdom of yesterday seems as kindergarten knowledge today. The great inventions and theories of today will seem as child's knowledge when you come into the abode of the all-knowing realm of the redeemed saints and angels.

For a while the greatest of earth knowledge seems so important, so essential, but the highest degrees of learning that the schools of earth can give you all amount to one grain of knowledge when compared to My infinite wisdom and knowledge. I look down on earth as humans are struggling in their halls of learning for a little more of earth's man-conceived knowledge and limited discoveries, and I pity them all. They strive so hard to attain a goal which tomorrow will be discarded as an old shoe.

The thing to strive for, which is eternal, is love. It does not just enter the brain; it enters the soul and beautifies it. That is what "edification" means, "to beautify."

Do not strive after the knowledge of the world, but rather after the beauty and durability of love. It is greater to be beautiful than to be puffed up.

October 18

ALL THINGS TO ALL MEN

Scripture Reading – I Corinthians 9:1-27

"To the weak became I as weak, that I might gain the weak: I am made all things to all men, that I might by all means save some." (I Corinthians 9:22)

To be able to adapt yourself to a situation is a very precious characteristic. Forget your nationality and customs when I send you to a nation. Lose your old identity. Try to fit in with the people so that you can become like them and walk in their shoes.

The key to greatness is not being different, it is identity. When I wanted to touch the world, I did not come to it as God, I came as "the son of man." It was only as I took upon Myself the identity of the human race that I was able to reach the heart of mankind.

So also I ask you to fit in with those to whom I call you. To the children be like a child, to the intellectual speak words of wisdom, to the traveller reminisce about the sights you have seen, to the Jew share your love for Israel, to the Arab remember them as children of Hagar, to the Hindu respect their reverence and zeal for religion. To the Chinese, the American, the city man or farmer, be what they can understand. And you will understand them also.

As you find others in the spirit, you can become all things to all men. It will help you to help them. They will receive you and you will reach them even as I reached them and brought them up to My level. It is in adapting yourself to their level that you can raise them to yours.

October 19

HOW TO ESCAPE TEMPTATION

Scripture Reading – I Corinthians 10:1-33

"There hath no temptation taken you but such as is common to man: but God is faithful, who will not suffer you to be tempted above that ye are able; but will with the temptation also make a way to escape, that ye may be able to bear it." (I Corinthians 10:13)

Everyone has to endure temptation. As long as you are in this world where Satan is the prince of the evil power and has charge over demonic activity, there will be many temptations put before you. You will be tempted in the same way as the Children of Israel were in the wilderness and as I was when I fasted forty days. It is not sinful to be tempted. But you do not need to fall. I call you to victory and not to defeat.

When Satan comes to tempt you and to discourage you, be not afraid or discouraged. I will be standing right there beside you to help you. Only turn to Me. There is a way to escape all temptation. I will take your hand and lead you from it. One of the great secrets of overcoming temptation is to flee from it. Do not try to endure it or fight your way through it. It is better to escape it, avoid it and turn away from it. I promised you I would "make a way of escape."

Guard your eyes. Much temptation comes through the eye gate. Put a watch over your mouth and take heed to what you hear and think. By being careful, you will escape much temptation.

October 20

SHOW YOUR APPRECIATION

Scripture Reading – I Corinthians 11:1-22

"Now I praise you, brethren, that ye remember me in all things, and keep the ordinances, as I delivered them to you." (I Corinthians 11:2)

It is a good thing to commend others for the good things they do. Commendation and praise is an encouragement to do even better.

Do not be afraid of making people proud or less diligent just because you praise them. Many of My children think that praise is false flattery. This is not true. It is an expression of recognition, gratitude and appreciation. If you praise others you will find it easier to praise Me.

Why don't you think right now of those who deserve your praise and start to show your appreciation to them? Don't only be appreciative of what people do for you, be grateful also for what they do for others. Give honour to whom honour is due. (Romans 13:7)

Paul praised the people of Corinth for two reasons. One: they remembered Paul. Always be grateful if you are not forgotten. Two: they kept the ordinances Paul had given them. Always be thankful when people are obedient and respectful to you for what you teach them and how you train them.

Give someone a word of praise and encouragement today. Let them know you see what they have done and that you appreciate it.

October 21

WHEN YOU ARE BETRAYED

Scripture Reading — I Corinthians 11:23,24

"For I have received of the Lord that which also I delivered unto you, That the Lord Jesus the same night in which he was betrayed took bread:" (I Corinthians 11:23)

When you are betrayed by those whom you call friends it is a dark night of your life. There is nothing that hurts more than being betrayed by someone who is close to you, someone who has called himself your friend, who has helped to carry your burden and shared the secrets of your soul.

But don't give up in this dark hour. Take courage, My beloved child. The secret of your strength to carry on is in this same verse. "Take bread." When your spirit is so crushed and the pain is overwhelming (for nothing hurts more than to be betrayed by a friend), "take bread."

It is only as you eat the bread of life, even My body which is broken for you, that you can receive strength to carry on. Join with Me in the Holy Communion of being broken as I was broken. Partake of My sufferings. Enter into the secret of My riven side and when you are torn and broken let My blood flow over your wounds and wash them clean so they will not fester and bring blood-poisoning to your soul.

Read My Word, not just with your head, but with your soul, and let My Spirit's life, which is in My Word, enter the deepest recesses of your being.

Paul said, "I received this truth from the Lord, and I have now delivered it unto you." Paul was often betrayed by those who were the closest to him. (Who was closer than Barnabas?) Paul received by impartation this truth and this healing and he passed it on to you. Now it is yours. In this dark night of your soul, eat My body, drink My blood.

"Then Jesus said unto them, Verily, verily, I say unto you, Except ye eat the flesh of the Son of man, and drink his blood, ye have no life in you. Whoso eateth my flesh and drinketh my blood, hath eternal life; and I will raise him up at the last day. For my flesh is meat indeed, and my blood is drink indeed. He that eateth my flesh and drinketh my blood, dwelleth in me, and I in him. As the living Father hath sent me, and I live by the Father: so he that eateth me, even he shall live by me." (John 6:53-57)

October 22

KNOW WHAT GOD WANTS YOU TO POSSESS

Scripture Reading – I Corinthians 12:1-11

"Now concerning spiritual gifts, brethren, I would not have you ignorant." (I Corinthians 12:1)

It is true, My child, that I want you to know the truth about the blessings and gifts that I have laid up for you.

I want you to have all the gifts and ministries that are possible for you to have. I want to freely give you all these precious gifts. It is not good to be ignorant concerning the gifts of the Spirit. How can you be at your best for Me in spiritual things if you do not know anything about them?

Many of My children are very ignorant about the gifts of the Spirit. All they know about is salvation. How can you grow into spiritual maturity if you do not understand the truths concerning My Spirit?

That is why My church never attains unto its full power. It is a church which does not possess its gifts. The church is like a bride who has received many beautiful wedding gifts but has never opened them to see what they are. She is walking about in unpressed garments because she does not know she has an iron. She never wears her bangles and jewels because she has never unwrapped them. And many other precious and useful gifts lie still in these wrappings.

Many precious gifts of the Spirit lie dormant because My ignorant bride is led by ignorant teachers. Satan has deceived them into thinking that ignorance is a sign of humility.

Stir up your soul to know and understand the workings of the Holy Spirit. And then believe Me for these gifts to operate in your life, that you might be a fruitful bride possessing all the gifts of the Holy Spirit in your life. My gifts for you are not all stored up for you in heaven. They are available for you right here on earth. Possess your possessions.

October 23

WE ARE ONE BODY

Scripture Reading — I Corinthians 12:12-31

"For by one Spirit are we all baptized into one body, whether we be Jews or Gentiles, whether we be bond or free;...But now are they many members, yet but one body. And the eye cannot say unto the hand, I have no need of thee: nor again the head to the feet, I have no need of you. Nay, much more those members of the body, which seem to be more feeble, are necessary: " (I Corinthians 12:13a,20-22)

You need each other. It saddens Me to see My children act as though they were self-sufficient. Don't be ashamed to reach out a hand for support or call for someone to help you. There is always someone who is waiting to do just that.

Neither should you think yourself better or more important than any other of My children who seem slower or less enthusiastic. That one who is groping for the way and looking for truth is as much a part of the body as you are.

I do not have two bodies, one Jewish and one Gentile, one Catholic and one Protestant, one white and one coloured. You are all equal in My sight. The one you look down on may be more precious and advanced in My Kingdom than the one you think is of great importance. See everyone as a part of the same body to which you belong. If one is injured, the pain of the injury should affect each of you.

Each member of the body is unique in that it has its own individual function. You cannot hold the pen with your nose or walk on your head or think with your liver. Some of the most important members of the body are the ones you do not see: the heart, the lungs, the stomach, etc. In fact, you **can** live without hands and feet and legs or arms, but not without the heart, and this is true of other parts.

Then there is the blood which is only seen when there is injury and suffering. This is like some of My children who live hidden and quiet lives, but as soon as there is suffering, they are there to give protection and help.

The Jews and Gentiles did not love each other. There was a great division in the early church. At times the situation became absolutely explosive and it grieved Me greatly. That is why Paul explained to them that they were one body, and must live in unity.

As you live in unity with others you help to make My body not only strong, but also beautiful. Even as the blood flows through every part of your being bringing life to all members of your body, so My blood flows through the different members of My body, even unto the tips of the fingers and the farthest extremities of the limbs.

October 24

LOVE IS GREATER THAN ALL

Scripture Reading — I Corinthians 13:1-3

"Though I speak with the tongues of men and of angels, and have not charity, I am become as sounding brass, or a tinkling cymbal. And though I have the gift of prophecy, and understand all mysteries, and all knowledge; and though I have all faith, so that I could remove mountains, and have not charity, I am nothing." (I Corinthians 13:1-3)

Talents, the gifts of the Spirit, mountain-moving faith, philanthropic giving and even martyrdom are all external things. The motive behind the operating of anyone of them can be a selfish one.

No one was a greater orator than Hitler. He swayed the masses. Even the clergy was convinced that he was "a man sent from God."

Gifts of the Spirit are given to man in the hour of his greatness, but when his own spirit becomes greedy and proud, he can still operate them to the very destruction of his soul. Because the "gifts and the callings of God are without repentance." (Romans 11:29)

The same is true of mountain-moving faith. What good is it to operate faith if faith will destroy your own soul? I said of Israel, I gave them the desire of their hearts but I sent leanness to their soul. (Psalm 106:15)

As for the giving of wealth, you can give to devils and demons. Many spend fortunes building temples to them. Others of My people give so that it be seen and they receive the praises of men, or they have a project of their own imagination which they feel compelled to support financially.

And then there is the one who dies for his cause. It may not even be My cause. Forced hunger strikes, suicide squads, terrorist raids, all these too give their lives for a "cause," but in doing so they have no motive of love.

And then, there is the one whom no one sees or notices, but who loves with that powerful, silent love. Whose every whisper is weighed with love, whose every act is born of the Spirit, who believes in Me for the good of others, who gives of his very living and who gladly lays down his life out of his love for others and for Me. This latter one is a saint and shall indeed be honoured in the court of heaven.

Love, love, love and it will grace every act you perform.

October 25

WHAT LOVE IS

Scripture Reading — I Corinthians 13:4-7

"Charity suffereth long, and is kind; charity envieth not; charity vaunteth not itself, is not puffed up, Doth not behave itself unseemly, seeketh not her own, is not easily provoked, thinketh no evil; Rejoiceth not in iniquity, but rejoiceth in the truth; Beareth all things, believeth all things, hopeth all things, endureth all things." (I Corinthians 13:4-7)

Willingness to suffer, kindness, humility, modesty, generosity, not being boastful, envious nor easily upset, having sorrow for sinners, love for truth, faith for all situations, endurance, hope, love for the truth, kind thoughts for others, a willingness to bear burdens, always abiding faithful, these are the virtues of true love.

Unless you have these qualities do not think too highly of yourself. A warm feeling for someone, a physical attraction, comradeship is not love. Love is much more than all of these. It is an overwhelming force lying resident in the heart even when everything works against it, rejects it, and even ridicules it.

True love is not conditional on circumstances. You need never work yourself up to love. It is a force which flows from My heart to yours and then from your heart to others. It carries its own strength to endure and to function in all situations.

My love for you has all of these great virtues. As you meditate upon these things, you will understand the greatness of the love that is available for you to possess for others. Why should you settle for less than the greatest, when you can possess this glorious heavenly virtue in its perfection, now? This is the way you will love in eternity, but the rewards are given for how you love now, and not how you will love when your spirit does not live in an imperfect atmosphere. It is here that you must be perfected in love. Reach out for it. It is yours.

October 26

WHEN WILL THE GIFTS OF THE SPIRIT BE OUTDATED

Scripture Reading — I Corinthians 13:8-13

"Charity never faileth: but whether there be prophecies, they shall fail; whether there be tongues, they shall cease; whether there be knowledge, it shall vanish away. For we know in part, and we prophesy in part. But when that which is perfect is come, then that which is in part shall be done away. When I was a child, I spake as a child, I understood as a child, I thought as a child: but when I became a man, I put away childish things. For now we see through a glass, darkly; but then face to face: now I know in part; but then shall I know even as also I am known. And now abideth faith, hope, charity, these three; but the greatest of these is charity." (I Corinthians 13:8-13)

Prophecies shall fail (stop), tongues shall stop, knowledge (as you know it) shall be outdated by advanced knowledge.

Everything you have and know is but an earnest of the inheritance. The greatest of man's knowledge is but a "drop of water from an ocean" when compared to the infinite knowledge that shall one day be yours.

When you prophesy, at best you can only prophesy in part, for although what you say may be "right on," there still is limitation in prophecy, for in no way can you prophesy over every living soul. And besides that, not all can receive it.

When you come into perfection, then you shall be as I am, knowing all things. And when everyone has reached this stage of development, what will be the use of prophecy? It will be useless in heaven. And when everyone speaks the same language of Beulah land, what will be the use of tongues then? Tongues are for a sign to those who do not believe. (I Corinthians 14:22) In the Kingdom there will be no unbelievers. Moreover, praying in tongues edifies yourself and prophecy edifies the church, but in heaven all shall be edified by the glory of God, for My Divine presence shall permeate all. What need will there be for gifts that were given for your earthly journey? Once you have arrived at the end of your journey, you can lay aside your "travelling aids."

You are still a child, but you are growing up and I challenge you to put away all those childish tricks and cute ways and all immature conduct. I want to bring you into spiritual maturity.

That does not mean you should stop prophesying or speaking in tongues, but it does mean that all prophecy and tongues will fall flat if you live an immature Christian life, and especially if you have no love!

You do not know half of what is awaiting you. At best you see it through a "smoked" window. But one day I shall draw aside the darkened glass. And then you shall see that the greatest thing in all your life is not gifts, but love.

October 27

DESIRE SPIRITUAL GIFTS ONLY TO BLESS OTHERS

Scripture Reading — I Corinthians 14:1-19

"Follow after charity, and desire spiritual gifts,...Even so ye, forasmuch as ye are zealous of spiritual gifts, seek that ye may excel to the edifying of the church." (I Corinthians 14:1a,12)

My child, in all things you should put others first and yourself last. Even in the kind of gifts that you desire My Holy Spirit to impart to you, be careful never to ask for something for self.

Let your love for others be so great that every motive and desire you have is only for the blessing and edification of others. Let My Spirit reach a lost and dying world through you.

Push your own critical spirit into the background and let your soul be permeated with My love and grace.

Never desire the gifts of the Spirit for any selfish reason, rather desire the gifts only so that others will be blessed.

Use these gifts only for the sake of others. Never "show off" the gifts of the Spirit. Unless you can bless others, be silent even in the church.

October 28

LET HIM BE IGNORANT

Scripture Reading – I Corinthians 14:20-39

"But if any man be ignorant, let him be ignorant." (I Corinthians 14:38)

My child, there are times when you have to stop "pushing" people. You can admonish and warn and teach and counsel and plead with people, but the end result will be a deaf ear. Some people don't want to know the truth. They prefer to believe a lie because then they can continue in their way of rebellion and self-will.

When this happens, there is nothing that either you or I can do with that person. Everyone is a free moral agent. I will not force anyone to do anything which they are not willing to do.

If you try to help that one who stubbornly refuses to be helped, you will become frustrated and grieved in spirit. Take your hands off. You have done what you could do. You counselled, admonished, prayed and grieved. Now, let that one continue in his self-inflicted ignorance.

There are times when I have dealt with you, admonished and warned you, but you have continued in your own wilful way, disregarding My warnings to you. Yet I have not forsaken you. I still love you. I still continue to bless you and use you and guide you. I have not turned My face from you because of your ignorance. So, you too continue to love that one who persists in their ignorant way. But don't try to change them. Let time and suffering teach them.

> Wait for My Spirit to speak to each soul;
> He knows each man's need, and what to do;
> Leave them with Him, if your voice they won't heed;
> The work of the Spirit is faithful and true.

October 29

"I DIE DAILY"

Scripture Reading — I Corinthians 15:1-31

"...I die daily." (I Corinthians 15:31)

There are different kinds of death.

1. There is that dying to the world and the things of the world.

2. There is that experience of being crucified with Me, where the old man in you lives no more. Your angers, lusts and all wrong passions that rule you have been crucified with Me and buried in baptism.

3. There is the actual physical death, when your spirit leaves the tabernacle wherein it has dwelt and the body is laid to rest.

4. There is the eternal death of the soul that has rejected salvation.

5. And then there is this death that Paul spoke about when he said, "I die daily."

This is an experience that is given only to those who are willing to follow all the way to Calvary. It is that painful experience that you go through every day when you are put to grief by others, and when you suffer because you see your own wretchedness and weakness.

To live the crucified life is not easy for the flesh. The old "you" does not want to submit to the victorious Christ within. The pains and sufferings you go through help to enable you to die daily.

Do not grieve because of your suffering. I allow a certain measure of pain every day to help you to die daily, that you might be raised in My glory.

October 30

CHANGED FROM EARTHY TO HEAVENLY

Scripture Reading — I Corinthians 15:32-56

"And as we have borne the image of the earthy, we shall also bear the image of the heavenly." (I Corinthians 15:49)

You inherited your natural body and physical life from your natural forefather, Adam. You received your spiritual life from Me, your second Adam. I am your spiritual life. From Adam you received your earthy inheritance with all its traits of good and evil. From Me you received your spiritual life. I birthed your born-again spirit through the travail of My suffering at Calvary. Adam's physical body resembled yours. You are your father's son, your mother Eve's daughter. You inherited your hair, eyes, smile, walk, measurements, shape and form from them, and not from some kind of monkey.

Now, not all that you received from Adam is good. Some is sinful, weak and rebellious. But I suffered travail to re-birth you and give you spiritual life, even the kind of spiritual life which is in My likeness.

As you die daily, your spirit is "sown" in its old dishonourable condition to be raised afresh in My glory. (vs. 43) Even as the earthy in you dies out, the heavenly is given birth.

From the days of your natural birth you have borne the likeness of your earthy parents, but as you pass through the daily dying experience you can become more and more like your spiritual Father. I have given you My eternal life, My peace and joy, glory and beauty. The "you" you see in the mirror now is not the eternally glorious person you shall yet be as you let Me work in you the daily dying experience.

Sown in dishonour and raised in glory, sown in weakness, raised in power, sown in the natural to be raised spiritually, sown corruptible, raised incorruptible, sown mortal, raised immortal, sown earthy, born heavenly.

"Behold, I shew you a mystery; We shall not all sleep, but we shall all be changed, In a moment, in the twinkling of an eye, at the last trump: for the trumpet shall sound, and the dead shall be raised incorruptible, and we shall be changed." (vs. 51,52) Await the sounding of the last trumpet; it is happening very soon now.

And this you know that, whether by the door of translation or the grave, you shall be changed into My likeness. This takes out the sting of death and the grave loses its power to hold the body of My righteous child.

October 31

KEEP ON; IT'S NOT IN VAIN

Scripture Reading — I Corinthians 15:57-58

"Therefore, my beloved brethren, be ye stedfast, unmoveable, always abounding in the work of the Lord, forasmuch as ye know that your labour is not in vain in the Lord." (I Corinthians 15:58)

This scripture has encouraged My servants and handmaidens more than any other. I have seen sheer strength and grace flow into their hearts many times as they have meditated on these words.

There have been many times in your own life too, My child, when you were so weary and under such attack of the evil one that you were ready to give up. Even now, when you see the complaining and disgruntled spirit that there is in man, you despair of doing anything more to bless and to help them. Very few really appreciate or are grateful to you for what you have done. Out of thirty, you do well if three will stop to say thank you before rushing on to do their own thing. Remember, only one out of ten lepers returned to thank Me for cleansing and healing them. And if they would not be grateful for such a great miracle, how do you expect anyone to appreciate what you have done for them?

Therefore, a man or woman who forsakes or regrets their high calling to please a lover or husband or wife or child or parents, is foolish. For in the end that one who was the hindrance will not be grateful for all the sacrifices that have been made for him, whereas the souls that were saved through your dedicated life will rejoice with you through eternity. And your greatest joy will be when they say, "I am in heaven because of you."

It is then that you will fully realize that your labour was not in vain by My standards. You will rejoice for every sacrifice you made. So do it all for Me. For then you will have eternal appreciation. Do not be discouraged. Continue what you are doing to help and train others. Be steadfast, unmovable from the goal of the high calling of God in Christ Jesus, always knowing that as you continue to serve Me in spite of all obstacles and discouragements, you are pleasing Me, and it is from Me alone you will receive your reward.

November 1

A GREAT DOOR AND MANY ADVERSARIES

Scripture Reading – I Corinthians 16:1-9

"For a great door and effectual is opened unto me, and there are many adversaries." (I Corinthians 16:9)

My beloved child, a closed door does not always mean that it is not My will or that I have another plan. It can mean that Satan is using his ways of keeping you from doing My will.

Do not give up as soon as you see a closed door. Believe Me to perform a miracle and open it up for you.

For all those who are called to do great things for Me there will always be many adversaries. The greater the door and the more effective your ministry is, the more you will face strong and evil adversaries who will do all in their power to upset and discourage you, so that you will give up.

My desire for you is to open great doors of ministry for you where your life will have a great affect on many others. I want you to light many candles in many dark places of the world.

Remember that if I have a plan for your life and you are willing at all costs to do My will, there is no impossible situation with Me. I will remove the most powerful and evil adversaries. I will render them helpless so that you will be given strength and grace to fulfil all My will with great joy and complete victory.

November 2

PLAY THE MAN!

Scripture Reading — I Corinthians 16:11-14

"Watch ye, stand fast in the faith, quit you like men, be strong. Let all your things be done with charity." (I Corinthians 16:13,14)

"Quit you like men!" What a challenge! As King David prepared to leave this world he gave his son Solomon the same charge, "shew thyself a man." "I go the way of all the earth: be thou strong therefore, and shew thyself a man;" (I Kings 2:2)

And then he goes on to tell him, how and in what way. "And keep the charge of the Lord thy God, to walk in his ways, to keep his statutes, and his commandments, and his judgments, and his testimonies, as it is written in the law of Moses, that thou mayest prosper in all that thou doest, and whithersoever thou turnest thyself:" (vs. 3)

There is no other way that you can be strong and show yourself a man! It is the secret of all strength. You are no stronger than the amount to which you are willing to obey Me and do the works which I command of you in My Holy Word.

"Watch ye!" Any soldier who is not alert is not worthy of his calling to be a soldier.

"Stand fast in the faith!" A soldier must have faith in the commands of the soldier who is his commanding officer.

"Quit you like men!" General William Booth, My soldier of the Salvation Army said, "My best men are women." A woman can have as great courage as a man.

"Be strong!" In My strength alone!

"Let all things be done in charity." Love is the power of your strength. The more you love, the stronger you are.

November 3

ADDICTED TO HOSPITALITY!

Scripture Reading – I Corinthians 16:15-24

"I beseech you, brethren, (ye know the house of Stephanas, that it is the firstfruits of Achaia, and that they have addicted themselves to the ministry of the saints,)...I am glad of the coming of Stephanas and Fortunatus and Achaicus: for that which was lacking on your part they have supplied. For they have refreshed my spirit and yours: therefore acknowledge ye them that are such." (I Corinthians 16:15,17,18)

"They have addicted themselves to the ministry of the saints." What wonderful words Paul could say about the house of Stephanas! But this would not have been possible without the open-heartedness of the women and their willingness to serve.

It is usually the women who make a home comfortable to be in and give it an air of hospitality. Besides, they have to do all the hard work of preparing meals and extra washing of bed linens and caring for their guest.

This is a calling. It is a character. "To be addicted" means it wasn't something they did now and then, but always. They loved to open their home to My servants. Everyone who came there felt at home, loved, wanted and a little bit spoiled.

I want you to become "addicted to the ministry of the saints." Let your home always be like the house of Stephanas and your heart like theirs. They were the first-fruits of Achaia. Sometimes it is not in the great things you do that you become a part of the first-fruits company, but in the seemingly small things. They also were generous of heart, giving where others could not give.

They refreshed the spirit of Paul. This is a beautiful gift of grace. Anyone can have it. You do not need to be rich or have a home where you can receive others, to be able to refresh another person's spirit. You only need to be refreshed yourself in My presence and take that refreshing with you to refresh the lives of those whom you meet. Do it today. Do it all day long. Be like water sprinkled on the wilting flowers.

November 4

COMFORTED TO COMFORT OTHERS

Scripture Reading – II Corinthians 1:1-24

"Blessed be God, even the Father of our Lord Jesus Christ, the Father of mercies, and the God of all comfort; Who comforteth us in all our tribulation, that we may be able to comfort them which are in any trouble, by the comfort wherewith we ourselves are comforted of God." (II Corinthians 1:3,4)

My Father is the Father of mercies and the God of all comfort. He does not delight to see you suffering, but He allows it so that your heart will be enlarged and you will be able to comfort others through experiencing His comfort.

He will comfort you in all tribulation. There is not a single tribulation experience where He will not comfort you. There are no heart breaks so great for Him that He cannot comfort and no hurts so deep that He cannot heal that inner tearing and rending. He even can lighten the blows and the shocks of betrayal which you have endured and He will dim the memory of them so that you can more easily forgive your enemies and your unfaithful friends.

Every experience My Father permitted Me to pass through was for My good and yours. Now, in your hour of suffering and betrayal you can be comforted. For as you look to Me, I am able to comfort and strengthen and help you. I too was betrayed by My close companions and wounded in the house of My friends. (Zechariah 13:6) The religious advisers and leaders deemed it necessary to put Me to death, calling Me many evil names, a blasphemer (Matthew 9:3), a seducer and an anarchist (John 19:12) who committed treason against the government. I accepted My cup of suffering, and My Father comforted Me so that I could comfort you in all of your suffering. Now, receive My comfort and go and comfort and understand others who suffer.

> Accept your cup of suffering
> From your Father's hand above,
> He knows just what is best for you,
> And He gives it with His love.

November 5

DON'T KEEP YOUR HEAVY SPIRIT

Scripture Reading – II Corinthians 2:1-5

"But I determined this with myself, that I would not come again to you in heaviness." (II Corinthians 2:1)

A continuously heavy spirit is very oppressing. I want you to keep balance in yourself. There are times when you will be so deeply hurt and grieved that you will feel as though you can never smile again. And there will be times when you will need to deal with a difficult and bad situation with all sobriety and sternness. (Sternness is not hardness.) Sin has to be dealt with in a firm way, but not only in a firm way, also with a broken heart.

Paul's heart was broken because of the sin in the camp. But when he had dealt with it firmly, he had the grace to lay it aside and go on in a positive and cheerful way.

Don't keep on mourning and feeling sad about that thing that broke your heart. Leave it with Me. When I was on earth, I told the people, "Be not of a sad countenance." (Matthew 6:16)

There are times when you will feel My grief and sorrow for a world of sin and suffering. You will weep like I wept at Lazarus' tomb. (John 11:34,35)

But there is so much pain and sorrow in many lives that your heavy spirit will only add to the weight of grief which others are already struggling under. "Heaviness in the heart of man maketh it stoop: but a good word maketh it glad." (Proverbs 12:25) I want you to spread cheer and joy. The last gift I gave My disciples was My joy. Joy is not determined by circumstances. You can have true joy in the midst of sorrow and difficulty. Reach out to Me for this joy. Give it to others. A continuously heavy spirit will make you so miserable no one will want to be with you. Cast it from you. Remember, I have given you "...beauty for ashes, the oil of joy for mourning, the garment of praise for the spirit of heaviness; that they might be called trees of righteousness, the planting of the Lord, that he might be glorified." (Isaiah 61:3)

November 6

FORGIVE, AND SATAN WILL BE DEFEATED

Scripture Reading — II Corinthians 2:6-11

"To whom ye forgive any thing, I forgive also: for if I forgave any thing, to whom I forgave it, for your sakes forgave I it in the person of Christ; Lest Satan should get an advantage of us: for we are not ignorant of his devices." (II Corinthians 2:10,11)

Paul wanted to test the believers in obedience. They were his spiritual children. He had a right to test their loyalty and obedience to him. He knew that if they would not obey him it was because they did not trust him and without this trust he could do nothing further to lead them. They were his sheep and he was their shepherd. Without trust and obedience you have mutiny on board. That is very dangerous. But they did obey Paul and dealt with the sin in the camp. I honoured them for this.

Paul had dealt severely with the sinful offender for their sake, and when the thing was corrected he was ready to forgive the man also because he was only grieved for their sake and he forgave for their sake. He did this for My sake.

There is greater power in forgiveness than in accusation. There is greater power in forgiveness than in all sin. Sin loses its sting to harm you when you forgive. Offences are cancelled when you forgive. Forgiveness is the greatest act of love which you can perform.

I have not only called you to teach love but to be love. This will demand forgiveness of all those who slander, disobey and wrongly accuse you. Don't say you cannot rise to those great heights. You can in Me; like Paul said, "I forgive in the person of Christ." It is in Me that you forgive. Hide in Me! Others of My great servants have been tried as you are and have overcome. Let neither praise nor criticism move you.

Remember Satan works by two ways, praise and criticism. If he cannot make you puffed up and proud, he will criticize you and try to destroy you.

To discern Satan's wiles you must live in My holy presence; otherwise you will fall victim of his wiles.

When you forgive you take the poison out of the viper's sting. If you don't forgive, the poison will enter your blood stream and it will kill you eventually. Many of My choice servants died that way. "And when ye stand praying, forgive,..." (Mark 11:25a)

November 7

A RESTLESS SPIRIT HINDERS THE SERVANT OF GOD

Scripture Reading – II Corinthians 2:12-13

"Furthermore, when I came to Troas to preach Christ's gospel, and a door was opened unto me of the Lord, I had no rest in my spirit, because I found not Titus my brother: but taking my leave of them, I went from thence into Macedonia." (II Corinthians 2:12,13)

Although Paul had My call upon his life to preach the glorious Gospel, and a door was open for him to minister in Troas, still he was hindered by his own restless and anxious spirit.

Satan would try to make your spirit anxious and restless so that you are not able to be at your best for Me. He always magnifies every situation and creates a tense and distrustful atmosphere. It is a common tactic of his to use people as a decoy so that you waste your time beating the air and fighting against imaginary enemies.

Titus was in My care. He was safe with Me. But Paul was overly anxious. You too must trust your brothers and sisters into My care. I am as close to that one who is absent from you as I am to you. My eye is on that one even now.

I have an important work for you to do. Why do you let Satan distract you from that which is of primary importance? Many souls were lost because Paul did not stay in Troas when the door was open to him.

The devil would have you lose out in winning those souls that I want you to reap. Forget about your Titus now; go back to preaching My Gospel.

November 8

CALLED TO TRIUMPH

Scripture Reading — II Corinthians 2:14-17

"Now thanks be unto God, which always causeth us to triumph in Christ, and maketh manifest the savour of his knowledge by us in every place. For we are unto God a sweet savour of Christ, in them that are saved, and in them that perish:" (II Corinthians 2:14,15)

You are called to triumph not in your own strength, but in Mine. I never failed to rise above every situation. Even as I triumphed over every demon and devil and death, so I give to you the victory which overcomes the world and all evil.

It is in the sweetness of My love alone that you can triumph, for every evil is grounded in hate. But as you let My perfect love flow through you, you will become a sweet fragrance in this love. I anoint you this morning to love and to forgive. Not just those who are easy to forgive, but those who crucify you and hang you on the cross.

Let this perfumed fragrance be upon you in such a way that all people, saved and perishing, will smell it today. Leave My fragrance which I give to you in the anointing oil waft out to all, whether they be good or evil.

November 9

NOT ALL CAN LOOK AT THE GLORY

Scripture Reading — II Corinthians 3:1-16

"But if the ministration of death, written and engraven in stones, was glorious, so that the children of Israel could not stedfastly behold the face of Moses for the glory of his countenance; which glory was to be done away: How shall not the ministration of the spirit be rather glorious?" (II Corinthians 3:7,8)

Let no one rob you of your glory. It is possible to lose it because of vexation of the soul. Moses lost it for only a little while and the terrible consequences were that he could not enter the Land of

Promise. All who lose My glory will never be able to get into the realm of the promises of God. They will be a skeleton of what they could be.

If Moses could have so much glory when he was only dealing with a covenant that was transitory, think how much glory you are capable of having in these days of grace in My Kingdom.

Moses put a veil over his face because My people could not gaze upon naked glory. There are times coming when the glory which I shall give you will be so great that you will have to veil Divine truth so that those who are in the camp, but who are not open to the truth that shines forth, will have to lose the opportunity of not only seeing My glory in My anointed ones, but also entering into My glory.

When you see people are afraid of glory, draw the veil over the revelation of Me in your life. They cannot bear it. I did not show the multitudes or even all My disciples My glory. I showed it only to Peter, James and John on the Mount of Transfiguration, and I showed it to them only once. But much later I showed it to John as I walked among the seven churches. So do not expect even the elect to be able to look full face into My glory.

November 10

LOOKING AT HIS GLORY WILL CHANGE YOU INTO HIS GLORY

Scripture Reading — II Corinthians 3:17,18

"But we all, with open face beholding as in a glass the glory of the Lord, are changed into the same image from glory to glory, even as by the Spirit of the Lord." (II Corinthians 3:18)

Yes, it is true that not many can look into revealed glory, but it is possible. The veil has been removed by Me. However, sad as it may be, many cannot see My glory nor receive it because of the veil that is before their eyes, even the veil of fleshly carnality and human reasoning.

There is liberty for you to look into My glory. You are free to climb the Mount of Transfiguration and so are all of My children, but not all are able, and so they themselves do not make it to the top.

I call you to remove the veil of flesh, and with an open face behold My glory. Even as Moses did when he cried, "Shew me thy glory." Moses saw only My backparts (outer rays of glory) and not the full intensity of it, but you are now in the age of "the Beloved Son." I came to remove your limitations and hindrances. I came to show you My glory. And if you will look into My glory, you shall be changed into that which you gaze upon.

If you look at carnal flesh with all its confusion and struggles and sinful ways, you shall become more and more a fleshly, struggling, carnal, corruptible creature. But I call you to look fully into My wonderful face, and the things of the world will grow strangely dim in the light of My glory and grace.

Then shall your own face be as Stephen's (even the face of an angel). And you shall enter into the glory which you have gazed upon. Moreover, the glory shall enter into you by the Spirit of God, Who shall dwell in you, changing and transforming you into My likeness.

November 11

HOW TO KEEP FROM FAINTING

Scripture Reading – II Corinthians 4:1-6

"Therefore seeing we have this ministry, as we have received mercy, we faint not; But have renounced the hidden things of dishonesty, not walking in craftiness, nor handling the word of God deceitfully; but by manifestation of the truth commending ourselves to every man's conscience in the sight of God." (II Corinthians 4:1,2)

I have given you your ministry. Neither has man given it to you nor have you in any way earned or worked for it. It is a vocation you have received from Me, your God. Because I have given it to you, you can have confidence in Me to have mercy upon you even in your weakness and failures. You need never faint (give up).

In these days as the trials and testings multiply, a very great strain is going to be put upon all who would truly serve Me. You will be tried and tested to the breaking point. But in the moment of your most extreme testing, I will give you strength so you need not faint.

But I must warn you, My beloved, that the key to your strength is your own soul's purity. Only as you completely fulfil the commands I gave through My servant, Paul, can you have strength to survive the coming fiery trials. The church was born in the fiery trials, it was cleansed and purified by fiery trials, and My bride will be prepared out of the church by fiery trials.

You must always, in all ways, renounce all hidden things of dishonesty. Keep your money matters and all business absolutely honest before God and man, so no one can ever bring a charge against you. Never be crafty or sneaky in any of your actions. Trust Me to lead you and to give you what is best. Never handle My Word deceitfully. Never serve Me for money. Never be motivated for the sake of profit.

Always be truthful and honest in your dealings in the sight of God and man and I will surely cause My blessing to rest upon you in such a way that you will be unmoved in the hour of greatest conflict. You will never faint nor give up.

November 12

EXCELLENT POWER: THE TREASURE IN EARTHEN VESSELS

Scripture Reading — II Corinthians 4:7-9

"But we have this treasure in earthen vessels, that the excellency of the power may be of God, and not of us." (II Corinthians 4:7)

"Excellency of power" (perfect and complete power) is poured into your vessel just when you need it, not before nor after. When you are in the hour of extreme testing, do nothing. Reach out to Me and let the excellency of My power pour into your being, body, soul and spirit. You will never fail in any test if you only look to Me to give you this excellency of power.

Though you are troubled on every side you will never become distressed, (exhausted or tired out by pain or suffering). You will be perplexed (bewildered and unable to understand the entanglement of a situation), but I will not let you despair. You will be persecuted by many, and oft-times even by those of your own household, but I will never forsake you.

You will be cast down, (thrown out of their company), but, though you suffer many wounds, you will never be destroyed. The excellency of My power will keep you from being crushed beyond repair, wounded beyond healing.

Reach out to Me and fill yourself with My excellent power, that you may be helped and delivered in trouble, persecution and every manner of rejection.

November 13

SUFFERING WORKS FOR YOUR GOOD

Scripture Reading — II Corinthians 4:10-15

"Always bearing about in the body the dying of the Lord Jesus, that the life also of Jesus might be made manifest in our body. For we which live are alway delivered unto death for Jesus' sake, that the life also of Jesus might be made manifest in our mortal flesh. So then death worketh in us, but life in you." (II Corinthians 4:10-12)

Yes, is it not too wonderful that death and dying works a good work in you? Accept every moment of hurt and suffering as a gift coming only from My hands, and never try to escape it.

Since when do those in leadership have the right to escape wounding? As I am, so are you in this world. (I John 4:17) I am your suffering Saviour. Where I am, My servant shall also be. (John 12:26) I am in the garden, weeping. You are called to walk in My footsteps of rejection, false accusation, humiliation and sorrow.

The "Via Dolorosa" is not only in the narrow streets of Jerusalem; it is also the way of life, narrow and separated, to which I call you and all those who would know Me in the power of My resurrection.

But it is for My sake you are always delivered to death. Therefore accept it as coming from My hands for your good. Let your body be the vehicle of My Holy Spirit's visitation to this earth.

November 14

DAILY RENEWAL — STRENGTH TO SUFFER

Scripture Reading — II Corinthians 4:16-18

"For which cause we faint not; but though our outward man perish, yet the inward man is renewed day by day. For our light affliction, which is but for a moment, worketh for us a far more exceeding and eternal weight of glory;" (II Corinthians 4:16, 17)

Your outward man and your inward man are really like two different parts of you. Terrible suffering and physical wounding can take place upon your outward man. But the inward man will never perish as long as it is renewed day by day through the indwelling presence of the Holy Spirit. Let men do to your outward body what they will; your inner self is safely hidden and protected under the covering of My Holy Spirit.

All suffering seems to be eternal and more than we can bear, but in comparison to My sufferings, it is counted as "a light affliction, which is but for a moment."

In comparison to the glorious result from suffering and the rewards that it gives, all of your suffering is as nothing. You need to compare your suffering with the rewards that will be given unto you. I know that from your side of the veil this is very difficult and almost impossible. It is only as the eternal rewards are revealed by the Holy Spirit that you can begin to fully appreciate the "far more exceeding and eternal weight of glory" which awaits you.

There are different degrees of glory, and not all who are called to endure vigorous and difficult training can undergo the restrictions such training imposes upon them. Many will fail in their life's highest calling and not even realize it because they will justify themselves. But I call you to accept all suffering as an example of what I can do through a yielded vessel.

And you can succeed because your inward man shall be renewed for each day. As your sufferings and testings for this day are, so shall be your renewal.

November 15

PREPARE YOUR BODY NOW

Scripture Reading — II Corinthians 5:1-9

"For we that are in this tabernacle do groan, being burdened: not for that we would be unclothed, but clothed upon, that mortality might be swallowed up of life." (II Corinthians 5:4)

Yes, My child, I understand your longing for release from the burden of your present body. Like Paul you say, "We who are in our present bodily form, groan with the burden of our fleshly body, not that we want to die, but that we might be translated, that our mortal body will be overtaken by abundant, eternal life."

And that is a good desire. Never become so satisfied with your present existence that you do not long for that perfect, eternal body which I have prepared for you.

As surely as I prepared your present body in your mother's womb, so I am preparing your future body.

But do not forget that, while you had nothing to do with the creation of your present body during the time when it was being fashioned in your mother's womb, you **do** have influence on your eternal body. All the love, the joy, the kindness, the gentleness, the peaceful and holy characteristics which you possess in this present body go into the making of your eternal body.

You will not be one person now and another person after dying. Five minutes after death you will be exactly what you are now. Dying does not perfect you.

So prepare your eternal body with great diligence and honesty. **Do not deceive yourself.** Labour to be accepted by Me that you may have a more glorious promotion.

> The glory that awaits you
> My child, you soon shall see;
> So wait, with patience for it,
> When translated you shall be;
> The body that's corrupted
> Transformed, from pain set free.

November 16

WE MUST ALL BE JUDGED

Scripture Reading – II Corinthians 5:10-15

"For we must all appear before the judgment seat of Christ; that every one may receive the things done in his body, according to that he hath done, whether it be good or bad. Knowing therefore the terror of the Lord, we persuade men;" (II Corinthians 5:10,11a)

My beloved child, it is true that you too shall appear before My seat of judgment. Because you love Me, you do not fear that terrible day. But still, I would exhort you to "labour to be accepted by Me." Do not take for granted that My blood will cleanse all your sins and therefore you have nothing to fear. Be sure, My blood **will** cancel all your sins, but what about your works? Your eternal position and rewards will be based on your works.

My blood cancels out all sins and everyone starts out equal in My sight. From there, each one determines what he shall be through eternity. The way you have lived, the love you have poured out upon others, the pure sacrifices you have made will all determine the way you shall be judged on this great day.

Paul knew My terror, so he tried to persuade all men to prepare for that great and dreadful day. With each day you live you are one day closer to that day. Therefore I say to you, My beloved, beware, for as much as I love you and appreciate all you have done for Me, you too will be standing for judgment on that day. In that hour I must be just in My judgment, and though I love you dearly, you will have to receive the just punishment. Therefore, be warned and warn others. Never live for yourself!

November 17

WAIT PATIENTLY FOR THE NEW CREATION TO BE FORMED IN OTHERS

Scripture Reading – II Corinthians 5:16-21

"Wherefore henceforth know we no man after the flesh: yea, though we have known Christ after the flesh, yet now henceforth know we him no more. Therefore if any man be in Christ, he is a new creature: old things are passed away; behold all things are become new." (II Corinthians 5:16,17)

My beloved child, I died and rose again to a new life. I live in My resurrected body. My fleshly body has been transformed through My suffering and death to become the body it now is. Not only is My body advanced to a higher degree, but My Spirit also has advanced to a higher level of understanding, love, compassion and mercy.

As you have been crucified together with Me, you too have entered a new way of life. Old things have passed away, all things have become new. Your old way of thinking and feeling was crucified. Now I am continuing to do a work in you to perfect both the dying to self and the new resurrection life which has been imputed to you. See others not as they once were or are now, but as they shall be when I have perfected them.

For this truth is not only for you. It is for all of My saints who have come to Me and asked to be born again. In some I have worked a greater degree of transformation than in others. Be patient for Me to work a work of perfection in them.

Your sensitivity and ability to feel pain and agonize over a situation is all a part of the crucified life being worked out in you. For every tinge of pain the glory will be greater. So bear your suffering. Be crucified with Me, that you may reign with Me.

November 18

GIVE NO OFFENCE TO THE MINISTRY

Scripture Reading — II Corinthians 6:1-4

"Giving no offence in any thing, that the ministry be not blamed: But in all things approving ourselves as the ministers of God, in much patience, in afflictions, in necessities, in distresses," (II Corinthians 6:3,4)

I want you to stop and meditate on the ways that My servant Paul said you could approve yourselves as ministers. There are too many who serve Me to their own advantage and honour.

You must always remember that the ministry is of the highest calling. Do all that you can to avoid bringing dishonour on My name and on the ministry.

You have no ministry; I am the one who has the ministry. I have called you to forsake your own ministry to work in My ministry. Never promote your own programme, nor your own ideas. Promote and talk about My plans and My vision and My burden. Very few of My servants have found it. They have dedicated their lives to Me and then become involved in their own programme or their part of My over-all plan. And soon there was envy and misunderstanding and strife.

Accept blame, false accusation, and all kinds of suffering, so that the ministry be not discredited. It is better that you suffer innocently like I did, than that the plan of the ages be brought to reproach through your life.

In the next few days we will look more closely into this portion of scripture, for it is one of the greatest for those who are called to be My disciples.

November 19

APPROVING YOURSELF IN PATIENCE, AFFLICTIONS, NECESSITIES, DISTRESSES

Scripture Reading – II Corinthians 6:4

"...in much patience, in afflictions, in necessities, in distresses," (II Corinthians 6:4)

Patience with the imperfections of others is one of the most difficult virtues to possess. It is also possible to become impatient with yourself. This is fatal. When you do that, you give up completely. Never lose heart with yourself or others. As long as people are human they will err. It is your prerogative to be God-like and forgive them seventy times seven. (Matthew 18:21, 22)

Do not become impatient with delays. Some people can stand all kinds of imperfections in others, but they cannot endure waiting for those who are slower than they are, both in the natural and in spiritual things. Never lose out because of impatience.

Afflictions: There are so many afflictions that will come upon the righteous, but I have promised to deliver you out of them all. (Psalm 34:19) No one had more afflictions than My servant David. But he had confidence that I would deliver him and I **always** did. I will always deliver you out of every affliction. Never give up. Every affliction seems to last forever, when, in fact, I have already planned the end of it. Nothing can happen to you which I have not permitted. I may not have engineered or planned it, but I permitted it for the downfall of one and the perfecting of the other.

Necessities: Not every need which you have will immediately be gratified. You must taste the sufferings of others. There are those who have so very many needs which never are met, and still they love Me. Your brothers and sisters cry for bread, for My Word, for freedom, for their loved ones, but they have accepted these necessities as a part of their perfecting and they do not complain. Never allow yourself to be spoiled by the blessings I have given you so that when you are deprived of them you will murmur and complain. When you murmur and complain you are turning your back on My testings in your life. And thereby the testings will increase.

Distresses: Distresses are those moments when you absolutely come to the end of yourself. It is then that you are "beyond yourself," like a child in the midst of the stormy ocean where no amount of swimming ability will save you. Then cast yourself completely on Me, abandon yourself totally to My mercy, for only a miracle can save you. You will be amazed how, in that moment, I will be there, walking on the water, reaching out to save you and calming the troubled seas around you. Look to Me and be saved.

November 20

APPROVING YOURSELF IN STRIPES, IMPRISONMENT, TUMULTS, LABOURS, WATCHINGS & FASTINGS

Scripture Reading — II Corinthians 6:5

"In stripes, in imprisonments, in tumults, in labours, in watchings, in fastings;" (II Corinthians 6:5)

Whippings and scars are badges of honour which I can only give to a few of My elect. So many of My children have never suffered (resisted) unto blood. (Hebrews 12:4) But I want you to prepare your spirit in such a way that, if you ever have to suffer stripes, you will do it with courage and gratitude that you have been chosen for this honour, knowing this, that if your spirit is right you will wear your badges of honour throughout eternity.

Imprisonment: Prisoners are a very select group of people. They are separated from society and their suffering is separation from loved ones and the loss of their freedom. But My prisoners are never separated from the society of the saints, angels and Myself. I will always be with you to communicate with you and comfort you. And you will still be as free as you are now, for even now you are not permitted to do anything which I do not permit you to do.

Tumults: Upsetting circumstances, confusion, disagreements, acts of subversion will touch your life as long as you are in this world. Rest in Me, knowing I will bring everything into My Divine order.

Labours: There are so many ways of serving Me. In every way you serve you give Me pleasure. In a great house there are many servants. The cook is as important as the chauffeur, and the gardener is as important as the housekeeper. Never think your work is more important than any of My other children's. Neither entertain the thought that it is less important. Be faithful in whatever I have called you to do.

Watchings: This is one of the most neglected of all aspects of serving Me. I am calling My children to keeping the night-watch with Me in prayers and intercessions. How can you be prepared to stop the adversary when you are not watchful and on the alert?

Fastings: More and more are beginning a life of fasting. This is the message of the hour. When you fast, remember My many children who are hungry in prisons and famine-stricken areas and even in poverty. Be united with them in this suffering.

> Can you not watch one hour,
> That you might victor be?
> The tempter's tricks beguile you
> From seeking only Me;
> In tumults, labours, fastings
> I will not forsake thee.

November 21

APPROVING YOURSELF BY PURENESS, KNOWLEDGE, LONG-SUFFERING, KINDNESS, THE HOLY GHOST & PURE LOVE

Scripture Reading — II Corinthians 6:6

"By pureness, by knowledge, by longsuffering, by kindness, by the Holy Ghost, by love unfeigned," (II Corinthians 6:6)

While not all of My children are called to endure stripes and imprisonment, all certainly are called to the following:

Pureness: The highest calling is purity of the body and spirit. When any of My children are pure in body, but not in spirit, they are contaminated. I call you to the purity which is in Me. "...the words of the pure are pleasant..." (Proverbs 15:26) I will listen when you call upon Me out of a pure heart. All the works of the pure in heart are right. (Proverbs 21:8) The scorner has no pureness of words. Everything he says is contaminated with a desire to bring strife and destruction. Mark him and have nothing to do with him. Be careful not to learn his ways. You will know who is pure and who isn't, for out of the abundance of the heart the mouth speaks. (Matthew 12:34) A fountain cannot produce both bitter and sweet waters. (James 3:11) "A good man out of the good treasure of the heart bringeth forth good things: and an evil man out of the evil treasure bringeth forth evil things." (Matthew 12:35)

Knowledge: This is the one thing Paul prayed for the Ephesians to have. He prayed earnestly "That the God of our Lord Jesus Christ, the Father of glory, may give unto you the spirit of wisdom and revelation in the knowledge of him: The eyes of your understanding being enlightened; that ye may know what is the hope of his calling, and what the riches of the glory of his inheritance in the saints, And what is the exceeding greatness of his power to us-ward who believe, according to the working of his mighty power,"
(Ephesians 1:17-19) This is the knowledge you should daily strive for. All other knowledge is carnal, and some is destructive. Be not inquisitive into evil. Satan would seek to fill you with wrong knowledge. His facts and figures may be correct, but if you eat from this tree, you will be destroyed.

Longsuffering: Longsuffering is the ability to endure your trials and testings over and over again. Just when you think you are getting respite and things are improving you find yourself in the midst of them again with the same old people bringing about the same old problems. When you can still keep the same spirit of compassion and mercy, that is longsuffering. As testings shall increase you will need it more and more.

Kindness: Everyone can be kind. You need not have great in-depth knowledge to be kind. A child is always kind. You must remember to be kind to all, not just one or two, but all. Let Me deal with those who are the trouble-makers. You be kind to them. It is not your duty to punish or judge anyone. Hand them over to Me. They were Mine before they were yours. I made them.

Unfeigned Love: Unfeigned (pure) love is not contaminated by the emotions you endure when you are put to the test. Pure love can love the betrayer, the thief, the son who plans the death of the father. (David loved Absalom with this pure love). Never turn off your river of love, no matter how much someone hurts you. If you do, you will become bitter. Love will heal the wounds which you are suffering from enemy and friend.

The Holy Spirit: Only through My Holy Spirit can you be holy in all these points and perfect in all these ways and the following. Let Him have full control of every faculty of your being continuously.

November 22

APPROVING YOURSELF BY TRUTH, THE POWER OF GOD, RIGHTEOUSNESS

Scripture Reading – II Corinthians 6:7

"By the word of truth, by the power of God, by the armour of righteousness on the right hand and on the left," (II Corinthians 6:7)

The Word of Truth: You would be shocked, My child, if you could see how many of My children are not completely honest. Many colour their words with partial lies or untruths of some kind. Let honesty and truth be an integral part of your life and I will bless and honour you. Let all that you preach be pure truth, and your words will reach the heart like a two-edged sword. Let your pen be dipped in truth and your writings will change lives and set captives free.

The Power of God: Lean completely on My power. You have no power. You are helpless in yourself against the great enemy of your soul. But if you look to Me and rely completely on the Holy Spirit, He will never fail you. This is His task. He is well qualified in spiritual warfare. Let Him fight all your battles for you.

The Armour of Righteousness on the Right Hand and on the Left: Righteousness is a quality which few possess any more. It is the doing of the right thing at the right time. It is the right use of your own life. Live only for Me. Never live for self. If you think for one minute that you can please yourself and do what you want to do, it is too long. Every faculty of your being, every thought, every ounce of strength must be put to My use. There can be no double standard. This is righteousness.

November 23

APPROVED BY THE WAY YOU SUFFER DISHONOUR, EVIL REPORT AND ACCUSATION

Scripture Reading – II Corinthians 6:8

"By honour and dishonour: by evil report and good report: as deceivers, and yet true;" (II Corinthians 6:8)

The pendulum always swings to two extremes. One day public opinion is totally for you, another day it is totally against you. Even the dearest friends can turn out to be the most dangerous foes. This is the way it was with Me, and if you will walk with Me, it will happen to you also.

In one place you are honoured and praised, and in the next you are rejected, talked against and dishonoured. You have to keep your balance. Do not let the high praises affect you, and then the dishonour won't phase you either. People are feeble. Always remember that. Bear the dishonour with patience and understanding, as long as it is not coming from Me: it is as empty as the honours people bestow on you.

Evil Report and Good Report: What you do with evil report will influence what others will do with it also. If you do not encourage evil report, you will have less evil report about yourself. Let others speak evil of you; if your heart is right, it will turn to pierce them. The good reports are coming eventually. I will both honour you and your report shall be given before the saints and angels when it is finally completed. Wait until then.

As Deceivers and yet True: You will be slandered and lied about and called names. You will be accused of deceiving others, leading them astray, a cultist and a fanatic, but as long as your heavenly record reads "TRUE", you will be proven to be what I already know that you are.

November 24

APPROVED BY BEING "A NOBODY," BY DYING TO SELF, AND BY CHASTENING

Scripture Reading – II Corinthians 6:9

"As unknown, and yet well known; as dying, and, behold, we live; as chastened, and not killed;" (II Corinthians 6:9)

As Unknown, and yet Well Known: If anything describes you it is this. Because you have poured out your life in a hidden way, you are known to multitudes of those in the outer reaches of the harvest field, but here, among your own, you are without honour. So it was with Me. The multitudes from Judea to Capernaum knew Me and awaited My coming, but in My own city of Nazareth I was a prophet without honour, rejected and despised. "Is not this Joseph's son?" (Luke 4:16-30)

As Dying, and Behold We Live: Dying daily and yet your flesh shrinks from it. Your spirit is grieved because I have called you to this high road of surrender. Embrace death to self and it will become the greatest blessing and joy of your life and in this dying-experience you will find the secret of your true life. It is like surrendering to sleep; in a moment the pain and hurt is gone and your dreams carry you into the realm of the subconciousness, a completely different realm than you are in when you are awake. So stop struggling, surrender to the Cross. Be crucified; give up your ghost (spirit), even into your Father's hands, and you will instantly be released from the agony of "dying." Your pain and suffering will cease as you cry out, "IT IS FINISHED!"

As Chastened and Not Killed: No chastening for the moment is pleasant, but because you are My child I want to correct you that I might perfect you. I lead you through the school of correction. There, you must quickly learn the lesson I am teaching you so that you can quickly graduate and come out. You may be severely chastened, but I will never kill you. Did I not say, "Withhold not correction from the child, for if thou beatest him with the rod, he shall not die"? (Proverbs 23:13) This rod that I use in your life to correct you is constructed to suit your need for **correction** and not to destroy you. The fact that I chasten you proves that I love you and you are My child. (Hebrews 12:8) Rejoice in that.

November 25

APPROVED BY REJOICING IN SORROW, TRUE RICHES IN POVERTY, POSSESSING ALL

Scripture Reading — II Corinthians 6:10

"As sorrowful, yet alway rejoicing; as poor, yet making many rich; as having nothing, and yet possessing all things." (II Corinthians 6:10)

Yes, you have been called to overcome your sorrow through rejoicing in Me. Your joy does not depend on your circumstances. I love you, that is your joy. All the sorrows in the world cannot take your smile away, My child. You have My joy. I am with you. You have broken through. Satan's power is destroyed. The victory has been won. It is a glorious victory. You will shortly see that I, the God of peace, have bruised Satan under your feet. (Romans 16:20) His work is defeated. Victory is yours!

As Poor, Yet Making Many Rich: Just look at the riches which I have given to you. You gave Me your full dedication. See how I have blessed you, so that today you can give of the richest blessings to multitudes. And the full extent of the blessings which shall pour from your life has never been fully realized. There is still much more to come. Only you must go through valleys to climb the high mountains.

As Having Nothing, Yet Possessing All Things: All things are yours through Me. I am your "all in all." Everything you need lies in

Me. Though you may feel like you have nothing, still, the blessings of heaven are at your fingertips. You possess all that I possess because you possess Me.

In all these ways you approve yourself as My minister, not by man-given credentials or human achievements, but by the overcoming life which is victorious in all trials and testings, weaknesses and victories. Let this be your example of perfection in serving Me.

November 26

LOVE, EVEN WHEN YOU ARE NOT LOVED

Scripture Reading – II Corinthians 6:11-18

"...our heart is enlarged. Ye are not straitened in us, but ye are straitened in your own bowels." (II Corinthians 6:11,12)

Love was the one thing the church of Corinth lacked, and because they did not have pure love sin entered into their lives. They did not live a life separated from the world. They were so mixed with the ways of the world that they were in agreement with the world.

Love calls for separation from all sin and darkness and uncleanness. It was sin that made the hearts of My children small. Evil and sin always close up the heart. Love expands it.

Paul loved them still, in spite of their sins, but they were feeling unloved. He said to them, "you still have a big place in our hearts, but you do not have any room in your hearts for us."

Always search your heart, lest you shut anyone out of your heart. It is a very sad thing for you to close up your heart to someone. The reason that they closed up their hearts was that they wanted the freedom to embrace the world. Their love for sin pushed out their love for God's anointed ones.

If you love the world you will find it hard to love My anointed ones. I call you to enlarge your heart to My children and to close it to the things of the world. Come out from the world. Do not touch the unclean thing. I will be your Father and you will be My child and I will enlarge your heart to love with pure love.

November 27

A HOLY LIFE AND A HOLY SPIRIT

Scripture Reading — II Corinthians 7:1-9

"Having therefore these promises, dearly beloved, let us cleanse ourselves from all filthiness of the flesh and spirit, perfecting holiness in the fear of God." (II Corinthians 7:1)

Paul is speaking about the promises of being My very own sons and daughters. (II Corinthians 6:18) It is because I have given you such a tremendous promise that you will be My son (My daughter), that you have so much to live up to. I have called you to a very high calling, the highest of the human race, to be My very own child, even the child of the King, a member of the royal family, a prince or princess.

Because of such a high calling you should daily work at cleansing yourself from all filthiness of the flesh and spirit. As a member of the royal family, you must live an exemplary life in purity and piety and perfect holiness.

I have given you My Holy Spirit to live in you and to help you to be perfected in all holiness. You are not able to do it without Him. He is all holiness. He is within your innermost spirit. He lifts you above your natural limitations into the Divine calling of being like Me. "Be ye perfect as I am perfect" is still the plan of the ages. (Matthew 5:48) I said to Abraham, "Walk before me, and be thou perfect," (Genesis 17:1) and I say it to you.

Many work on outward signs of holiness, but on the day when your spirit stands before the Judgment Seat to receive its rewards it will be the spirit which shall be judged, for you are called to the gathering of "...the general assembly and church of the firstborn, which are written in heaven, and to God the Judge of all, and to the spirits of just men made perfect," (Hebrews 12:23)

Strive not only to be perfected yourself, but to present every man perfect in Christ Jesus. (Colossians 1:28) True holiness is none other than perfection.

November 28

THE RIGHT AND THE WRONG SORROW

Scripture Reading — II Corinthians 7:10-16

"For godly sorrow worketh repentance to salvation not to be repented of: but the sorrow of the world worketh death." (II Corinthians 7:10)

Yes, there are two kinds of sorrow. The first is the working of the Holy Spirit in your life. It is feeling My heartbreak and weeping My tears. You have prayed, "Let my heart be broken with the things that break the heart of God." So I have allowed it to happen. Be careful that you are not so overwhelmed with My sorrows, which I have for those who grieve Me and who are wrong, that it imbitters your soul. No one on earth is treated as wrongly as I, yet I love and forgive those who grieve Me. Do not hold a grudge against anyone for My sake. Let your sorrow be My sorrow, for that is a godly sorrow. It is the pure search-light that sees its own faults more clearly than its brother's.

Do not allow Satan to affect you with the sorrow of self-pity. If you do, it will work death to your spiritual life. Repent daily, from your heart, for your sins, and keep your own heart pure. Let My Spirit reprove, rebuke and exhort you, so that My glorious work of grace and redemption might be perfected in your life.

November 29

FIRST TO GOD, THEN TO OTHERS

Scripture Reading — II Corinthians 8:1-24

"And this they did, not as we hoped, but first gave their own selves to the Lord, and unto us by the will of God." (II Corinthians 8:5)

"For ye know the grace of our Lord Jesus Christ, that, though he was rich, yet for your sakes he became poor, that ye through his poverty might be rich." (II Corinthians 8:9)

I am your example. The church of Macedonia is also a perfect example of giving. First, they gave themselves completely to Me. Then they shared what they had with others, especially with Paul and his companions. Do you remember the hospitable spirit of Lydia? (Acts 16:15)

November 30

GIVE GENEROUSLY – REAP GENEROUSLY

Scripture Reading – II Corinthians 9:1-15

"But this I say, He which soweth sparingly shall reap also sparingly; and he which soweth bountifully shall reap also bountifully." (II Corinthians 9:6)

This is the true law of prosperity. It starts with you. Like the farmer will reap according to how he has sown, so you also will reap as you sow. Of course there are also two conditions for reaping.

1. You must have faith that I am a good Father who will keep My promises to reward you according to your giving by putting My blessings upon what you have done.

2. You must give with the right attitude. Never give begrudgingly, stingily, of necessity, for the purpose of getting it back or buying someone's friendship.

Give because you feel My love in your heart, prompting you to give, and it will give you joy and great reward, both in this world and in the world to come. Giving is always recorded in the book of life and it will be remembered eternally. It is one thing which everyone can do to get My attention and approval, because I take special note of all givers and love them in a special way.

December 1

REFUSE WRONG IMAGINATIONS

Scripture Reading – II Corinthians 10:1-18

"For though we walk in the flesh, we do not war after the flesh: (For the weapons of our warfare are not carnal, but mighty through

God to the pulling down of strong holds;) Casting down imaginations, and every high thing that exalteth itself against the knowledge of God, and bringing into captivity every thought to the obedience of Christ;" (II Corinthians 10:3-5)

Paul knew that his great battles were not in the flesh realm, but in the spiritual realm and so he fought his battle through the power of the Holy Spirit. He saw too that Satan worked through people's imaginations, pride and their disobedience towards Me.

He was correct, and this is the way every wise soldier of the cross must do spiritual warfare.

Never use the fleshly tactics of warfare. Beseech the wayward, the proud and boastful ones, the disobedient ones, the ones who would disdain and debase you, with My "meekness and gentleness." (vs. 1)

Beloved, never enter into carnal warfare. And never do any warfare in a carnal way. If you do, you may lose. You certainly will lose in your own testing even if you win the outward battle. Remember, there are always two battles waging at the same time; one is Satan's attempt to destroy My plan and the other is Satan's attempt to destroy you. Never be so concerned with the first battle that you yourself lose out in the testing.

Do warfare in the spiritual realm by casting down imaginations. Satan works through the imaginations of the proud and the undisciplined. When someone exalts himself against My perfect will he becomes a ready tool of Satan. He puts in that one's imagination every kind of suggestion for the destruction of My workings in lives and through lives.

Never let Satan use your imagination. He will bring confusion, pain, false accusations against My children and Me, and boastful thinking of superiority into your mind. After filling your mind with this, it will enter your heart and destroy your spirit.

Cast out all imaginations except the meditation on heavenly things. Bring every thought into captivity. Thoughts of accusation, of resentment, of self-pity, of suspicion, of romanticizing over past relationships, of dreaming up new love affairs, of wanting this or that. Bring every thought into captivity and you shall win a mighty victory against Satan's wiles.

December 2

GLORY IN INFIRMITIES

Scripture Reading — II Corinthians 11:1-33

"If I must needs glory, I will glory of the things which concern mine infirmities." (II Corinthians 11:30)

Paul's credentials were not his education, his Israelite blood, his missionary trips, his sermons or the miracles which I did through his life, and Paul knew this. He knew that his true credentials were his life of suffering. His decorations read:

— Two hundred stripes, (save five)
— Three times beaten with rods
— One time stoned (even unto death)
— Three times ship-wrecked
— Dangerous journeys, innumerable
— Dangers from robbers, heathen, relatives in the cities, in the wilderness, on the sea, among false brethren
— Weariness, pain, night vigils, hunger, thirst, fasts, heat and cold
— The great burden of the churches always lying heavily upon his heart.

He said if one person fell away it grieved him deeply. He was a true shepherd. He suffered all these things as he went out again and again to bring comfort and My Word to My children.

He never bragged about his high birth or his apostleship. He only gave glory to Me that he was counted worthy to suffer for Me and My children. Let your attitude be the same. Say with My servant Paul, "If I must needs glory, I will glory of the things which concern mine infirmities (suffering)." (vs. 30)

December 3

THINGS NOT LAWFUL FOR A PERSON TO TALK ABOUT

Scripture Reading — II Corinthians 12:1-6

"And I knew such a man, (whether in the body, or out of the body, I cannot tell: God knoweth;) How that he was caught up into paradise, and heard unspeakable words, which it is not lawful for a man to utter." (II Corinthians 12:3,4)

There are certain things that you can never talk about. Many of My children have had tremendous experiences in which they saw and heard the secrets of heaven, but My Holy Spirit has not permitted them to talk about it.

Not everyone is ready or able to accept the supernatural. Many, many good, but shallow, children of Mine limit My ability to rend the veil and bring man into My Divine presence where the supernatural becomes the natural to him.

Paul heard unspeakable things which he could not tell about. You will be trusted with glorious revelations and words of truth which it would be unwise to share with others.

Nobody tells all his secrets to everyone he meets, and I, too, cannot tell all my secrets to everyone, so if I tell them to you, do not share them with others. Keep My secrets. It is not an indication of disloyalty between you and a friend when you do not share with that one the secret which I have revealed to you.

There are revelations of the eternal world so glorious that if you were to share them with others, even some of the most religious and zealous of My children would turn against you and repudiate or destroy you. It is hard for man to believe in the supernatural and it is difficult for him to believe that I would do something more or reveal something more to someone else than I have done for him, and so, in religious jealousy, he rejects the fact that I could communicate with another of My children on a higher plane, so he rejects it all and discredits that one who was "caught up into paradise." (vs. 4)

Because of his reaction it will even harm him, so be careful not to cause him to stumble because of My revelation to you. Share some secrets, keep others. Do not speak without My permission. Ask Me to set a watch before your mouth, and keep the door of your lips. (Psalm 141:3)

December 4

THE MESSENGER OF SATAN IN YOUR LIFE

Scripture Reading — II Corinthians 12:7-21

"And lest I should be exalted above measure through the abundance of the revelations, there was given to me a thorn in the flesh, the messenger of Satan to buffet me, lest I should be exalted above measure. For this thing I besought the Lord thrice, that it might depart from me." (II Corinthians 12:7,8)

Because of the double portion blessings and revelations in the life of Paul I had to give him a double portion of trials and testings. This is true about every one of My servants whom I have mightily anointed.

If you could see the terrible trials and testings in the lives of My children you would know who is the most highly favoured. The greater the honour and glory, the greater the trials and testings which are permitted in that life. That is why Paul could say, "I will glory in my infirmities."

I did not test Paul or tempt him; I allowed a messenger of Satan to buffet him. Paul was not permitted to tell all about it because there are many different messengers of Satan. This messenger was an angel under the command of Satan who was dispatched to the scene of Paul's life to stir up people against him and destroy both him and the work which I had called him to do. Satan has many ways of working against My chosen ones. Don't you ever think for one moment that you are immune from satanic warfare. As surely as he attacked Paul and David, Abraham and Esther (and he even met Me in the wilderness when I had fasted), he will come after you. In that hour keep calm, be still and know that I am God. Rest in the covering of My blood and put a watch over your heart, your mind and your mouth.

And have trust in Me. I know you. I understand you, I will help you. I am holding your hand now, My child. My grace is sufficient for you, for my strength shall be perfectly manifested through your life even though you feel weak; for in the moments you feel the most weak and helpless, that is when I take over and carry you across the difficult passage, and so you are the strongest then, for you are resting in My arms while I face your adversary for you.

December 5

MAKE SELF-EXAMINATION

Scripture Reading — II Corinthians 13:1-14

"Examine yourselves, whether ye be in the faith; prove your own selves. Know ye not your own selves, how that Jesus Christ is in you, except ye be reprobates?" (II Corinthians 13:5)

"Finally, brethren, farewell. Be perfect, be of good comfort, be of one mind, live in peace; and the God of love and peace shall be with you." (vs. 11)

It is good to stop and take inventory of yourself and make self-examination. You must be absolutely honest with yourself. Never deceive yourself. Be sure that all you do is in obedience to the laws of the true faith which you have accepted.

I am living within you. I want to live My life through you, therefore you must live by the law of "Him who dwelleth within and whose temple you are." Never live contrary to the laws of My life.

As Paul closes his glorious letter to the church, he gives the admonition which I now give to you.

Be perfect (with Me inside of you this is possible).

Be of good comfort (with the Holy Spirit filling you this is possible).

Be of one mind (if you put on the mind of Christ, you will have one mind).

Live in peace. As much as you are able, strive to live at peace with your fellowman. With the God of peace standing, ready to bruise Satan under your feet shortly, this is possible. (Romans 16:20)

And the God of love and peace shall be with you.

December 6

DELIVERED FROM THE WRATH TO COME BY HIS COMING

Scripture Reading — I Thessalonians 1:1-10

"And to wait for his Son from heaven, whom he raised from the dead, even Jesus, which delivered us from the wrath to come." (I Thessalonians 1:10)

Yes, I am coming again. The great tribulation has even now begun and it is going to get worse and spread slowly over nation after nation until the whole world will be enveloped in the flame of persecution fires, but be of good hope, I am coming too. I want you to always have this hope in your heart.

Before the outpouring of My wrath and judgment upon this world which has rejected My love and mercy, I will deliver you and all who love and serve Me and who are waiting for Me.

I have promised you, even in this scripture, that I already have determined by My foreknowledge to deliver you from the wrath to come. As I delivered Noah and Lot in the day of wrath, and Elijah from the far reaching tentacles of Jezebel, so I will deliver you. I have spoken the word. Nothing can reverse it. It is forever settled in heaven. Fear not. Only rejoice and tell others, that they may also rejoice and not be fearful.

December 7

THE LIVES WE HAVE BLESSED ARE OUR JOY AT HIS COMING

Scripture Reading — I Thessalonians 2:1-20

"For what is our hope, or joy, or crown of rejoicing? Are not even ye in the presence of our Lord Jesus Christ at his coming? For ye are our glory and joy." (I Thessalonians 2:19,20)

My children can either be a blessing or a burden, both to you and to Me. The church of Corinth was a great heartache and burden to Paul. (II Corinthians 12:20,21) He said he was afraid that when he would come to them, he would find them involved with debates, envyings, wraths, strifes, backbitings, whisperings, swellings (haughtiness, pride) and tumults. He was very grieved with them because they accused him of being spiritually weak (II Corinthians 10:10), not loving them (II Corinthians 12:15), of being a fool (II Corinthians 11:16), his speech being contemptible (provoking, despised, of least esteem), (II Corinthians 10:10),, of preaching for gain (II Corinthians 11:8,9) and many other slanderous and cruel things. But the church of Thessalonica was different. It was Paul's hope, his joy, his crown of rejoicing and his glory.

Though you may be called to leadership, you cannot make people be what they do not want to be, so that they will automatically give you joy and hope, glory and rejoicing. People are free moral agents. Under training and discipline and correction the true character will emerge. No amount of charm or love or diplomacy on your part can change them. I can't even change them Myself, if they are not willing to be changed. It is only by them letting Me take over in their lives. Only if they are living in Me they become a new creature.

At My coming all will be manifested. Think what great joy will be yours when you will see the victorious translation and rapture of those who have been fully trained and prepared under your care and love.

Then indeed, as they receive their rewards, you will find in these precious, spiritual children the greatest joy, glory and crown of rejoicing that you have ever experienced.

Paul awaited that day when they would rise out of Corinth, Salonica, Philippi, Ephesus, Antioch, and all the places where he had so faithfully laboured.

And when I do return to this earth, Paul together with other triumphant saints, is coming with Me to welcome you and yours home.

December 8

WE ARE PREPARED BY LOVE FOR HIS COMING

Scripture Reading — I Thessalonians 3:1-13

"To the end he may stablish your hearts unblameable in holiness before God, even our Father, at the coming of our Lord Jesus Christ with all his saints." (I Thessalonians 3:13)

When Paul wrote this letter to the Thessalonian Christians he was filled with the revelation of My second coming. I had made this glorious truth very real to him.

The truth of My coming is one which you must ever keep before My people. Many are not prepared in love and true holiness of heart. So I call you to a ministry of preparing others for My coming.

Paul never told the saints to prepare in the natural, but he told them to be ready in the spirit for My coming. And this is of the greatest importance of all. The key to preparation is, "Increase in love toward one another and toward all men." Satan is trying to rob you of the greatest gift which you have to give, love.

I gave you a baptism of love when I filled you with My Holy Spirit, and I would refresh you and re-anoint you with this love. Love can suffer rebuke, rejection, rebuttal and still continue to be manifest. Don't dry up and wither away when you are hurt. Love! Love can change the hardest heart.

It is time for you to have an increase of My love. Ask Me for only one thing, a fresh baptism of love. I am coming soon and I want to find your heart established in true holiness, which is even My pure love poured out through your heart for Me and for all men. Only through loving with perfect love can you be unblamable in holiness. This is the only true holiness, even My perfect love.

I am coming soon with **all** My saints. Those who have just recently left you are already preparing for the return journey back to earth with Me. Prepare your heart also by love. The most glorious meeting awaits us all in the near future when I come with all My saints. (vs. 13)

December 9

WE ARE JOINED WITH OUR LOVED ONES AT HIS COMING

Scripture Reading — I Thessalonians 4:1-18

"But I would not have you to be ignorant, brethren, concerning them which are asleep, that ye sorrow not, even as others which have no hope. For if we believe that Jesus died and rose again, even so them also which sleep in Jesus will God bring with him. For this we say unto you by the word of the Lord, that we which are alive and remain unto the coming of the Lord shall not prevent them which are asleep. For the Lord himself shall descend from heaven with a shout, with the voice of the archangel, and with the trump of God: and the dead in Christ shall rise first: Then we which are alive and remain shall be caught up together with them in the clouds, to meet the Lord in the air: and so shall we ever be with the Lord." (I Thessalonians 4:13-17)

What words of comfort these should be to you who have suffered and known deep sorrow! You need not grieve any longer for those things which you have lost, those loved ones who have departed. Your mourning must cease. Do not look back at the past with its mistakes. Do not look inward at yourself with all your weakness. Do not look at others with all their failures. Look to heaven, I am coming! Never lose the joy and expectancy of My coming. Let no one rob you of this vital truth.

Everything you have lost for My sake or the Gospel's you will gain back in the hour of My coming. All your beloved and precious loved ones, who have died in Me, will come together with Me to welcome you home. And they shall be as you have known them, for before you see them their graves will split open, their bodies translated and glorified will be united with their spirits, for I have said that you who are alive and yet remain unto the coming of the Lord shall not take precedence over them which are asleep.

I shall descend with a shout, and with the shout of the mighty archangel who shall be in command of this mass resurrection and ascension. The heavenly trumpet shall give the sound that shall enable you to break earth's gravity and you shall be caught up in the clouds to meet Me in the air. And we shall never more part, neither will there be any separation from your loved ones. Be comforted! Be prepared!

December 10

NOT IGNORANT CONCERNING HIS COMING

Scripture Reading — I Thessalonians 5:1-11

"But of the times and the seasons, brethren, ye have no need that I write unto you. For yourselves know perfectly that the day of the

Lord so cometh as a thief in the night. For when they shall say, Peace and safety; then sudden destruction cometh upon them, as travail upon a woman with child; and they shall not escape." (I Thessalonians 5:1-4)

The early church knew by My instructions to My disciples that My return was a secret known only to the Father and that I would come "as a thief in the night." (Matthew 24:42-44; Luke 12:39,40)

I gave many signs of My coming, but the main one is "unpreparedness of mankind and sudden destruction and judgment upon the earth."

For those who are not expecting My coming I will return as unexpectedly as a thief comes in the night. The "night" of scripture speaks of the dark days that have begun and will increase in intensity, just like a woman in travail. The true sign of My coming is the darkness of the age.

But many will be working and striving for peace. There will be peace-conferences, peace treaties and peace talks, for concerned people will try to stop the holocaust that is appearing on the horizon.

In those days, sudden destruction shall come upon the earth, and as a babe leaping out of his mother's womb, the Church triumphant, the Bride who has made herself ready, shall be raptured out of the womb of the earth which shall then enter into the agony of My outpoured wrath, and she shall be united with her beloved through eternity.

Therefore, My Bride, prepare yourself, watch, be sober, put on the breastplate of faith and love and the helmet of salvation. For the Father has not appointed you to wrath, but to salvation through Me, your Saviour. (vs. 6-9)

December 11

BLAMELESS IN BODY, SOUL AND SPIRIT AT HIS COMING

Scripture Reading – I Thessalonians 5:12-28

"And the very God of peace sanctify you wholly; and I pray God your whole spirit and soul and body be preserved blameless unto the coming of our Lord Jesus Christ." (I Thessalonians 5:23)

Paul knew how very important it was for the bride to be sanctified in spirit, soul and body, for this is the only way that you can be blameless. The bride is not only blood-bought, she is blood-washed and blood-empowered to live a holy, spotless life.

> Would you be free from your burden of sin?
> There is pow'r in the blood, pow'r in the blood;
> Would you o'er evil a victory win?
> There's wonderful pow'r in the blood.
>
> Chorus:
> There is pow'r, pow'r, wonder-working pow'r
> In the blood of the Lamb;
> There is pow'r, pow'r, wonder-working pow'r
> In the precious blood of the Lamb.
>
> Would you be free from your passion and pride?
> There is pow'r in the blood, pow'r in the blood;
> Come for a cleansing to Calvary's tide—
> There's wonderful pow'r in the blood.

Yes, it is only by bringing every impurity in spirit, soul and body to Me day by day, that My blood can cleanse it away and sanctify you wholly, so that you will be that "wife who has made herself ready." (Revelation 19:7)

December 12

THE SINNER WILL BE JUDGED AND THE RIGHTEOUS WILL BE GLORIFIED AT HIS COMING

Scripture Reading — II Thessalonians 1:1-12

"And to you who are troubled rest with us, when the Lord Jesus shall be revealed from heaven with his mighty angels, In flaming fire taking vengeance on them that know not God, and that obey not the gospel of our Lord Jesus Christ: Who shall be punished with everlasting destruction from the presence of the Lord, and from the glory of his power; When he shall come to be glorified in his saints, and to be admired in all them that believe (because our testimony among you was believed) in that day." (I Thessalonians 1:7-10)

Is your heart troubled? Has the evil one disturbed your peace and shaken your soul? Is everything twisted and in disorder? Then this message is to you. I am calling you to rest. Rest by standing fast, supported by My constancy.

You need only to stand still and look up into the heavens and there you will see that I am getting ready to return to you.

With Me come not only the saints and your loved ones but the armies of heaven who have been given a flaming sword and who are commissioned to punish with vengeance all those who obey not the gospel (the truth I have given). All rebellious ones shall be punished with everlasting destruction by being eternally banned from My presence and the loss of the glory of My power.

But to you, My saints, it shall be the day of your glorification when you are chosen as My Bride. For you are betrothed to Me and on that day we will drink the bridal cup of the new wine together as we seal our vows through eternity.

December 13

THE WICKED SHALL BE DESTROYED BY THE BRIGHTNESS OF HIS COMING

Scripture Reading — II Thessalonians 2:1-17

"For the mystery of iniquity doth already work: only he who now letteth will let, until he be taken out of the way. And then shall that Wicked be revealed, whom the Lord shall consume with the spirit of his mouth, and shall destroy with the brightness of his coming:" (II Thessalonians 2:7,8)

My beloved one, you are filled with sadness as you see iniquity abounding on every hand. And many around you are believing the lies of the wicked one who gains ground through lawless hearts who love not the truth, that they might be saved. "And for this cause God shall send them strong delusion, that they should believe a lie: That they all might be damned who believed not the truth, but had pleasure in unrighteousness." (vs. 11,12)

It gives Me sorrow to see even My own children being deceived and led astray, because I know how terrible their end will be. You should pity them and weep for them, for they will go from darkness to darkness, from deception to deception, from iniquity to iniquity. And as they do, they make room for the anti-Christ and prepare the way for his coming, even as My righteous Bride prepares the way for My coming. But as long as you are here, you still are a deterrent to the full workings of Satan. Your very presence is the salt of the earth, the light on the lampstand which puts some restraint on their satanic workings and makes them miserable in their sinning so that they hate you.

But when I come they will be made powerless because their evil instigator, the wicked one himself, shall be destroyed by the brightness of My coming. My light (which you are a reflection of) will destroy all his power to work because he works in darkness and in secret, and in that day every work shall be disclosed and made manifest. Yea, it shall be shouted from the housetops (Luke 12:3), and every hypocrite shall be revealed.

This day has already begun. My judgment has begun in the earth. Many who walked with you into My house shall forsake you and Me and turn to their wicked way because they refuse correction and guidance. Let them be! **You** follow Me and walk in holiness. Stand fast and hold the traditions that you have been taught by the teachers of holiness. Remember, there are not two Gospels. There is but one, and that is the Gospel of holiness and righteousness.

December 14

DIRECT YOUR HEART INTO LOVE AND PATIENCE
—WAITING FOR HIS COMING—

Scripture Reading — II Thessalonians 3:1-18

"And the Lord direct your hearts into the love of God, and into the patient waiting for Christ." (II Thessalonians 3:5)

My beloved child, there are so many activities that crowd in upon your life and take precedence, and most of them are of vital importance; but I would have you put your heart to the most vital of all. First, direct your heart into the love of God.

The love of God is like a great big snow bank, soft and fluffy. If you land upon it, you will be safe.

Picture a plane being forced to land. The pilot knows that if he can make his emergency landing in a certain place, there is every chance of all being saved.

My child, the only safe landing place in the emergencies of your life is to head your "plane" (your heart) into the love of God, "Love Field."

But there is one more thing of great importance that will take place as you do this. You will be enabled to receive Divine patience from above. The only way you can have patience is through love.

The patience I am calling you to possess will enable you to wait for Me. Wait, not only for My coming again, but wait for Me to step into every situation of your life and bring Divine order out of chaos.

When chaos struck this planet and everything was without form and void, I stepped down upon this scene and in six days created a perfect habitation. I can do it again in your life. When I have finished training and testing you I will step into your life and in "six days" (a few short days) I will perfect all that concerns you. So direct your heart into the love of God and into patiently waiting for Me.

December 15

HUMILITY, THE KEY TO GREATNESS

Scripture Reading – II Chronicles 26:1-23

"...and as long as he sought the Lord, God made him to prosper....But when he was strong, his heart was lifted up to his destruction." (II Chronicles 26:5,16)

My beloved, this is the simple, but powerful, key to success and prosperity. King Uzziah's mother and father had taught him the importance of obedience to God and of seeking the Lord, but his father too had failed in the end, and this spirit of pride and self-reliance was in the royal family.

Many people who are humble and led by My Spirit change after they come into a place of power and leadership. Their whole personality alters and they are not careful to seek My will in all things. It is dangerous to become great, for power "goes to the head" and destroys many who have it.

My heart grieves for those whom I have taken from the sheep cotes, from following the sheep, and made rulers over My people, only to see them forget from whence they have come and what great things I have done for them and from whence they have been lifted up.

As long as they are small in their own eyes they are able to know the gentle ways of the Spirit of God, but when they attain unto leadership, popularity, power and fame, they are under great temptation. Then it is that many completely change so that another heart is given to them. This happened to Saul (I Samuel 13:9-14; 15:17-35), to Solomon (I Kings 11:1-13), to Nebuchadnezzar, (Daniel 4:28-37) and to many others. Even John and James **were** tempted in this way. (Luke 9:54)

In Thyatira there was a woman (Revelation 2:18-23) who called herself a prophetess, and she had known Me at one time, but her heart was lifted up because of My gifts which I had given her, and she became a proud and rebellious woman who caused many to be led astray. Pray much for those in secular and religious leadership, for they are under great temptation. Satan stands always at their side seeking how to destroy them, and he uses **pride** as a tool.

December 16

LET GOD TURN EVIL INTO GOOD

Scripture Reading — Psalm 21:1-13

"For they intended evil against thee: they imagined a mischievous device, which they are not able to perform." (Psalm 21:11)

My precious, beloved one. I have seen your broken heart. I have felt the terrible agony which you have endured. Your love, your patience, your long-suffering has been tested to the uttermost. Also your courage is now being tested as you face the raging wolves of silent hate and revenge.

But fear not! No weapon that is formed against you shall prosper. You are My anointed one. I love you. I have formed you in the furnace of affliction. I will not cast you off nor cease from hearing your cry. Your enemy which rose up against you is defeated. This day you have broken through his stronghold. You have broken his alliance, you have divided his tongue, you have taken the prey.

I will now shake his kingdom and undo his stronghold. All your words cannot assail him, but *tswum* (fasting) can. Now be silent in this regard, nor make comment to the ones concerned. Behold I set a seal over your mouth, for Satan would seek to bring you into conversation. But I will now talk, I, the Lord God, will speak on your behalf and it shall suffice. And you shall indeed rejoice in all My goodness and stand in awe.

December 17

YOU ARE A PATTERN IN GRACE AND SUFFERING

Scripture Reading — I Timothy 1:1-20

"Howbeit for this cause I obtained mercy, that in me first Jesus Christ might shew forth all longsuffering, for a pattern to them which should hereafter believe on him to life everlasting." (I Timothy 1:16)

Paul called himself "the chiefest of sinners." (vs. 15) He never forgot to wonder at My grace which reached into his sinful, blasphemous and cruel life and which forgave and transformed him completely.

Paul knew he was saved for two reasons, to serve and to suffer. Now, in writing to his "son in the faith" he reveals that he was permitted to suffer for a very special reason, "that in me first Jesus Christ might shew forth all longsuffering, for a pattern to them which should hereafter believe on him to life everlasting."

My child, there are two ways to interpret this scripture.

The first one is that I took the cruellest sinner, the one who hated Me the most and fought Me the hardest, and saved him and made him My faithful follower, so that no one would ever after be able to say, "I am too great a sinner. God could not save me."

The second one is that I allowed Paul to suffer so greatly for My name's sake so that he could be a pattern for all believers of all times, giving the example of suffering, courage and strength that they can have to be able to endure all the hard trials that come into their lives.

Remember, My beloved child, you too are an example in both ways. I chose you to show the world how I could save you, a rebellious sinner, and fill your heart with such love and devotion to Me that all would marvel at that love and devotion which they would see exemplified through your willingness to suffer for Me and the high calling which I have put upon your life. Remember, many eyes are watching your courage in suffering. Because you are strong, it will also give them strength.

December 18

LOVE QUALIFIES TO BE OUR MEDIATOR

Scripture Reading – I Timothy 2:1-15

"For there is one God, and one mediator between God and men, the man Christ Jesus;" (I Timothy 2:5)

This is one of the most powerful scriptures in the New Testament. It tells you that you can come straight to Me without appealing to any other saint, or lesser "god." Are you not happy for this wonderful open door, this access into My presence? It means that no matter where you are, or how terrible a sinner you are, all you need to do to reach the highest courts of heaven is to come in My name, even the wonder-working name of "Jesus." I have given you My name so that you can ask anything in My name and I will do it. It is loved and honoured in the highest courts of heaven. It is feared in the lowest depths of hell. Speak My name on the uttermost planets of space and then the planets will vibrate with response, for they know I created them in the beginning.

What is your greatest need, My beloved child? Come to the Father to obtain all your needs through My wonder-working name. I love you. I died for you. That is why My name has authority with the Father.

If you love someone deeply, even deeply enough to die for that one, and then you come to the Father to petition concerning that one, He will hear you because He knows your love and your purity of heart towards that one. But if you hate someone, think not that the Father will or can hear your "prayers" for that one. Love is the mediator. That is why the Father hears Me. I love. Love is never refused. Love qualifies Me to be a mediator for the chiefest of sinners. Come to the Father, not with gifts of oratory and reasoning, but **love**.

December 19

GOD IS STILL MANIFEST IN THE FLESH

Scripture Reading — I Timothy 3:1-16

"And without controversy great is the mystery of godliness: God was manifest in the flesh, justified in the Spirit, seen of angels, preached unto the Gentiles, believed on in the world, received up into glory." (I Timothy 3:16)

My child, this mystery of godliness did not end when My son was received up into glory; it still continues today in your life and the lives of all of My precious and beloved overcomers. I am made manifest to the world through your flesh. You ask, "how can this be?" It happens every time you let Me live in your being and have full control of your life. Every time you do what I would do, I am being made manifest in your flesh.

"Justified in the Spirit," My Holy Spirit is with you to guide you through this day and every day. He will vindicate every right thing that He does through your life. You do not justify or vindicate My workings through you; the Holy Spirit will surely do this.

"Seen of angels," means guarded by angels. Yes, My angels are with you constantly. You could not sleep in safety if you did not have the protection of the constant vigil of angels, for when you sleep you are unable to defend yourself from any danger, physical or spiritual, in any way. Many angels are standing beside you in the hour of the night protecting you from evil spirits who would attack your unprotected mind.

"Preached unto the Gentiles," Every time you bear witness of Me to the unsaved, you are fulfilling this work which My Son began when He was on earth.

"Believed on in the world." Many believe because of your life and your witness, just like they did because of Jesus' life and witness before the religious and wicked.

"Received up into glory." The last way you will fulfil My workings through you is the way in which you will come home into My eternal abode. The grace with which you say good-bye to the world is as important as the way you have lived your life.

December 20

THE AUTHORITY OF THE LAYING ON OF HANDS

Scripture Reading – I Timothy 4:1-16

"Neglect not the gift that is in thee, which was given thee by prophecy, with the laying on of the hands of the presbytery." (I Timothy 4:14)

This is one of the great authorities imputed by the Holy Spirit to those in spiritual leadership. They have the right to act in My name and under My guidance and inspiration in giving My Word and imparting My gifts to those whom I am calling out to serve Me.

Paul used his apostolic authority to touch the lives of many young men. Timothy was not the only one whom he laid hands on and imparted gifts upon.

This authority to lay hands on those whose lives are dedicated and whom I am going to use in a special way is a gift which has not been used by the church, except in ordination services, but even then, it was not accompanied by prophecy.

The church has lost its power and anointing, therefore it had nothing to impart. But a new day has come. I give My spiritual leaders the anointing and the authority to lay hands on the "called out ones" and to impart to them spiritual gifts and anointings.

Hands have been laid on you. Words of prophecy have been spoken over you. Stir up that spirit of slumber within you and begin to walk in faith to fulfil the Word of God which was spoken over you. You have a part to play to fulfil that word of prophecy. No "magic carpet" will sweep you to the nation of your calling. All of hell will fight you and if you do nothing about it you will never get there. I have commanded you, rise up and begin to act.

December 21

YOUR MOTHERS, YOUR SISTERS AND DAUGHTERS

Scripture Reading — I Timothy 5:1-25

"Rebuke not an elder, but intreat him as a father; and the younger men as brethren; The elder women as mothers; the younger as sisters, with all purity." (I Timothy 5:1,2)

In this generation of disrespect for elders and dishonour for all men, I am calling for respect and honour among My people. I will not tolerate the dishonour and disrespect which is prevalent in the world, nor will I allow it to enter into the lives of My people. It is an abomination unto Me.

Everyone who shows disrespect for the elderly is marked. There will be strong and severe judgment upon all who break this holy and righteous law.

I want you to see Me in every life, but even much more, in the lives of the women. Many of My elderly daughters are forgotten and unloved by their family and the church. I am giving you a great compassion for these women who have suffered so greatly. You will find your heart is filled with love for them. This is the working of My Holy Spirit in you.

If a sister is older than you by fifteen or more years look upon her as a mother and honour her. If she is younger than you by fifteen or more years, look upon her as your daughter. If she is in between these ages, look upon her as your sister. Love them as though they were a part of your family, for indeed they are, even a part of your eternal heavenly family.

Treat women with great respect and honour and all purity, and they will respond to this love, for they have been deeply hurt and many are suffering and are forgotten by those whom they love. There are so many wounds that need healing.

December 22

GAIN IS NOT GODLINESS

Scripture Reading — I Timothy 6:1-21

"Perverse disputings of men of corrupt minds, and destitute of the truth, supposing that gain is godliness: from such withdraw thyself." (I Timothy 6:5)

My child, you have come to an age of madness where there are all kinds of false, erroneous beliefs, and one of them is that My people actually believe that to prosper and get gain is a sign of godliness. They have lost sight of what the true riches really are. A man's bank account, accumulation of houses and lands and much property does not indicate that he is a godly man. The Psalmist said, "Behold, these are the ungodly who prosper in the world; they increase in riches." (Psalm 73:12)

While it is true that in some lives I bless My people by multiplying their finances, still this does not indicate that the man with three cars and a $100,000 house is more godly than the man who stands all day over a factory furnace and comes home to a rented cottage.

My people do not know what true riches are. My Word says, "...godliness with contentment is great gain." (vs. 6) If you are content and happy, live a godly life, walk in humility, give of your finances to Me and bear witness to a lost and dying world, you are blessed. If you have those who love you, good health, a happy spirit, you are blessed. You can even lose all these things, the friendship of dear ones, your husband, wife, parents, children, health and home, but if you love Me and I am your everything, you are blessed.

You brought nothing into this world, and you will take nothing out. And no matter how much you may gain of earthly riches and good gifts, your most blessed moment will be when you stand stripped of all earth's richest gifts at the pearly gate where the only true riches are laid up for those who love Me, and you hear Me say to you, "...Well done, thou good and faithful servant: thou hast been faithful over a few things, I will make thee ruler over many things: enter thou into the joy of thy lord." (Matthew 25:21)

December 23

SERVING WITH A PURE CONSCIENCE

Scripture Reading – II Timothy 1:1-6

"I thank God, whom I serve from my forefathers with pure conscience, that without ceasing I have remembrance of thee in my prayers night and day;" (II Timothy 1:3)

My child, it is a great thing to be able to say that you serve Me with a pure conscience. There are so many of My servants and handmaidens who do not have a clean and pure conscience. There are hidden sins in their lives, sins that keep them from having that deep inner peace. To know that there is "nothing between your soul and your Saviour" is one of the most important and precious treasures that you can have.

One of the things that gave Paul the strength to live a holy life lies in the words "from my forefathers." He pointed out to Timothy to remember his faith that was first in his grandmother, Lois, and his mother, Eunice. Timothy's faith was not something that was given to him in the moment when he was born again, but it began in the godly life of his mother and grandmother. Always be grateful for godly parents and grandparents. Remember that they have walked in holiness through hard years and hard times and that you have inherited the blessing of the righteous which I promised would go down into the third and fourth generation. Their prayers, their holiness and their dedication is the greatest wealth that they could pass on to you. It is greater than all the riches of the earth and the blue blood of nobility. Treasure the true treasures of life. That which you have inherited from them will help you to walk in purity and holiness all the days of your life.

December 24

HE HAS GIVEN YOU POWER, LOVE AND SANITY

Scripture Reading – II Timothy 1:7-11

"For God hath not given us the spirit of fear; but of power, and of love, and of a sound mind." (II Timothy 1:7)

Satan is the instigator of fear. He would seek to torment you with every kind of fear, fear of the dark, of people, of poverty, of losing your reputation, of being stranded, of insanity, of people hating you, of evil men, of wild beasts, of heights or depths, of heat or cold, of accident, of losing loved ones, of rejection and even of death. There are so many ways he would torment you and worry you.

He sends a messenger of Satan after My children to buffet and upset them. He wants you to lose your mind, to get upset, to anger you and rob you of your peace and happiness.

All these aggravating and upsetting things are not of Me. They are of the evil one, even your enemy and Mine.

I have given you power over him and his demons to bind him. He cannot fill your heart with anger and hate because it is filled with My love and My Divine understanding. You can find your worst enemy in the spirit and you can even have compassion on him. Hating him will not solve anything. It will only accomplish what Satan set out to do from the beginning.

I have given you every weapon you need to fight against him and defend yourself from his attacks. I have given you power over him, even My power. I have given you love to guard your heart from evil and hate vibrations which would destroy your soul, and I have given you a sound mind, healthy nerves, so that you will not suffer a nervous breakdown or go insane. Your mind has My protection. I love you and will do you good all the days of your life. Fear not! I am with you. I will hold your right hand and guide you.

December 25 – Christmas

BE IT UNTO ME ACCORDING TO THY WILL

Scripture Reading – Luke 1:26-56

"And Mary said, Behold the handmaid of the Lord; be it unto me according to thy word. And the angel departed from her." (Luke 1:38)

My beloved, this is the perfect attitude that is needed in order to be used by Me. Many want to serve Me, but they only want to serve Me according to **their** will, and not according to **My** will.

When your life is yielded to Me completely there are absolutely NO limitations. I can do anything, for My angels always work to do My will. So it is that when you volunteer and surrender to do My will, you have the mighty angels working with you to cause it to come to pass.

Mary never doubted for one moment My greatness and ability to fulfil the word that I had commanded Gabriel to say to her.

Today I speak, not only by angels, but by My prophets, My Word and My Spirit who dwells within you. If you believe, you will prosper. You will see My perfect will fulfilled in your life.

Nothing belongs to anyone. Everything you see is only on loan to those who seem to possess it for a little while. The only eternal thing is what you, yourself, become in your eternal spirit. The ornaments of the spirit and the gemstones of the soul are eternal. As you become more and more like Me, through yieldedness to My will, you are acquiring the true treasures which will never pass away and like Mary of old, you will be great in My Kingdom.

December 26

HE WILL KEEP YOU IN "THAT DAY"

Scripture Reading – II Timothy 1:12-14

"...and am persuaded that he is able to keep that which I have committed unto him against that day." (II Timothy 1:12)

Everybody's "that day" is different. There are many "that days" in every person's life. It is a day of trials and testings, even a desperate day when all hell seems to be arrayed against your soul.

Every trial and testing is different and some are much greater than others. I want to lift you up above all of these trials so that you will as it were, "fly over them."

You do not need to wade through all the filthy muck and mire of this polluted generation. I will give you grace, even My grace to rise above every one of your adversaries. Do not stoop to their level to do battle with them.

So many of My children fear the day of persecution which is coming upon the world. It is a day of fiery trials. Many of My children have already laid down their lives for My sake and the Gospel's. It is a great victory to die for Me. A glorious homecoming awaits the soul of the one who dies in the Lord.

There are many different trials. One person's "that day" is one of torture and imprisonment, another's is sickness and suffering, another's is divorce or the death of a life-long partner. No matter how hard your day of testing is, or how long it lasts, I will surely keep you and bring you safely through it so that you do not need to deny Me or fall away from My grace, or betray another of My precious children. Take courage. I am with you. I will not fail you nor forsake you, even when your feet stand in the waters of the river of death.

December 27

ALL ARE TURNED AWAY FROM ME

Scripture Reading — II Timothy 1:13-18

"This thou knowest, that all they which are in Asia be turned away from me; of whom are Phygellus and Hermogenes." (II Timothy 1:15)

It is hard to believe that in the end all of Paul's popularity was reversed. This great apostle who had walked with Me, preached My Word with power and with signs following, finds himself forsaken by all of his former converts and companions. He goes through his Gethsemane experience all alone.

And indeed, there is no other way that you can go through your "Gethsemane." Your dearest and nearest disciples will "fall asleep" only a stone's throw from you in the hour of agony and trial. And do not condemn them, for it is needful for every one of My children to pass through that hour of solitude when the only companion you have is Myself. For then you will turn your eyes upon Me and you will be drawn closer to Me.

The poet of Song of Solomon said, "Who is this that cometh up from the wilderness, leaning upon her beloved?" (Song of Solomon 8:5) As My Bride comes into perfection she will not be leaning on friends or loved ones, but on Me, her eternal beloved.

So I have to take you too in the last days of your life down that lonely path where I am your everything, your all in all.

There are many Phygelluses and Hermogeneses in this world who are used by Satan to turn people against My precious children. And I let it happen because I want to bring you closer to Me.

Phygellus means "escape" and Hermogenes means "born talker." Watch out for those who escape responsibilities and will not carry the burden and also be careful of those "born talkers." They will work a work of destruction with their evil tongues and turn many away from My anointed end-time "Pauls."

Do not put your confidence in flesh. The one who praises you the most today will forsake you tomorrow.

December 28

HARD TRAINING FOR A GOOD SOLDIER

Scripture Reading — II Timothy 2:1-13

"Thou therefore endure hardness, as a good soldier of Jesus Christ." (II Timothy 2:3)

Soldiers are trained in boot camps to endure a rigorous life-style. Everything changes when you join the army. Your clothes, your relationships with your family, your food, your privacy is gone, your independence, everything. They even cut your hair so that when you look in the mirror you know that old things are passed away and all things are new. I say unto you, get yourself in line and submit to Me as I train you to a different life. I want you to realize that I, the Captain of your salvation, have full control of all your life and you can "get no leave" and "take no furloughs" without a "pass" from Me. You are on permanent duty, day and night. It is not easy, nor can it be, for if I allow the training to be slacked off you will not be the strong and hardened (toughened up) soldier that I need to train others who will later be the new recruits in your charge.

The Holy Spirit is your drill sergeant. He puts you through the paces. Be sure that you do all that He demands of you and do not resent the strong and difficult training that you must experience. He knows you better than you know yourself and He knows just how much you can endure. It is all for your good. He cannot plan for your destruction, only for your promotion.

You are My soldier. Always remember that you cannot take leave without permission from Me, or go AWOL. Your behaviour must be exemplary because you represent the Kingdom of God on earth. There are places out of bounds for you, and don't you dare go where I do not permit you to go.

The loneliness of being separated from loved ones and the pain of leaving the comforts of your home to spend long weeks and months out on the battlefield will not be easy. But to become a general in the army you must be proven. There are no "promotions" for favourites. You will have to "climb up" the hard way. Be faithful, be loyal, endure.

December 29

PURGED TO BE A VESSEL OF HONOUR

Scripture Reading – II Timothy 2:14-26

"But in a great house there are not only vessels of gold and of silver, but also of wood and of earth; and some to honour, and some to dishonour. If a man therefore purge himself from these, he shall be a vessel unto honour, sanctified, and meet for the master's use, and prepared unto every good work." (II Timothy 2:20,21)

My beloved, you are a vessel in My great house. I have many vessels. When you first became My child, you were a vessel of clay. But because of My touch in your life you were changed to be a vessel of glory and honour and praise. Vessels of clay are used for common household tasks. You would not find gold or silver being used as slop-buckets, toilet bowls or chamber pots. But even so, all those vessels are needful.

However, you have the opportunity for promotion. Clay is never covered in gold or silver, it is too breakable. But wood is overlaid with gold and silver. I instructed Moses to make the furniture of the tabernacle with wood and overlay it with gold and silver that it might become fit to adorn My house.

When you were a sinner, you were a vessel of clay, but when you came to Me, I made of you a vessel of wood, like the trees of the forest for strength and beauty.

As you let Me work My work in your life, I am overlaying you with silver or with gold. The silver speaks of My redemptive work in you and the gold speaks of My Deity, My very likeness being stamped in your being. The closer you come into My likeness, the more precious you are. I said, "I will make a man more precious than fine gold; even a man than the golden wedge of Ophir." (Isaiah 13:12) I have the prerogative to overlay you with silver or with gold. The silver vessels were used in My house too. It is up to you. If you will dedicate yourself to My highest purity, My highest honour for your life, I will make you a vessel of gold.

Purge yourself of every unclean act. You know what your own weaknesses and hindrances are. My Spirit deals with each one according to that one's need. If you are unclean, I cannot use you as a vessel of glory. You will be smelly and hidden in a corner. It is up to you to be that vessel of gold or silver which can adorn the shelves of glory and be on display throughout eternity. Let My grace finish My perfect work in you.

December 30

WHY THE GODLY SUFFER PERSECUTION

Scripture Reading – II Timothy 3:1-17

"Yea, and all that will live godly in Christ Jesus shall suffer persecution." (II Timothy 3:12)

This is the hour of persecution. It must come to purify My children. Do not be overcome by it. Prepare for it!

These are perilous times. Men are lovers of selves. Self-preservation and perversions of all kinds lie in the hearts of the people. Every vile thing that Paul mentions in this letter to Timothy is prevalent in these days. There never has been a day of such multiplied evil as there is now. Covetousness, boastfulness, pride, blasphemy, disobedience to parents, ingratitude, and unholy people are not only in the world, much of it is in the church. Did I not say of those who commit all these listed evils, that they have "a form of godliness, yet deny the power thereof"?

There is power to live above all of these evils. There is also power to live the life of a martyr.

Do not be shocked that you must suffer persecution even from those who you thought loved and respected you. This is a day when every hidden evil in every heart shall be revealed. Many who seemed to be so nice and friendly, so godly, are really without natural affection; they make a promise today and break it tomorrow. They accuse you falsely, they are inconsistent, savage, traitors of a cause, highminded, lovers of pleasures more than lovers of God and they despise those who are good. (II Timothy 3:2-4)

If they despise those who are good, how can you expect them to love you when you cannot run with them nor live their life style. I have commanded you "from such turn away." That means you are to have nothing to do with them. What fellowship has light with darkness?

And when you live a holy, godly life, they will hate you. You will suffer persecution and feel the hatred of those who hate good. For when you are righteous you will become the object of everything they hate.

Rejoice therefore when you are persecuted for it is a sign of who you really are in Me.

December 31

I HAVE FINISHED MY COURSE

Scripture Reading — II Timothy 4:1-22

"I have fought a good fight, I have finished my course, I have kept the faith:" (II Timothy 4:7)

What glorious words! What a finale!

Paul was always concerned that he might one day fail his Lord.

When he was on his way to Jerusalem for the last time he expressed the longing to be able to finish his life's calling according to the blue print for his life.

Today, My beloved child, I want to congratulate you and give you a heavenly pat on your back. You have just completed a long and difficult assignment. You can shout triumphantly "Mission Accomplished!" There have been times when you have been discouraged and sorely tried. If a broken heart could bleed, you would have bled from the heart.

But no one can point to the wounds of the heart and say "This is where it hurts!" No one can see the dreadful slash which the sword has made. And there is no visible blood.

But in spite of the hurts and the unanswered questions and the rejection, you have gone on, refusing to look back and I honour you, My child. You have been obedient to the plan. Maybe others failed but you never did. No, not for a moment did you fail to take that step of obedience and sacrifice. All you have done, all you have given has been duly recorded by My angels. And now we close the book. Do not fret about what you think might have been different. Others may have failed to hear My voice, but you didn't. The course is finished. VICTORY!

> Tis finished, yes, tis finished!
> Oh, hear the victory cry!
> My soldier has just crossed the bar
> To dwell with Me on high.
>
> The course he ran is finished,
> The battle has been won;
> His faith has conquered dragons
> And now his work is done.
>
> Welcome to the city
> The hosts of heaven are here;
> To greet My worthy soldier,
> And wipe away each tear.

GWEN SHAW'S AUTOBIOGRAPHY!

UNCONDITIONAL SURRENDER—*Gwen Shaw*. The life story of Gwen R. Shaw, lovingly known as "Sister Gwen" to thousands of people in over one hundred nations. You will laugh and cry with her as you feel the heartbeat of a great woman of God who has given all to Him, asking only for souls in return. Your life will be challenged as you walk with her through mission field after mission field. You will never be the same when you read how God pours out His Spirit and confirms His Word. ....Hardcover #U106-82 $19.95
..........................video NTSC (North American format) #GSL-99 $20.00
..........................video PAL (European format)   #GSLP-99 $20.00

DAILY DEVOTIONALS BY GWEN SHAW

DAILY PREPARATIONS FOR PERFECTION —*Gwen Shaw*. This daily devotional comes to you exactly as the Holy Spirit spoke to the author's heart in her own private devotions. You will feel that Jesus is speaking to you every time you open it. It is loved by all; read and re-read ....Paperback #D101-32 $12.50

DAY BY DAY—*Gwen Shaw*. The author's daily devotional book based on the Psalms will give you an inspiring word directly from the Throne Room each day to fill your heart with praise to God. It was a great comfort to the author herself after the fire in 1990 that destroyed so much. (Also available in French) ....Hardcover #D101-38 $18.50

FROM THE HEART OF JESUS—*Gwen Shaw*. This devotional book is like no other. It will take you back to Bible days and you will walk and talk with Jesus and His disciples as he ministered to the people, as He suffered and died and as He rose again from the dead. These words from the heart of Jesus will go straight to your heart, bringing comfort, peace encouragement and hope! 923 pages Hardcover ....
....#F102-11 $29.95

GEMS OF WISDOM — A daily devotional based on the book of Proverbs — *Gwen Shaw*. In the Proverbs you will find instruction for upright living, honesty, justice and wisdom. Every word in the Proverbs applies to today's problems as when they were first written. If you are going through great difficulties and facing problems which seem to have no solution, you will find the answer in these Proverbs. You'll have a Proverb and an inspired writing about it for each day of the year
....Hardcover #G105-49 $25.95

IN THE BEGINNING — A daily devotional based on the book of Genesis — *Gwen Shaw*. The Book of Genesis is perhaps the most important Book in the Old Testament. It is the foundation stone of all knowledge and wisdom. Deep and wonderful truths hidden in the pages of Genesis are revealed in this devotional book. You'll be amazed at the soul-stirring writings inspired by the well-known stories of Genesis............ ....#I115-47 **$27.95**

CLASSIC ANOINTED BIBLE STUDIES

BEHOLD THE BRIDEGROOM COMETH!—*Gwen Shaw*. A Bible study on the soon return of Jesus Christ. With so many false teachings these days, it is important that we realize how imminent the rapture of the saints of God really is ....#B100-37 **$6.50**

ENDUED WITH LIGHT TO REIGN FOREVER — *Gwen Shaw*. This deeply profound Bible study reveals the characteristics of the eternal, supernatural, creative light of God as found in His Word. The "Father of Lights," created man in His image. He longs for man to step out of darkness and into His light..#E101-71 **$6.00**

GOD'S END-TIME BATTLE-PLAN—*Gwen Shaw*. This study on spiritual warfare gives you the biblical weapons for spiritual warfare such as victory through dancing, shouting, praising, uplifted hands, marching, etc. It has been a great help to many who have been bound by tradition ....#G102-35 **$8.00**

IT'S TIME FOR REVIVAL—*Gwen Shaw*. A Bible Study on Revival that not only gives scriptural promises of the end-time Revival, but also presents the stories of revivals in the past and the revivalists whom God used. It will stir your heart and encourage you to believe for great revival..#I103-24 **$7.75**

OUR MINISTERING ANGELS—*Gwen Shaw*. A scriptural Bible study on the topic of angels. Angels will be playing a more and more prominent part in these last days. We need to understand about them and their ministry ....#O104-87 **$7.50**

POUR OUT YOUR HEART—*Gwen Shaw*. A wonderful Bible study on travailing prayer. The hour has come to intercede before the throne of God. The call to intercession is for everyone, and we must carry the Lord's burden and weep for the lost so that the harvest can be brought in quickly ....#P105-16 **$3.75**

REDEEMING THE LAND—*Gwen Shaw*. This important teaching will help you know your authority through the Blood of Jesus to dislodge evil spirits, break the curse, and restore God's blessing upon the land. A Bible study on spiritual warfare ....#R108-61 $9.50

THE FINE LINE—*Gwen Shaw*. This Bible study clearly magnifies the "fine line" difference between the soul realm and the spirit realm. Both are intangible and therefore cannot be discerned with the five senses, but must be discerned by the Holy Spirit and the Word of God. A must for the deeper Christian..............................#F101-91 $6.00

THE POWER OF THE PRECIOUS BLOOD—*Gwen Shaw*. A Bible study on the Blood of Jesus. The author shares how it was revealed to her how much Satan fears Jesus' Blood. This Bible study will help you overcome and destroy the works of Satan in your life and the lives of loved ones ....#P105-18 $4.00

THE POWER OF PRAISE—*Gwen Shaw*. When God created the heavens and earth He was surrounded by praise. Miracles happen when holy people praise a Holy God! Praise is the language of creation. If prayer can move the hand of God, how much more praise can move Him!..#P400-66 $5.00

YE SHALL RECEIVE POWER FROM ON HIGH *Gwen Shaw*. This is a much needed foundational teaching on the Baptism of the Holy Spirit. It will enable you to teach this subject, as well as to understand these truths more fully yourself..#Y107-37 $5.00

YOUR APPOINTMENT WITH GOD—*Gwen Shaw*. A Bible study on fasting. Fasting is one of the most neglected sources of power over bondages of Satan that God has given the Church. The author's experiences are shared in this Bible study in a way that will change your life ....#Y107-40 $4.50

IN-DEPTH BIBLE STUDIES

FORGIVE AND RECEIVE—An In-Depth Bible Study on Philemon for the Serious Student of God's Word—*Gwen Shaw*. This Bible Study is a lesson to the church on the much-needed truths of forgiveness and restoration. The epistle to Philemon came from the heart of Paul who had experienced great forgiveness.....#F102-01 $7.00